PENGUIN  CLASSICS

PENGUIN ENGLISH POETS
GENERAL EDITOR: CHRISTOPHER RICKS

THE CANTERBURY TALES:
THE FIRST FRAGMENT

GEOFFREY CHAUCER was born in London, the son of a wine-merchant, in about 1342. He became a page to the Countess of Ulster, and an esquire in the royal household. When he was captured fighting in France, Edward III paid part of his ransom.

Chaucer's first literary achievement was a translation of the opening of *Le Roman de la Rose*, a long allegorical poem of courtly love. He wrote his early poem *The Book of the Duchess* for John of Gaunt. His literary perspectives opened further when on the king's business he visited Italy and read Dante, Petrarch and Boccaccio. Besides his languages, he had interests in philosophy, astronomy and science. Among his greater works are *The Parliament of Fowls* and *Troilus and Criseyde*.

Chaucer held a succession of public offices in the royal service, eventually moving to Kent, where he was an MP and a Justice of the Peace. In the 1390s he worked on his *Canterbury Tales*, and in 1399 he took a lease on a house in the garden of the Lady Chapel of the Abbey at Westminster. He was buried in the Abbey a year later.

MICHAEL ALEXANDER is Berry Professor of English Literature at the University of St Andrews. His verse translations, *The Earliest English Poems* and *Beowulf*, are both published in Penguin Classics. He has published poetry of his own, and is Associate Editor of *Agenda*. He has anthologized, edited and written on modern and medieval poetry. Recent publications include *Sons of Ezra: British Poets and Ezra Pound*, and the Penguin English Poets edition of the text of *Beowulf*.

GEOFFREY CHAUCER

The Canterbury Tales: The First Fragment

THE GENERAL PROLOGUE, THE KNIGHT'S TALE,
THE MILLER'S TALE, THE REEVE'S TALE,
THE COOK'S TALE

A Glossed Text

Edited by MICHAEL ALEXANDER

PENGUIN BOOKS

PENGUIN BOOKS

Published by the Penguin Group
Penguin Books Ltd, 27 Wrights Lane, London w8 5TZ, England
Penguin Books USA Inc., 375 Hudson Street, New York, New York 10014, USA
Penguin Books Australia Ltd, Ringwood, Victoria, Australia
Penguin Books Canada Ltd, 10 Alcorn Avenue, Toronto, Ontario, Canada M4V 3B2
Penguin Books (NZ) Ltd, 182–190 Wairau Road, Auckland 10, New Zealand

Penguin Books Ltd, Registered Offices: Harmondsworth, Middlesex, England

This edition first published 1996
10 9 8 7 6 5 4 3 2 1

Chaucer's text is that of *The Riverside Chaucer*, General Editor Larry D. Benson
Copyright © Houghton Mifflin Company, 1987

All editorial matter in this edition copyright © Michael Alexander, 1996
All rights reserved

The moral right of the editor has been asserted

Set in 10/12.5pt Bembo Monotype
Typeset by Datix International Limited, Bungay, Suffolk
Printed in England by Clays Ltd, St Ives plc

For Mary

CONTENTS

EDITOR'S ACKNOWLEDGEMENTS

I am grateful to Houghton Mifflin Company, Boston, MA for their kind permission to use Chaucer's text from *The Riverside Chaucer*, General Editor Larry D. Benson, first published in 1987; here reprinted from the Oxford University Press paperback edition of 1988.

I should also like to thank my family for their patience, Christopher Ricks for his logical vigilance, Felicity Riddy and George Jack for reading and commenting on the Introduction, Dorothy Black, Frances Mullan and Jane Sommerville in the Office of the School of English at the University of St Andrews, and the University for granting research leave.

M. J. A.

INTRODUCTION

The First Fragment of the *Canterbury Tales* begins with Chaucer's General Prologue, and is followed by the Tales of the Knight, Miller, Reeve and Cook, each with its Prologue. It is the most complete of the ten Fragments of the *Canterbury Tales*, and the most often read.

Readers of the General Prologue to the *Canterbury Tales* often feel the wonder expressed by John Dryden: 'Here is God's plenty. We have our forefathers and great-grand-dames all before us, as they were in Chaucer's days.' The first Tale, the Knight's, was admired by Shakespeare, who drew on it for *A Midsummer Night's Dream* and other plays. The remaining tales of the First Fragment have always had readers. On Boxing Day 1801, Dorothy Wordsworth recorded in her journal, 'After tea we sate by the fire comfortably. I read aloud – The Miller's Tale.' The audience was her brother, and Mary Hutchinson, whom he was shortly to marry. Wordsworth recalls reading the Reeve's Tale at Cambridge: 'Beside the pleasant Mills of Trompington/I laughed with Chaucer.'

This poet, who has never lost his ability to surprise and delight readers, was for a long time called the Father of English poetry. He was certainly the founder of modern English verse. He naturalized the iambic pentameter in English, and wrote it with a wonderful ease. Chaucer also imported other verse-forms, and seems to have invented the rhyming pentameter couplet. Technical accomplishments of such consequence count for much, although it is the quality, range, variety and humanity of Chaucer's writing that make him the most complete poet in Middle English. But to call him the Father of English poetry is to set aside all the poetry composed in English for seven centuries before him, *Beowulf* for example. It is true that the older English language was dethroned at the Conquest and that it re-emerged transformed, partly through the influence of French. After Chaucer wrote, the language changed in less fundamental ways, so that he is indeed one of the earlier English poets who are now intelligible, though he is not the first.

If one implication of calling Chaucer the Father of English poetry is that there was no English poetry before him, another is that the real achievements in English poetry came after him. Renaissance triumphs were indeed to conceal the achievement, and even the existence, of Old English verse, and also of the profusion of Middle English verse before Chaucer. The notion that Chaucer somehow created English poetry – that English Literature began *because* Chaucer wrote so well that English became the literary language of England – is a fancy which appealed to G. K. Chesterton. It is true that Chaucer, so far as we know, wrote only in English, whereas his friend John Gower wrote in English, French and Latin. It is true also that Chaucer brought the flexibility and elegance of modern European writing into English verse. He was the first great modern European poet to write in English. But in 1363 Parliament was summoned in English, and English would have become the literary language of England without Geoffrey Chaucer.

Excellent poet though he is, the reason that we can read Chaucer with some ease is due less to his genius and to his lucid and engaging style than to the fact that the standard written English of today developed directly from a London English closely related to the English he wrote. *Piers Plowman*, a work which, like the *Canterbury Tales*, survives in many manuscripts, is composed in an alliterative measure and in a West Midlands dialect. This great poem has become hard to read, and has been less read, whereas Chaucer has been read in every generation.

In modern times the *Canterbury Tales* has become the most widely enjoyed of Chaucer's writings, although it is less perfect and less moving than his *Troilus and Criseyde*. Towards the end of that 'tragedye', Chaucer had prayed that God would enable him to write some comedy. His prayer was granted. The Tales are a collection of stories, supposedly told by a varied company of some thirty pilgrims as they ride along the road from London to Canterbury. Some of the pilgrims tell tales written earlier in Chaucer's literary career, but he is thought to have devised the fiction of the pilgrimage with its tale-telling game in about 1387, and to have worked on it on and off until his death in 1400.

There had been omnibus collections of stories before, such as the Arabian *Thousand and One Nights* and, in the generation before Chaucer, Boccaccio's *Decameron*. In this work, which Chaucer may have known or known of, ten beautiful young people tell one tale a day for ten days in a garden above Florence while the Black Death rages in the city below. But Chaucer devised for his Tales a frame which has two sources of narrative energy – the Pilgrimage itself, and the competitiveness of the tale-telling game. Although the pilgrims exist to tell the tales, no other collection has tellers so varied, and in none do the tellers come to life and speak so vividly. At times the vigorous interaction between the tellers upstages the tales. Chaucer himself tells the Tale of Sir Topaz, a parody of popular romance so dreadful that the Host of the Tabard stops Chaucer with an extremely rude comment on his rhyming. Chaucer then tells a second tale, a serious moral allegory in prose. Although the Host had proposed that each pilgrim should tell two tales on the way to Canterbury and two on the way back, Chaucer is the only pilgrim to tell two stories (neither of which would have won the prize).

The eighty or more surviving manuscripts of the *Canterbury Tales* suggest that it was left in a form in which the narrative is not continuous, but is in sections which are not linked to each other. These 'Fragments' are not in the same order in each manuscript. The best manuscripts have ten Fragments, some of them incomplete. Some tales are themselves incomplete, as are several of Chaucer's other works. The *Canterbury Tales* is, however, provided with a conclusion, when the Host explicitly asks the Parson to tell the last tale.

A look at the contents of the *Canterbury Tales* may suggest their variety. The First Fragment, with its General Prologue, Knight's Tale, Miller's Prologue and Tale, Reeve's Prologue and Tale and Cook's Prologue and Tale, has 4422 lines. The longest Fragment, VII, has great variety in its parts: the Shipman's Tale, the Prioress's Prologue and Tale, Chaucer's own Tales, of Sir Thopas (cut short by the Host) and of Melibee, the Monk's Prologue and Tale (also cut short by the Host) and the Nun's Priest's Prologue, Tale and Epilogue. This complex Fragment runs to 4652 lines. Most Fragments contain two tales. Two Fragments consist of a single pilgrim's prologue and tale.

In the ten Fragments, there are twenty-three Tales, four of them unfinished, variously accompanied by Introductions, Prologues and Epilogues. There is always some linking matter between tales. The tales swim in a river of narrative more lively than is suggested by the terms 'framework' and 'link'. There is vast variety of genre: between the General Prologue and the Retraction the tales include fabliaux, romances, moral allegories, saints' lives, animal fables, tragedies, tales of tricks and hoaxes, a sermon, and a penitential treatise in prose. Within the prologues and tales Chaucer's discourse varies spectacularly: there are apologias, hymns, diatribes, learned disquisitions, discussions of *gentillesse* and of the roles of the sexes in marriage, farcical and indecent jokes, boasts and confessions, arguments, fallings-out, and, after an attempt to sell a pardon to the Host, a violent quarrel, halted by the Knight.

Some parts of the *Canterbury Tales* are unfinished, but the work has a conclusion. The unity of a common aim is also provided by the Pilgrimage to the shrine of the *hooly blisful martir* in Canterbury, beyond which lies what the Parson calls 'thilke parfit glorious pilgrymage,/That highte Jerusalem celestial'. Smaller unities are provided by debates in tales and links on marriage. Irreligious quarrels erupt between economic competitors: envy and avarice and vanity burst out under the influence of anger, humiliation and drink. Vice is not confined to the lay pilgrims. Chaucer often changes key by the use of contrast and humour. He tells us that many a true word is spoken in jest, but also that play and game should not be taken in earnest.

As they go on, the diversity of the *Tales* becomes more evident than their unity, which is far from classical, and only locally organic. *Tales* is plural and 'a Canterbury tale' meant 'a traveller's tale, a tall story such as pilgrims tell'. And although Dante's *Commedia* and Chaucer's *Troilus* have a beautiful formal symmetry, other medieval works, such as Chaucer's *Legend of Good Women* and Monk's Tale, are bundles of stories of a single type. Many medieval manuscripts are miscellanies rather than 'works', and some are magazines mixing fact and fiction with as much unity as the *Reader's Digest*. Chaucer probably meant the Host's 120-Tale scheme to look grandiose. Had he been obliged to fulfil the scheme, he would have thrown in plenty of chaos.

Whatever the unity or variety of the *Canterbury Tales*, the sequencing of the First Fragment indicates to the audience that they should expect some surprises in the narrative of the *Tales* as a whole. As the first fragment, it contains Chaucer's own preamble, his description of the pilgrims, and his account of the tale-telling game. The tales and links of the Knight, Miller and Reeve form a unified sequence of three complete tales, with a fourth which, although it stops short, is designed as part of that sequence. The 4422 lines of the Fragment contain hardly any of the false starts or signs of imperfect revision found in other fragments. Indeed, the First Fragment is as finished, and as artistically purposeful, as anything in the *Tales*. The Prologue is 'general' in that it introduces all but one of the tellers of the tales. The catalogue of pilgrims was praised by William Blake as well as Dryden as an inclusive picture of human nature; it is certainly a miniature social encyclopedia. The two tales that follow are as good as any later. The First Fragment touches the secular heights and depths, but has no tales by clerics: no piety, no inter-clerical rivalry. The links of this Fragment are lively enough, though lacking the extreme disruptiveness which breaks out later. Yet the First Fragment remains the best-finished piece of narrative in the *Tales*. It is surprising that though its parts have been separately edited, it seems not to have been edited as a unit on its own.

The choice of the First Fragment as a unitary piece of writing to be read on its own was the starting-point of this edition. The advantage of the edition is to be found in its format. The text, set on the 'noble' right-hand page, is faced by very full glosses set on the left-hand page. The policy is to gloss word by word, not phrase by phrase, although occasionally a whole line has had to be glossed. Formal language teaching has declined in British schools, and students require more help with the language of older texts. And even the most expert reader of Chaucer may need help. The very closeness to modern English of Chaucer's English can hide differences. At the end of the portrait of the Knight we read *His hors were goode*. A gloss tells the reader that *hors* means 'horses', though at least one editor took it as singular. But even the most helpful gloss is the servant of the text and of the reader. In this edition the text stands on its own without marginal or superscript signals. There are full notes at the end, those most immediately helpful to the reader being indicated by an asterisk to a gloss at the nearest convenient point. The editor stands on the shoulders of previous editors of Chaucer, especially as regards the text. After some work and deliberation, it was decided to reproduce the text and editorial punctuation of the Riverside Chaucer, rather than produce a text which would differ only in minor details from the standard text.

This edition allows the First Fragment to be read as a whole, and its articulation to be seen. The sequence is as follows. The General Prologue opens with April prompting the movement of pilgrims from all over England to the shrine of St Thomas at Canterbury. Chaucer falls in with a party of twenty-nine pilgrims, at the Tabard Inn, Southwark, and by talking to them makes himself one of their company. In the famous gallery of portraits, he anatomizes the Estates: *bellatores*, *oratores*, *laboratores*; those who fight, those who pray and those who work. He puts himself with the rascals at the end. The Host then persuades the pilgrims to take part in the tale-telling game. He will judge which tale is *of best sentence and moost solaas*, and the pilgrims will obey him. The prize is a free dinner for the winner (at the Tabard, paid for by the others). Much of this does not come to pass, but next morning they do ride out, and the Host has the Knight tell the first tale.

The Knight tells an elaborate tale, found in Boccaccio, of Palamon and Arcite and their love for Emelye, a chivalric romance set in an ancient Athens ruled by Duke Theseus. The young Theban cousins become rivals for the hand of the princess they see from their prison window; she does not know they exist. Arcite is released, Palamon escapes, and, meeting by chance in a grove, they agree to fight. Their mortal duel is halted by Theseus, out hunting. He mercifully appoints that they should fight properly in a grand tournament, one hundred a side, Emelye to marry the winner. One year later, the lists are built, and the three young people pray to their gods: Venus seems to accept Palamon's plea to have Emelye, but signifies a delay. Diana tells Emelye that she may not remain a virgin (her first request), but must marry. Mars promises Arcite 'Victory'. The cousins get what they ask for, and in the event Emelye gets her second request, *hym that moost desireth me*. The promises of Mars and Venus are reconciled by Arcite winning the tournament, but, as he rides up to claim Emelye, an infernal fury starts out of the ground, causing his horse to throw him. After an eloquent and pathetic speech, Arcite dies in the arms of Emelye. There follows a solemn funeral, but after years of mourning Theseus advises in a philosophical speech that Palamon and Emelye should marry, which they do. Chivalry has made the best of a bad job.

The *gentils* like this tale, and the Host invites the Monk to tell the next. But the drunken Miller insists on matching the Knight's noble tale. He tells how John, a rich old carpenter, was cuckolded by his student lodger Nicholas, who pretends to foresee a Second Flood, and persuades John to provide three tubs in which to survive it. When John is snoring in his 'ark' and Nicholas and

John's young wife Alison are in bed together, another admirer, Absalom, comes to the window and asks Alison for a kiss. She sticks her bottom out of the window, and in the darkness Absalom kisses her arse. Returning with a hot iron, Absalom begs one more kiss. This time Nicholas sticks his rear out of the window. Branded by the hot iron, he yells out 'Help! Water!' John wakes, thinks that the Flood has come, cuts the rope and falls to the ground, breaking his arm. The Oxford students agree that John is *wood*, mad. Most of the pilgrims laugh.

The Reeve, a carpenter and an old lecher, retaliates with a tale of the cuckolding of a proud miller by two Cambridge students, John and Alan. Symkyn the miller is proud of his marriage to the illegitimate daughter of a parson. The lads are determined that he will not cheat them of any of their corn. He outwits them, but lets them stay the night. While Symkyn snores, Alan gets into bed with his daughter. John, not to be outdone, takes the cradle and places it beside his bed, so that Symkyn's wife mistakes her way in the dark, and gets into bed with John. The miller's women enjoy their guests. At dawn Alan gets into the miller's bed and tells him how he has enjoyed the miller's daughter, three times. In the ensuing fight in the dark, the miller's wife mistakenly hits him on the head with a staff and knocks him out. The students return to college in triumph, with their flour and a loaf the miller had stolen from them.

The drunken Cook, helpless with laughter, insists on telling a tale about a London apprentice. Ignoring the Host's gibes about the rotten food that he sells, the Cook embarks on the tale of the riotous Perkyn Revelour. Dismissed at last by his master, Perkyn moves in with a *compeer* who is married to a wife. She keeps a cook-shop for the sake of appearances, but, as the Cook's last line tells us, she *swyved for hir sustenance*, or fucked for a living. Thus ends the First Fragment.

The First Fragment introduces the pilgrims and launches the tale-telling competition. After a noble start, the game degenerates into a rogues' competition to see who can be most entertainingly rude about the sex-lives of the others. When the Cook's Tale breaks off, it is clear that the freshness of the April opening – with its *blisful* saint, conviviality, high hopes, and a worthy knight recounting an Athenian romance to pilgrims early in the morning – has returned, via the cheerful cuckolding of elderly artisans by young intellectuals, to a London brothel. The Host's plan to divert the pilgrims (and ensure their return to the Tabard) has diverted the pilgrimage. In Fragment IX, the Host wakes the Cook, who is asleep on his horse. The Manciple tells the Cook that he is stinking drunk. In his anger the Cook falls off his horse; but unlike Arcite survives. With Canterbury in sight, the Host asks the Parson to tell the last tale. But by the end of the First Fragment, the dawn Pilgrimage to the *hooly blisful martir* is already turning into a long night at the Rat and Badger.

Dr Johnson wrote in his *Preface to Shakespeare* that his author was 'so much more careful to please than to instruct that he seems to write without any moral purpose'. Matthew Arnold thought Chaucer, though 'free, shrewd, benignant', lacking in 'high seriousness'. Many since Arnold have tried to find Chaucer's moral viewpoint (though John Ruskin thought he taught the purest theological truth). On his deathbed Arcite asks:

'What is this world? What asketh men to have?
Now with his love, now in the colde grave,
Allone, withouten any compaignye.'

These agonized cries are followed not long after by the Miller's Tale. The Miller begins by repeating 'Allone, withouten any compaignye': a joke about Nicholas's lack of *compaignye*, shortly to be supplied by Alison, whose breath smells as sweet as mead, or as a hoard of apples laid in hay or heath. Perhaps Chaucer's Catholic audience did not look for moral guidance in Canterbury tales. As for lack of moral purpose, Dr Johnson had already found one defence for Shakespeare by arguing that his plays show life as we find it. For, in 'the real state of sublunary nature', the 'course of the world' is such that 'at the same time, the reveller is hasting to his wine, and the mourner burying his friend . . .'

If we seek for an analogy for the First Fragment's bringing together of love and death, and of the grave and the tavern, we need look no further than a work which took some hints from it. In this comedy of love, the confused agonies of noble young lovers in a wood near Athens are succeeded by artisans rehearsing for a play competition. Their winning play, to be played before Duke Theseus on his wedding-night, is a travesty of the tragedy of Pyramus and Thisbe, in which Thisbe says (to the wall which separates her from Pyramus):

> 'My cherry lips have often kissed thy stones,
> Thy stones with lime and hair knit up in thee.'

A Midsummer Night's Dream is, like the mechanicals' play, 'very tragical mirth'. The imaginative and the gross faces of love, and its tragic and absurd outcomes, parody each other in a manner and a sequence which owe much to the tales of the First Fragment.

This summary of the tales does not suggest the skill of their telling; but a rich humanity begins to appear as soon as we meet the pilgrims. Chaucer needed tellers for his tales, and took them from Estates satire, and the thirteenth-century French poem *Le Roman de la Rose*. But the pilgrims come to life as soon as they open their mouths – and disagree. The historian is tempted to think that Chaucer's purpose in the Prologue was not to set his tales in a larger fiction, but to hold a mirror up to medieval society. But Chaucer did not know that he lived in the Middle Ages, or that he had a duty to history. He told stories and knew that these stories were not true. He was not recording the colourful mores of a people in need of reform. A lay writer on secular themes, one of the first in English, he was making what we call literature. In his portraits Chaucer drew on Latin and French traditions of writing on the medieval Estates, writing which satirized social abuses. The General Prologue can be useful to the historian. But its purposes are fictional and metaphysical, showing the composition, ideals and practices of human society, and the laughable vanity of most of its members, especially the rich and the dishonest among laity and clergy. Chaucer does indeed show what Dryden called 'God's plenty'. Satirical and historical the Prologue may be, but its genre is Christian comedy.

Chaucer's method in the Prologue is one of ironical praise. He does not reprove obstinate vice, as medieval satirists like Langland did, and as his own Parson does. On the contrary, Chaucer the pilgrim admires the Prioress's table manners and the Monk's beautiful boots. And when the fat and worldly Monk disputes the text which says that a monk out of his cloister is not worth an oyster, Chaucer agrees: 'And I seyde his opinion was good.' His irony is almost invisible in his enthusiasm. His disciple Lydgate testified that Chaucer 'seide alweie the beste'. Chaucer the pilgrim is disarming:

> So hadde I spoken with hem everichon
> That I was of hir felaweshipe anon.

His way is to make himself agreeable, win the confidence of his companions and allow them to speak for themselves. The portraits are speaking portraits, in which the pilgrims, good, bad and silly, give themselves away. Readers too have succumbed to the charm of this inviter of confidences.

Chaucer was a diplomat and a customs officer. He was a King's man, neither merchant nor gentry, but a 'new man'. He was a court poet and a city poet. By the time of the *Tales* he was well-known to audiences, many of whom could not read; he was in that sense a popular poet. He read widely himself, in philosophy and science as well as in literature; and the learned read him. Born in the Vintry, the wine-merchants' street, he knew London. He sailed to and rode through France, Italy and Spain in the King's service, and lived through the Black Death, the French war, the Popes' captivity at Avignon, the Peasants'

Revolt, and the deposition and murder of Richard II. Chaucer tells us strictly nothing about these upheavals, although his writing has a quick, unsettled tone. His standards, if they can be guessed from his work, are Christian, human and ethical rather than political. His Parson and Plowman show that he shared the ideals of his age. He knew the world, and treated it with loving humour but also with detached irony. He writes with humorous respect of the Knight and the Clerk of Oxenford, but was also drawn to anatomize vanity, dishonesty, hypocrisy and greed in others. The Chaucerian chuckle is not always cosy. He notes that the Doctor was 'but esy of dispense' (slow to spend money), for 'He kepte that he wan in pestilence.' Chaucer was a humorist not a reformer and his humour is humane; but his eye is deadly. It was Chaucer who wrote of 'the smylere with the knyf under the cloke', and it was of Chaucer's Man of Law that we read

> Nowher so bisy a man as he ther nas,
> And yet he semed bisier than he was.

Chaucer also wrote that 'Glosynge is a glorious thyng, certeyn.' Glosses can help the reader to get at the poet's sense as he or she goes along. But I must ask the reader to read Chaucer aloud, preferably with friends – as I once had the pleasure of hearing it done in Nevill Coghill's rooms in Merton College by Coghill, Norman Davis, John Burrow and Lena Davis. Following this introduction is a note on how the pronunciation of Chaucer's English affects the reading of his verse.

Michael Alexander
St Andrews
March 1995

A NOTE ON CHAUCER'S
ENGLISH AND VERSE

Glosses help with sense, not sound. The quickest way into the verse is to listen to a good reading, and imitate it. There are several recordings which offer scholarly reconstructions of Chaucer's English (see Further Reading). The phonetic values are reasonably reliable, and if other aspects of vocalization are less certain, we can be confident that we understand the bases of Chaucer's verse.

Pronunciation. The dialects of Middle English show much variation. There was no national literary standard English; and even in London usage and spelling were not fully standardized. What follows is not an account of the language, but a set of hints. In general, each letter is distinctly pronounced, as in modern Italian and Spanish; *r* is trilled. In *knyght*, *k* is pronounced, and *gh* is sounded as in Scots *loch*. When the letter *y* is a vowel it has the sound of modern *i*, either short as in *sit* or long as in *machine*. The word *ye*, meaning 'eye', is disyllabic; the first syllable is a long *i*, the second a neutral vowel, like that given by English speakers to the first sound of *about*. All consonants are pronounced, except initial *h* in words from French like *hostelrye* and *honour*. Vowels are pronounced with purer continental values than the diphthong vowels of Modern English. Thus *condicioun* has four syllables.

The inflectional system of Old English had decayed, with many endings reduced to *-e*, the neutral vowel of the first sound of *about*. In some cases and some dialects, this final *e* was not pronounced in speech. Chaucer took advantage of this disappearing

final *e* in his versification. In the first line of the Fragment, the
final *e* of *soote* is pronounced. In line 3, final *e* is not sounded in
veyne, as it is elided before *in*. Final *e* is sounded in *sweete* (5),
tendre, *yonge* and *sonne* (6), but not in *Thanne* (12), where it is
scribal. In lines 671–2 of the General Prologue Chaucer rhymed
Rome and *to me* where *to* is stressed, so that *Rome* must have two
syllables. As a general rule, sound the final *e* at the end of the
line, but not within the line except when it is required by the
metre. It is normally elided before vowels and words like *honour*.
A similar convention seems to be observed in the enunciation of
French classical verse.

The verse. The First Fragment is written throughout in five-
beat lines rhyming in couplets; some later tales are in stanzas or
in prose. Although this five-beat line beginning with an off-beat,
now called the iambic pentameter, had appeared occasionally
before Chaucer, it had not been rhymed. Chaucer began writing
verse in the four-beat couplet long established in English, but he
was the first to develop the five-beat line, which does not break
into balancing halves. He had as models both the decasyllabic
French line and the hendecasyllabic Italian line. Lines ending
with final *e* (which, according to our general rule above, is
always to be pronounced at the end of the line), are hendecasyl-
lables, for example, line 2: 'The droghte of March hath perced to
the roote'. The five beats normally come in an iambic pattern,
but, as is usual in later verse, variation, reversal and substitution
are permitted.

The grammar of Chaucer's English is too large a field to
plough here, but it may be helpful to mention two points. In the
present indicative tense the third person singular ends in -*eth*, the
third person plural in -(*e*)*n*. Finally, the second person pronouns
preserve a distinction lost in modern English: the singular *thou* is
used familiarly – to an intimate, to God, and to an inferior. The
plural is more formal: *ye* (you) is nominative, and *yow* accusative
or dative.

FURTHER READING

Edition

Benson, Larry D. (general editor), *The Riverside Chaucer* (Boston, 1987; Oxford, 1988, paperback). This is the 3rd edn of F. N. Robinson's *The Works of Geoffrey Chaucer* (2nd edn, 1957) and is now the standard edition.

Background

Bryan, W. F. and Dempster, Germaine (eds), *Sources and Analogues of Chaucer's Canterbury Tales* (1941, repr. New York, 1958)

Lewis, C. S., *The Discarded Image: An Introduction to Medieval and Renaissance Literature* (London, 1964, repr. 1971)

Pearsall, Derek, *Geoffrey Chaucer: A Life* (London, 1993)

Criticism

Blamires, Alcuin, *The Canterbury Tales* (The Critics Debate) (London and Atlantic Highlands, NJ, 1987)

Boitani, Piero (ed.), *Chaucer and the Italian Trecento* (Cambridge, 1983)

Boitani, Piero, and Mann, Jill, *The Cambridge Chaucer Companion* (Cambridge, 1988)

Bowden, Muriel, *A Preface to the Canterbury Tales* (2nd edn, New York and London, 1967)

Brewer, Derek, *Chaucer: Poet as Storyteller* (London, 1984)

Burrow, John, *Essays on Medieval Literature* (Oxford, 1984)

Cooper, Helen, *The Structure of the Canterbury Tales* (London and Athens, GA, 1983)

—, *The Canterbury Tales* (Oxford Guides to Chaucer) (Oxford, 1989)

Donaldson, E. Talbot, *Speaking of Chaucer* (London, 1970)

Elliott, Ralph W. V., *Chaucer's English* (London, 1974)

Howard, Donald R., *The Idea of the Canterbury Tales* (Berkeley, Los Angeles and London, 1976)

Kolve, V. A., *Chaucer and the Imagery of Narrative: The First Five Canterbury Tales* (Stanford and London, 1984)

Mann, Jill, *Chaucer and Medieval Estates Satire: The Literature of Social Classes and the General Prologue to the Canterbury Tales* (Cambridge, 1973)

Muscatine, Charles, *Chaucer and the French Tradition* (Berkeley and Los Angeles, 1957)

Pearsall, Derek, *The Canterbury Tales* (London, Boston and Sydney, 1985)

Robertson, D. W., Jr, *Preface to Chaucer* (Princeton, 1962)

Recordings

The General Prologue, read by Nevill Coghill, Norman Davis, John Burrow, 1982, ARGO 1091

—, read by George Sayer, TWC 8

Knight's Tale, read by Trevor Eaton, 1982, THES 625

—, read by John Burrow, TWC 1/2

Miller's Tale, read by Norman Davis, TWC 3

—, read by Trevor Eaton, 1987, THE 595

Reeve's Tale, read by Trevor Eaton, 1992, THE 606

Cook's Prologue and Tale, read by Trevor Eaton, THE 626

The Canterbury Tales:
The First Fragment

* An asterisk, placed at the nearest point in the glosses, indicates a note immediately helpful to the reader. The Notes, beginning on page 261, also include notes giving supplementary information; these are not indicated by an asterisk in the glosses.

his his, its   *shoures soote* sweet showers
droghte dryness*   *perced* pierced
veyne vein (of sap)   *swich licour* liquid such (that)
Of which vertu by its power   *flour* flower
5   *Zephirus* god of the west wind; breeze   *eek* also
Inspired breathed life into   *holt* grove   *heeth* field
croppes shoots, new leaves   *yonge* young*
Has run (the second) half of his course in Aries*
smale foweles little birds
10   *ye* eye
So much does Nature prick them in their hearts*
longen folk to goon people long to go
palmeres pilgrims*   *straunge strondes* foreign shores
To distant shrines known in various lands
15   *every shires ende* the corner of every county
wende make their way
blisful martir blessed martyr (St Thomas à Becket)*   *seke* seek
hem hath holpen helped them*   *seeke* sick
Bifil it happened   *seson* season
20   *Southwerk* Southwark   *Tabard* Tabard Inn*   *lay* stayed

corage spirit

GENERAL PROLOGUE

Here bygynneth the Book of the Tales of Caunterbury.

    Whan that Aprill with his shoures soote
The droghte of March hath perced to the roote,
And bathed every veyne in swich licour
Of which vertu engendred is the flour;
5 Whan Zephirus eek with his sweete breeth
Inspired hath in every holt and heeth
The tendre croppes, and the yonge sonne
Hath in the Ram his half cours yronne,
And smale foweles maken melodye,
10 That slepen al the nyght with open ye
(So priketh hem nature in hir corages),
Thanne longen folk to goon on pilgrimages,
And palmeres for to seken straunge strondes,
To ferne halwes, kowthe in sondry londes;
15 And specially from every shires ende
Of Engelond to Caunterbury they wende,
The hooly blisful martir for to seke,
That hem hath holpen whan that they were seeke.
    Bifil that in that seson on a day,
20 In Southwerk at the Tabard as I lay
Redy to wenden on my pilgrymage
To Caunterbury with ful devout corage,
At nyght was come into that hostelrye
Wel nyne and twenty in a compaignye

25   Of various sorts of people fallen by chance
     felaweship fellowship
     wolden wished to
     chambres bedrooms   *wyde* spacious
     And we were made very comfortable in the best way
30   *to reste* setting
     hem everichon every one of them
     That I became part of their company
     made forward (we) made agreement
     ther as as   *devyse* shall tell
35   *nathelees* nonetheless
     Er before   *pace* proceed
     Me thynketh it it seems to me   *resoun* proper order
     condicioun state, circumstances
     ech of hem each one of them
40   And of what occupation and rank they were
     eek also   *array* dress
     than wol then will
     KNYGHT knight*   *worthy* respected, brave

45   *riden out* go on campaign   *chivalrie* prowess
     Trouthe integrity   *fredom* magnanimity
     lordes werre the war of his feudal superior
     ferre further
     In Christendom as well as in heathen lands*
50
     Alisaundre Alexandria (Egypt)*   *wonne* taken
     bord bigonne sat at the head of the table of honour
     Above (knights of) all nations in Prussia*
     He had ridden on campaign in Lithuania* and in Russia
55   *degree* rank
     In Granada also he had been at the siege
     Algezir Algeciras   *Belmarye* Benmarin, i.e. Morocco*
     Lyeys Ayash (Turkey)   *Satalye* Antalya (Turkey)*
     Grete See Mediterranean
60   *armee* military expedition

25 Of sondry folk, by aventure yfalle
In felaweshipe, and pilgrimes were they alle,
That toward Caunterbury wolden ryde.
The chambres and the stables weren wyde,
And wel we weren esed atte beste.

25 And shortly, whan the sonne was to reste,
So hadde I spoken with hem everichon
That I was of hir felaweshipe anon,
And made forward erly for to ryse,
To take oure wey ther as I yow devyse.

35   But nathelees, whil I have tyme and space,
Er that I ferther in this tale pace,
Me thynketh it acordaunt to resoun
To telle yow al the condicioun
Of ech of hem, so as it semed me,

40 And which they weren, and of what degree,
And eek in what array that they were inne;
And at a knyght than wol I first bigynne.

A KNYGHT ther was, and that a worthy man,
That fro the tyme that he first bigan

45 To riden out, he loved chivalrie,
Trouthe and honour, fredom and curteisie.
Ful worthy was he in his lordes werre,
And therto hadde he riden, no man ferre,
As wel in cristendom as in hethenesse,

50 And evere honoured for his worthynesse;
At Alisaundre he was whan it was wonne.
Ful ofte tyme he hadde the bord bigonne
Aboven alle nacions in Pruce;
In Lettow hadde he reysed and in Ruce,

55 No Cristen man so ofte of his degree.
In Gernade at the seege eek hadde he be
Of Algezir, and riden in Belmarye.
At Lyeys was he and at Satalye,
Whan they were wonne, and in the Grete See

60 At many a noble armee hadde he be.

Tramyssene Tlemcen (western Algeria)
lystes thries lists three times   *ay* always
ilke same
65   *Somtyme* once   *Palatye* Balat (Turkey)*
Agayn against
And always he had an outstanding reputation
worthy brave   *wys* wise, prudent
port bearing, manner
70   *vileynye* rudeness
maner wight kind of person
verray true   *parfit* complete   *gentil* noble*
array equipment
hors horses   *gay* gaily attired
75   *fustian* coarse cotton cloth   *gypon* over-tunic
bismotered marked, spotted   *habergeon* coat of mail
late recently   *viage* expedition

SQUIER (e)squire, beginner in knighthood*
80   *lovyere* lover   *lusty* zestful   *bacheler* aspirant to knighthood*
crulle curly   *presse* curler

of evene lengthe well-proportioned
delyvere agile
85   *somtyme* for a time   *chyvachie* cavalry expedition
Flaundres Flanders*
born hym conducted himself   *space* space of time
his lady grace his lady's favour
Embrouded embroidered   *meede* meadow
90   *reede* red
floytynge playing the flute

koude knew how to
95   *endite* write (the words for a song)
Juste joust   *purtreye* draw

At mortal batailles hadde he been fiftene,
And foughten for oure feith at Tramyssene
In lystes thries, and ay slayn his foo.
This ilke worthy knyght hadde been also
65   Somtyme with the lord of Palatye
Agayn another hethen in Turkye;
And everemoore he hadde a sovereyn prys.
And though that he were worthy, he was wys,
And of his port as meeke as is a mayde.
70   He nevere yet no vileynye ne sayde
In al his lyf unto no maner wight.
He was a verray, parfit gentil knyght.
But for to tellen yow of his array,
His hors were goode, but he was nat gay.
75   Of fustian he wered a gypon
Al bismotered with his habergeon,
For he was late ycome from his viage,
And wente for to doon his pilgrymage.
    With hym ther was his sone, a yong SQUIER,
80   A lovyere and a lusty bacheler,
With lokkes crulle as they were leyd in presse.
Of twenty yeer of age he was, I gesse.
Of his stature he was of evene lengthe,
And wonderly delyvere, and of greet strengthe.
85   And he hadde been somtyme in chyvachie
In Flaundres, in Artoys, and Pycardie,
And born hym weel, as of so litel space,
In hope to stonden in his lady grace.
Embrouded was he, as it were a meede
90   Al ful of fresshe floures, whyte and reede.
Syngynge he was, or floytynge, al the day;
He was as fressh as is the month of May.
Short was his gowne, with sleves longe and wyde.
Wel koude he sitte on hors and faire ryde.
95   He koude songes make and wel endite,
Juste and eek daunce, and weel purtreye and write.

hoote passionately   *nyghtertale* night-time
sleep slept
lowely humble   *servysable* willing to serve
100   *carf* carved
YEMAN yeoman, free-born servant*   *he* the Knight   *namo* no more
hym liste it pleased him
he the Yeoman
pecok with flights made from peacock feathers
105   *bar ful thriftily* bore very properly
He knew well how to care for his equipment like a true yeoman
His arrows did not fall short with sagging feathers

not heed close-cropped head   *broun* dark brown
110
bracer archer's arm-guard
bokeler buckler, shield
gay bright
Harneised ornamented
115   *Cristopher* image of St Christopher*   *sheene* bright
bar bore   *bawdryk* baldrick, shoulder strap
forster forester, gamekeeper   *soothly* truly
PRIORESSE head of a priory of nuns*
symple unaffected   *coy* shyly reserved
120   *ooth* oath   *but* only   *Seinte Loy* St Eloi, St Eligius*
cleped called
soong the service dyvyne sang the liturgy*
Entuned intoned   *ful semely* in a most seemly manner
fetisly gracefully
125   In the manner of Stratford at Bow*
unknowe unknown
At mete at table*   *with alle* indeed
leet allowed

130   *koude* knew how to   *kepe* take care
fille fell
She took great delight in courtly manners

So hoote he lovede that by nyghtertale
He sleep namoore than dooth a nyghtyngale.
Curteis he was, lowely, and servysable,
100 And carf biforn his fader at the table.
      A YEMAN hadde he and servantz namo
At that tyme, for hym liste ride so,
And he was clad in cote and hood of grene.
A sheef of pecok arwes, bright and kene,
105 Under his belt he bar ful thriftily
(Wel koude he dresse his takel yemanly;
His arwes drouped noght with fetheres lowe),
And in his hand he baar a myghty bowe.
A not heed hadde he, with a broun visage.
110 Of wodecraft wel koude he al the usage.
Upon his arm he baar a gay bracer,
And by his syde a swerd and a bokeler,
And on that oother syde a gay daggere
Harneised wel and sharp as point of spere;
115 A Cristophcr on his brest of silver sheene.
An horn he bar, the bawdryk was of grene;
A forster was he, soothly, as I gesse.
      Ther was also a Nonne, a PRIORESSE,
That of hir smylyng was ful symple and coy;
120 Hire gretteste ooth was but by Seinte Loy;
And she was cleped madame Eglentyne.
Ful weel she soong the service dyvyne,
Entuned in hir nose ful semely;
And Frenssh she spak ful faire and fetisly,
125 After the scole of Stratford atte Bowe,
For Frenssh of Parys was to hire unknowe.
At mete wel ytaught was she with alle;
She leet no morsel from hir lippes falle,
Ne wette hir fyngres in hir sauce depe;
130 Wel koude she carie a morsel and wel kepe
That no drope ne fille upon hire brest.
In curteisie was set ful muchel hir lest.

over upper

hir coppe her cup   *ferthyng* spot the size of a farthing

135

after hir mete she raughte she reached for her food

sikerly certainly   *greet desport* fine deportment

port bearing, manner

And took pains to represent the manners

140   *estatlich* dignified*

And to be held worthy of respect

conscience moral sense

pitous compassionate

saugh saw

145

Of smale houndes some little dogs

flessh meat   *wastel-breed* fine white bread

soore sorely, bitterly   *oon* one

men smoot someone hit   *yerde* stick   *smerte* smartly

150

Her wimple was pleated in a very proper manner*

tretys well formed

therto moreover

sikerly surely   *fair forheed* lovely forehead

155   *spanne* stretch between thumb and little finger   *trowe* believe

hardily certainly   *undergrowe* not fully grown

Ful fetys very elegant   *was war* noticed

smal slender

peire of bedes set of beads, rosary   *gauded* decorated*

160   *sheene* beautiful

write engraved   *A* a capital A*

Amor vincit omnia Love conquers all*

chapeleyne assistant   *preestes thre**

165   MONK*   *a fair for the maistrie* a surpassingly fine one

outridere a rider-out, supervisor   *venerie* hunting*

A fine figure of a man, good enough to make an abbot

deyntee fine

Hir over-lippe wyped she so clene
That in hir coppe ther was no ferthyng sene
135 Of grece, whan she dronken hadde hir draughte.
Ful semely after hir mete she raughte.
And sikerly she was of greet desport,
And ful plesaunt, and amyable of port,
And peyned hire to countrefete cheere
140 Of court, and to been estatlich of manere,
And to ben holden digne of reverence.
But for to speken of hire conscience,
She was so charitable and so pitous
She wolde wepe, if that she saugh a mous
145 Kaught in a trappe, if it were deed or bledde.
Of smale houndes hadde she that she fedde
With rosted flessh, or milk and wastel-breed.
But soore wepte she if oon of hem were deed,
Or if men smoot it with a yerde smerte;
150 And al was conscience and tendre herte.
Ful semyly hir wympul pynched was,
Hir nose tretys, hir eyen greye as glas,
Hir mouth ful smal, and therto softe and reed.
But sikerly she hadde a fair forheed;
155 It was almoost a spanne brood, I trowe;
For, hardily, she was nat undergrowe.
Ful fetys was hir cloke, as I was war.
Of smal coral aboute hire arm she bar
A peire of bedes, gauded al with grene,
160 And theron heng a brooch of gold ful sheene,
On which ther was first write a crowned A,
And after *Amor vincit omnia.*

Another NONNE with hire hadde she,
That was hir chapeleyne, and preestes thre.
165 A MONK ther was, a fair for the maistrie,
An outridere, that lovede venerie,
A manly man, to been an abbot able.
Ful many a deyntee hors hadde he in stable,

rood was riding   *heere* hear
170   *Gynglen* jingle

Where this lord was in charge of the house
reule Rule   *Maure* Maurus   *Beneit* Benedict*
somdel streit somewhat strict
175   *ilke* same   *leet* let   *pace* pass away
And observed the liberty of modern times
yaf gave   *of* for   *pulled hen* plucked hen (thing of little worth)*

Ne nor   *recchelees* heedless (of discipline)*
180   *til* to   *waterlees* out of water

thilke that

What why! (an exclamation)   *wood* mad
185   *alwey* always   *poure* pore over
swynken work
Austyn bit St Augustine commands*
Let St Augustine keep his hard work to himself!
prikasour hunter on horseback   *aright* indeed
190
prikyng tracking (*prick* spoor)
lust pleasure
seigh saw   *purfiled* finely sewn
grys a grey squirrel fur
195   *festne* fasten
of . . . pyn a very elaborate pin fashioned in gold
love-knotte elaborate device   *gretter* larger
balled bald   *glas* glass, or glaze
enoynt anointed with oil
200   *poynt* physical condition
stepe prominent or bright   *heed* head
Which gleamed like the flames under a cauldron
souple supple, uncreased
prelaat prelate, churchman

And whan he rood, men myghte his brydel heere

170 Gynglen in a whistlynge wynd als cleere
And eek as loude as dooth the chapel belle
Ther as this lord was kepere of the celle.
The reule of Seint Maure or of Seint Beneit –
By cause that it was old and somdel streit

175 This ilke Monk leet olde thynges pace,
And heeld after the newe world the space.
He yaf nat of that text a pulled hen,
That seith that hunters ben nat hooly men,
Ne that a monk, whan he is recchelees,

180 Is likned til a fissh that is waterlees –
This is to seyn, a monk out of his cloystre.
But thilke text heeld he nat worth an oystre;
And I seyde his opinion was good.
What sholde he studie and make hymselven wood,

185 Upon a book in cloystre alwey to poure,
Or swynken with his handes, and laboure,
As Austyn bit? How shal the world be served?
Lat Austyn have his swynk to hym reserved!
Therfore he was a prikasour aright:

190 Grehoundes he hadde as swift as fowel in flight;
Of prikyng and of huntyng for the hare
Was al his lust, for no cost wolde he spare.
I seigh his sleves purfiled at the hond
With grys, and that the fyneste of a lond;

195 And for to festne his hood under his chyn,
He hadde of gold ywroght a ful curious pyn;
A love-knotte in the gretter ende ther was.
His heed was balled, that shoon as any glas,
And eek his face, as he hadde been enoynt.

200 He was a lord ful fat and in good poynt;
His eyen stepe, and rollynge in his heed,
That stemed as a forneys of a leed;
His bootes souple, his hors in greet estaat.
Now certeinly he was a fair prelaat;

205   *forpyned goost* spirit wasted by suffering
       roost roast meat*
       palfrey horse   *berye* berry*
       FRERE friar, brother*   *wantowne* attractive
       lymytour friar licensed to beg in a district*   *solempne* imposing, impressive
210   *ordres foure* four orders (of friars)*   *kan* knows
       muchel much   *daliaunce* sweet-talking
       maad arranged
       cost expense*
       post pillar, support
215   *famulier* intimate
       With franklins throughout his district*
       eek also   *worthy* prosperous

       curat parish priest (not curate)*
220   *licenciat* licensed to hear confessions
       swetely sweetly   *confessioun* confession*

       esy lenient   *yeve* give   *penaunce* penance*
       Where he knew that he would get a good contribution
225   For to give to a poor order
       yshryve shriven, absolved of sin*
       he yaf a man gave   *he . . . avaunt* the friar dared assert
       wiste knew   *repentaunt* truly penitent
       so . . . herte is so hard-hearted
230   He is not able to weep, though he feels very sorry
       preyeres prayers
       moote yeve must give
       typet tippet, tip of the hood   *farsed* stuffed
       pynnes pins   *wyves* women
235   *murye note* pleasant singing voice
       koude knew how to   *rote* stringed instrument
       In singing ballads he took the prize outright
       flour-de-lys lily
       Therto in addition   *champioun* champion*

240

205   He was nat pale as a forpyned goost.
A fat swan loved he best of any roost.
His palfrey was as broun as is a berye.
   A FRERE ther was, a wantowne and a merye,
A lymytour, a ful solempne man.
210   In alle the ordres foure is noon that kan
So muchel of daliaunce and fair langage.
He hadde maad ful many a mariage
Of yonge wommen at his owene cost.
Unto his ordre he was a noble post.
215   Ful wel biloved and famulier was he
With frankeleyns over al in his contree,
And eek with worthy wommen of the toun;
For he hadde power of confessioun,
As seyde hymself, moore than a curat,
220   For of his ordre he was licenciat.
Ful swetely herde he confessioun,
And plesaunt was his absolucioun:
He was an esy man to yeve penaunce,
Ther as he wiste to have a good pitaunce.
225   For unto a povre ordre for to yive
Is signe that a man is wel yshryve;
For if he yaf, he dorste make avaunt,
He wiste that a man was repentaunt;
For many a man so hard is of his herte,
230   He may nat wepe, althogh hym soore smerte.
Therfore in stede of wepynge and preyeres
Men moote yeve silver to the povre freres.
His typet was ay farsed ful of knyves
And pynnes, for to yeven faire wyves.
235   And certeinly he hadde a murye note:
Wel koude he synge and pleyen on a rote;
Of yeddynges he baar outrely the pris.
His nekke whit was as the flour-de-lys;
Therto he strong was as a champioun.
240   He knew the tavernes wel in every toun

And every innkeeper and barmaid
Better than a leper or a beggar-woman*

It suited not, by virtue of his office
245 *sike* sick
honest honourable   *avaunce* be advantageous
swich poraille such poor people
vitaille victuals
over al, ther as in general, wheresoever
250 *lowely* humbly
nas was not   *vertuous* effectual

ferme payment   *graunt* licence (to beg)
haunt territory
sho shoe (worthless object)
'*In principio*' In the beginning*
255 *ferthyng* farthing, fourth part of a penny
purchas takings   *rente* payment for the licence
rage play   *right a whelp* just a puppy
love-dayes days for out-of-court settlements*
cloysterer cloister-dweller (such as a monk)
260 *cope* priest's top-garment
maister Master of Arts
double worstede double-woven woollen cloth   *semycope* short cape
That was as round as a bell from the (foundry) mould
lipsed lisped   *for his wantownesse* as a whim
265

songe sung
aryght just
sterres stars

270 *MARCHANT* merchant*
mottelee cloth woven with a parti-coloured design   *hye* in a high saddle
Flaundryssh Flemish   *bever* beaver
fetisly neatly
resons opinions   *solempnely* impressively

And everich hostiler and tappestere
Bet than a lazar or a beggestere,
For unto swich a worthy man as he
Acorded nat, as by his facultee,
245 To have with sike lazars aqueyntaunce.
It is nat honest; it may nat avaunce,
For to deelen with no swich poraille,
But al with riche and selleres of vitaille.
And over al, ther as profit sholde arise,
250 Curteis he was and lowely of servyse;
Ther nas no man nowher so vertuous.
He was the beste beggere in his hous;
252^a [And yaf a certeyn ferme for the graunt;
252^b Noon of his bretheren cam ther in his haunt;]
For thogh a wydwe hadde noght a sho,
So plesaunt was his 'In principio,'
255 Yet wolde he have a ferthyng, er he wente.
His purchas was wel bettre than his rente.
And rage he koude, as it were right a whelp.
In love-dayes ther koude he muchel help,
For ther he was nat lyk a cloysterer
260 With a thredbare cope, as is a povre scoler,
But he was lyk a maister or a pope.
Of double worstede was his semycope,
That rounded as a belle out of the presse.
Somwhat he lipsed, for his wantownesse,
265 To make his Englissh sweete upon his tonge;
And in his harpyng, whan that he hadde songe,
His eyen twynkled in his heed aryght
As doon the sterres in the frosty nyght.
This worthy lymytour was cleped Huberd.
270   A MARCHANT was ther with a forked berd,
In mottelee, and hye on horse he sat;
Upon his heed a Flaundryssh bever hat,
His bootes clasped faire and fetisly.
His resons he spak ful solempnely,

275 *Sownynge in* tending to   *wynning* profit
      He wanted the sea to be guarded at any price
      Middelburgh Dutch port   *Orewelle* Orwell, nr Ipswich*
      koude knew how to   *sheeldes* écus, units of exchange*
      bisette employed
280 *wight* creature*   *dette* debt*
      estatly dignified   *governaunce* conduct
      bargaynes lending and borrowing   *chevyssaunce* dealing*
      For sothe truly   *with alle* indeed
      noot (ne woot) do not know
285 *CLERK* university student reading for Orders*
      unto . . . ygo devoted himself to*
      leene lean
      he he himself   *undertake* promise
      holwe emaciated   *therto sobrely* gravely withal
290 *overeste* topmost   *courtepy* short cape
      geten . . . benefice not yet got himself a living*
      office secular position
      hym was levere he would rather
      clad bound
295
      fithele fiddle   *sautrie* psaltery*
      al be although   *philosophre* philosopher; also alchemist
      cofre chest*
      hente get
300
      bisily gan . . . preye earnestly did pray
      hem them   *scoleye* study in the university Schools
      cure care   *heede* notice
      Noght o not one
305 *in forme and reverence* in due form and with respect
      quyk pregnant   *hy sentence* elevated content
      Sownynge in tending to

      SERGEANT OF THE LAWE lawyer for the Crown*   *war* shrewd
310 *Parvys* the porch of St Paul's Cathedral*

275   Sownynge alwey th'encrees of his wynnyng.
       He wolde the see were kept for any thyng
       Bitwixe Middelburgh and Orewelle.
       Wel koude he in eschaunge sheeldes selle.
       This worthy man ful wel his wit bisette:
280   Ther wiste no wight that he was in dette,
       So estatly was he of his governaunce
       With his bargaynes and with his chevyssaunce.
       For sothe he was a worthy man with alle,
       But, sooth to seyn, I noot how men hym calle.

285   A CLERK ther was of Oxenford also,
       That unto logyk hadde longe ygo.
       As leene was his hors as is a rake,
       And he nas nat right fat, I undertake,
       But looked holwe, and therto sobrely.
290   Ful thredbare was his overeste courtepy,
       For he hadde geten hym yet no benefice,
       Ne was so worldly for to have office.
       For hym was levere have at his beddes heed
       Twenty bookes, clad in blak or reed,
295   Of Aristotle and his philosophie
       Than robes riche, or fithele, or gay sautrie.
       But al be that he was a philosophre,
       Yet hadde he but litel gold in cofre;
       But al that he myghte of his freendes hente,
300   On bookes and on lernynge he it spente,
       And bisily gan for the soules preye
       Of hem that yaf hym wherwith to scoleye.
       Of studie took he moost cure and moost heede.
       Noght o word spak he moore than was neede,
305   And that was seyd in forme and reverence,
       And short and quyk and ful of hy sentence;
       Sownynge in moral vertu was his speche,
       And gladly wolde he lerne and gladly teche.

          A SERGEANT OF THE LAWE, war and wys,
310   That often hadde been at the Parvys,

swich so

Justice judge   *assise* (county) court of assizes

315   By open (royal) letter and with full jurisdiction

science knowledge   *renoun* reputation

fees and robes yearly grants*   *many oon* many a one

purchasour buyer of land   *noon* not one

fee symple unrestricted ownership*   *in effect* in the upshot

320   *been infect* be invalidated

nas was not

termes terms or Term books   *caas* cases   *doomes* judgements

William the Conqueror   *were falle* had happened

325   *koude endite* knew how to draft   *thyng* contract

pynche find fault*

And he knew by rote every statute in its entirety

rood rode   *hoomly* simply   *medlee* parti-coloured*

ceint belt   *barres smale* narrow stripes

330   *array* dress

FRANKELEYN franklin, country landowner*

dayesye daisy

His temperament was sanguine*

morwe morning   *sop in wyn* piece of bread in wine*

335   *delit* delightfulness   *wone* custom

Epicurus owene sone Epicurus' own son*

That who (i.e. Epicurus)   *pleyn delit* pleasure itself

verray felicitee parfit true, complete happiness

He kept a great household

340   *St Julian* patron of hospitality   *contree* part of the world

after oon of the same standard (the best)

envyned provided with wine

bake baked (in a pie)   *mete* food

plentevous plentiful

345   *snewed* snowed*

Ther was also, ful riche of excellence.
Discreet he was and of greet reverence –
He semed swich, his wordes weren so wise.
Justice he was ful often in assise,

315 By patente and by pleyn commissioun.
For his science and for his heigh renoun,
Of fees and robes hadde he many oon.
So greet a purchasour was nowher noon:
Al was fee symple to hym in effect;

320 His purchasyng myghte nat been infect.
Nowher so bisy a man as he ther nas,
And yet he semed bisier than he was.
In termes hadde he caas and doomes alle
That from the tyme of kyng William were falle.

325 Therto he koude endite and make a thyng,
Ther koude no wight pynche at his writyng;
And every statut koude he pleyn by rote.
He rood but hoomly in a medlee cote,
Girt with a ccint of silk, with barres smale;

330 Of his array telle I no lenger tale.
    A FRANKELEYN was in his compaignye.
Whit was his berd as is the dayesye;
Of his complexioun he was sangwyn.
Wel loved he by the morwe a sop in wyn;

335 To lyven in delit was evere his wone,
For he was Epicurus owene sone,
That heeld opinioun that pleyn delit
Was verray felicitee parfit.
An housholdere, and that a greet, was he;

340 Seint Julian he was in his contree.
His breed, his ale, was alweys after oon;
A bettre envyned man was nowher noon.
Withoute bake mete was nevere his hous,
Of fissh and flessh, and that so plentevous

345 It snewed in his hous of mete and drynke;
Of alle deyntees that men koude thynke,

After the sondry according to the varying

partrich partridge   *muwe* pen, cage
350   *breem* bream   *luce* pike   *stuwe* fish-pond
Wo unhappy   *but if* unless   *his* ?the cook's
Poynaunt piquant   *geere* gear, utensils
table dormant standing table*

355   He presided at sessions of the county court*
knight of the shire MP for the county*
anlaas dagger   *gipser* purse*
Heeng hung   *morne* morning
shirreve sheriff   *contour* auditor of the shire*
360   *vavasour* feudal landholder (vassal's vassal)
HABERDASSHERE retailer of hats etc.
WEBBE weaver   *DYERE* dyer   *TAPYCER* tapestry-weaver*
o one   *lyveree* distinctive attire, here of a guild
solempne dignified   *greet* important*
365   *hir* their   *geere* gear, equipment   *apiked* picked out, trimmed
chaped mounted
wroght made
everydeel in every part
ech each   *burgeys* burgess, citizen
370   *yeldehalle* guildhall*   *deys* dais, platform
Everich each   *kan* knows
shaply suitable   *alderman* alderman, civic officer
catel property   *rente* income
eek also   *wolde* would be willing   *assente* testify
375   *elles* otherwise   *were* would be
ycleped addressed as
goon go   *vigilies* the vigils of feast days   *al before* in front of everyone
roialliche ybore royally carried*
COOK   *nones* nonce, occasion
380   *marybones* marrowbones
poudre-marchant spice-powder   *tart* sharp   *galyngale* a sweet spice*
knowe assess*

After the sondry sesons of the yeer,
So chaunged he his mete and his soper.
Ful many a fat partrich hadde he in muwe,
350 And many a breem and many a luce in stuwe.
Wo was his cook but if his sauce were
Poynaunt and sharp, and redy al his geere.
His table dormant in his halle alway
Stood redy covered al the longe day.
355 At sessiouns ther was he lord and sire;
Ful ofte tyme he was knyght of the shire.
An anlaas and a gipser al of silk
Heeng at his girdel, whit as morne milk.
A shirreve hadde he been, and a contour.
360 Was nowher swich a worthy vavasour.

AN HABERDASSHERE and a CARPENTER,
A WEBBE, a DYERE, and a TAPYCER —
And they were clothed alle in o lyveree
Of a solempne and a greet fraternitee.
365 Ful fressh and newe hir geere apiked was;
Hir knyves were chaped noght with bras
But al with silver, wroght ful clene and weel,
Hire girdles and hir pouches everydeel.
Wel semed ech of hem a fair burgeys
370 To sitten in a yeldehalle on a deys.
Everich, for the wisdom that he kan,
Was shaply for to been an alderman.
For catel hadde they ynogh and rente,
And eek hir wyves wolde it wel assente;
375 And elles certeyn were they to blame.
It is ful fair to been ycleped 'madame',
And goon to vigilies al bifore,
And have a mantel roialliche ybore.

A COOK they hadde with hem for the nones
380 To boille the chiknes with the marybones,
And poudre-marchant tart and galyngale.
Wel koude he knowe a draughte of Londoun ale.

koude knew how to   sethe seethe, boil
mortreux stews
385   thoughte me seemed to me
shyne shin   mormal ulcer*
blankmanger a thick chicken mousse   with equal to
SHIPMAN sailor*   wonynge . . . weste dwelling far to the west
woot know   Dertemouthe Dartmouth, Devon
390   rouncy carthorse   kouthe knew how
faldyng coarse woollen cloth
laas cord, lanyard

hewe hue
395   felawe companion
ydrawe carried as cargo; also drawn off, removed
From Bordeaux-way while the merchant slept*
nyce scrupulous   keep notice
hyer hond upper hand, victory
400   hem them, the losers*
craft skill   rekene reckon
stremes currents   hym bisides near at hand
herberwe harbourage   moone lunar position   lodemenage navigation*
There was no one like him from Hull to Cartagena*
405   wys to undertake prudent in undertakings

Gootlond Gotland, a Baltic island   Fynystere Cape Finisterre, Spain
cryke creek   Britaigne Brittany
410   barge trading sailing vessel   Maudelayne Magdalen*
DOCTOUR OF PHISIK physician*

To speke if we speak
grounded instructed   astronomye astrology
415   kepte watched   deel amount (of time)
In houres at the astronomical hours   magyk natureel science*
He knew well how to find the Ascendant in favourable position*
ymages talismanic figures*

He koude rooste, and sethe, and broille, and frye,
Maken mortreux, and wel bake a pye.
385 But greet harm was it, as it thoughte me,
That on his shyne a mormal hadde he.
For blankmanger, that made he with the beste.

A SHIPMAN was ther, wonynge fer by weste;
For aught I woot, he was of Dertemouthe.
390 He rood upon a rouncy, as he kouthe,
In a gowne of faldyng to the knee.
A daggere hangynge on a laas hadde he
Aboute his nekke, under his arm adoun.
The hoote somer hadde maad his hewe al broun;
395 And certeinly he was a good felawe.
Ful many a draughte of wyn had he ydrawe
Fro Burdeux-ward, whil that the chapman sleep.
Of nyce conscience took he no keep.
If that he faught and hadde the hyer hond,
400 By water he sente hem hoom to every lond.
But of his craft to rekene wel his tydes,
His stremes, and his daungers hym bisides,
His herberwe, and his moone, his lodemenage,
Ther nas noon swich from Hulle to Cartage.
405 Hardy he was and wys to undertake;
With many a tempest hadde his berd been shake.
He knew alle the havenes, as they were,
Fro Gootlond to the cape of Fynystere,
And every cryke in Britaigne and in Spayne.
410 His barge ycleped was the Maudelayne.

With us ther was a DOCTOUR OF PHISIK;
In al this world ne was ther noon hym lik,
To speke of phisik and of surgerye,
For he was grounded in astronomye.
415 He kepte his pacient a ful greet deel
In houres by his magyk natureel.
Wel koude he fortunen the ascendent
Of his ymages for his pacient.

420 *Were it* whichever of (the four elemental qualities)
     humour a bodily fluid*
     verray true *parfit* complete *praktisour* practitioner
     The cause once diagnosed, and the source of his disease,
     He at once gave the sick man his remedy
425
     drogges drugs *letuaries* electuaries, medical syrups
     hem i.e. doctor and apothecary *wynne* gain*
     newe to bigynne newly begun
     Esculapius the legendary father of medicine*
430 *Deyscorides* . . . *Rufus* ancient Greek authorities*
     Ypocras Hippocrates *Haly* a Persian *Galyen* Galen*
     Serapion, Razis Arab writers *Avycen* Avicenna*
     Averrois Averroes *Damascien, Constantyn*
     Bernard . . . *Gatesden* . . . *Gilbertyn* three recent British authorities*
435 *mesurable* moderate

     sangwyn red *pers* blue
440 *taffata, sendal* kinds of silk
     but esy of dispence slow to spend money
     that what *wan* gained *pestilence* the plague*
     For since *cordial* medicine for the heart*
     special particular
445 *WIF* woman *OF biside BATHE* from near Bath*
     Except that she was a bit deaf, which was a pity
     swich an haunt such a practice, skill
     She surpassed them [weavers] of Ypres and Ghent*

450 Who should go up at the Offertory* before her
     ther dide any did so *wrooth* angry
     charitee loving-kindness, Christian love
     Her linen head-coverings (*coverchiefs**) were very finely woven
     dorste swere dare swear *weyeden* weighed

He knew the cause of everich maladye,
420 Were it of hoot, or coold, or moyste, or drye,
And where they engendred, and of what humour.
He was a verray, parfit praktisour:
The cause yknowe, and of his harm the roote,
Anon he yaf the sike man his boote.
425 Ful redy hadde he his apothecaries
To sende hym drogges and his letuaries,
For ech of hem made oother for to wynne –
Hir frendshipe nas nat newe to bigynne.
Wel knew he the olde Esculapius,
430 And Deyscorides, and eek Rufus,
Olde Ypocras, Haly, and Galyen,
Serapion, Razis, and Avycen,
Averrois, Damascien, and Constantyn,
Bernard, and Gatesden, and Gilbertyn.
435 Of his diete mesurable was he,
For it was of no superfluitee,
But of greet norissyng and digestible.
His studie was but litel on the Bible.
In sangwyn and in pers he clad was al,
440 Lyned with taffata and with sendal.
And yet he was but esy of dispence;
He kepte that he wan in pestilence.
For gold in phisik is a cordial,
Therefore he lovede gold in special.
    A good WIF was ther OF biside BATHE,
But she was somdel deef, and that was scathe.
Of clooth-makyng she hadde swich an haunt
She passed hem of Ypres and of Gaunt.
In al the parisshe wif ne was ther noon
450 That to the offrynge bifore hire sholde goon;
And if ther dide, certeyn so wrooth was she
That she was out of alle charitee.
Hir coverchiefs ful fyne weren of ground;
I dorste swere they weyeden ten pound

455   *weren* were
       hosen stockings
       streite yteyd tightly laced   *moyste* supple

460   *at chirche dore* in front of the door of the church*
       Withouten not counting
       But there is no need to speak of that just now
       thries thrice*
       passed crossed   *straunge strem* foreign sea or river
465   *Boloigne* Boulogne-sur-Mer, a shrine of the Virgin*
       In Galicia at Santiago and at Cologne*
       She knew a lot about wandering along (or off) the road
       Gat-tothed with teeth widely spaced*   *soothly* truly
       amblere an ambling horse   *esily* comfortably
470   *Ywympled wel* with a large wimple
       As broad as a buckler or a shield
       foot-mantel over-skirt   *large* loose (i.e. the skirt)
       spores spurs*
       carpe talk
475   *of love* for love-sickness*   *per chaunce* by chance
       the olde daunce the whole art, the ins and outs*

       povre PERSOUN poor parson   *TOUN* village

480

       parisshens parishioners
       Benygne gracious   *wonder* wonderfully

485   *swich* such   *ypreved* proven   *ofte sithes* often times
       He was very loath to excommunicate for non-payment of tithes*
       yeven give   *out of doute* in fact

       offryng money given at the Offertory of the Mass   *substaunce* stipend
490

455 That on a Sonday weren upon hir heed.
Hir hosen weren of fyn scarlet reed,
Ful streite yteyd, and shoes ful moyste and newe.
Boold was hir face, and fair, and reed of hewe.
She was a worthy womman al hir lyve:
460 Housbondes at chirche dore she hadde fyve,
Withouten oother compaignye in youthe –
But thereof nedeth nat to speke as nowthe.
And thries hadde she been at Jerusalem;
She hadde passed many a straunge strem;
465 At Rome she hadde been, and at Boloigne,
In Galice at Seint-Jame, and at Coloigne.
She koude muchel of wandrynge by the weye.
Gat-tothed was she, soothly for to seye.
Upon an amblere esily she sat,
470 Ywympled wel, and on hir heed an hat
As brood as is a bokeler or a targe;
A foot-mantel aboute hir hipes large,
And on hir feet a paire of spores sharpe.
In felaweshipe wel koude she laughe and carpe.
475 Of remedies of love she knew per chaunce,
For she koude of that art the olde daunce.

    A good man was ther of religioun,
And was a povre PERSOUN OF A TOUN,
But riche he was of hooly thoght and werk.
480 He was also a lerned man, a clerk,
That Cristes gospel trewely wolde preche;
His parisshens devoutly wolde he teche.
Benygne he was, and wonder diligent,
And in adversitee ful pacient,
485 And swich he was ypreved ofte sithes.
Ful looth were hym to cursen for his tithes,
But rather wolde he yeven, out of doute,
Unto his povre parisshens aboute
Of his offryng and eek of his substaunce.
490 He koude in litel thyng have suffisaunce.

asonder apart
lefte neglected
meschief misfortune
ferreste furthest   *muche and lite* great and small
495

tho those

500   *iren* iron*
foul corrupt
lewed untaught, lay
take keep pay attention
shiten covered in excrement
505

He did not rent out his living
Nor left his sheep stuck in the mire (of sin)
Seinte Poules St Paul's Cathedral, London
510   To get himself a chantry for souls*
bretherhed guild   *withholde* retained as chaplain
kepte watched   *folde* sheepfold
myscarie come to destruction*
mercenarie hireling
515

despitous contemptuous
daungerous ne digne disdainful nor haughty
discreet courteous
fairnesse attraction
520

But unless
lough estat low position
snybben rebuke   *for the nonys* therefore

525   *waited after* expected, looked for
spiced over-scrupulous

Wyd was his parisshe, and houses fer asonder,
But he ne lefte nat, for reyn ne thonder,
In siknesse nor in meschief to visite
The ferreste in his parisshe, muche and lite,
495 Upon his feet, and in his hand a staf.
This noble ensample to his sheep he yaf,
That first he wroghte, and afterward he taughte.
Out of the gospel he tho wordes caughte,
And this figure he added eek therto,
500 That if gold ruste, what shal iren do?
For if a preest be foul, on whom we truste,
No wonder is a lewed man to ruste;
And shame it is, if a preest take keep,
A shiten shepherde and a clene sheep.
505 Wel oghte a preest ensample for to yive,
By his clennesse, how that his sheep sholde lyve.
He sette nat his benefice to hyre
And leet his sheep encombred in the myre
And ran to Londoun unto Seinte Poules
510 To seken hym a chaunterie for soules,
Or with a bretherhed to been withholde;
But dwelte at hoom, and kepte wel his folde,
So that the wolf ne made it nat myscarie;
He was a shepherde and noght a mercenarie.
515 And though he hooly were and vertuous,
He was to synful men nat despitous,
Ne of his speche daungerous ne digne,
But in his techyng discreet and benygne.
To drawen folk to hevene by fairnesse,
520 By good ensample, this was his bisynesse.
But it were any persone obstinat,
What so he were, of heigh or lough estat,
Hym wolde he snybben sharply for the nonys.
A bettre preest I trowe that nowher noon ys.
525 He waited after no pompe and reverence,
Ne maked him a spiced conscience,

But the teaching of Christ and of . . .

*PLOWMAN**

530 Who had pulled many a cart-load of dung
     swynkere worker
     pees peace *charitee* love
     hoole whole*
     thogh . . . smerte whether it pleased or pained him
535 And then his neighbour just as himself
     dyke and delve make ditches and dig
     wight creature
     hire payment

540 *propre swynk* own labour *catel* possessions*
     tabard short sleeveless outer garment *mere* mare
     REVE steward
     SOMNOUR summoner (to the church court)
     MAUNCIPLE buyer of provisions *namo* no more
545 *MILLERE** *carl* churl, fellow *for the nones* indeed

     proved was shown *over al* everywhere
     have win *ram* ram (the prize)
     short-sholdred thick-necked *knarre* knot (in wood)
550 *nolde heve of harre* would not heave off hinge
     a rennyng one single charge *heed* head
     berd beard *sowe* sow

     Upon the cop right on top
555 *werte* wart *toft of herys* tuft of hairs
     sowes erys sow's ears
     nosethirles nostrils
     bar bore
     greet big *forneys* oven furnace
560 *janglere* talker *goliardeys* (ribald) joker*
     harlotries dirty jokes
     stelen steal *tollen* take toll *thries* thrice

But Cristes loore and his apostles twelve
He taughte; but first he folwed it hymselve.
    With hym ther was a PLOWMAN, was his brother,
530 That hadde ylad of dong ful many a fother;
A trewe swynkere and a good was he,
Lyvynge in pees and parfit charitee.
God loved he best with al his hoole herte
At alle tymes, thogh him gamed or smerte,
535 And thanne his neighebor right as hymselve.
He wolde thresshe, and therto dyke and delve,
For Cristes sake, for every povre wight,
Withouten hire, if it lay in his myght.
His tithes payde he ful faire and wel,
540 Bothe of his propre swynk and his catel.
In a tabard he rood upon a mere.
    Ther was also a REVE, and a MILLERE,
A SOMNOUR, and a PARDONER also,
A MAUNCIPLE, and myself – ther were namo.
545   The MILLERE was a stout carl for the noncs;
Ful byg he was of brawn, and eek of bones.
That proved wel, for over al ther he cam,
At wrastlynge he wolde have alwey the ram.
He was short-sholdred, brood, a thikke knarre;
550 Ther was no dore that he nolde heve of harre,
Or breke it at a rennyng with his heed.
His berd as any sowe or fox was reed,
And therto brood, as though it were a spade.
Upon the cop right of his nose he hade
555 A werte, and theron stood a toft of herys,
Reed as the brustles of a sowes erys;
His nosethirles blake were and wyde.
A swerd and a bokeler bar he by his syde.
His mouth as greet was as a greet forneys.
560 He was a janglere and a goliardeys,
And that was moost of synne and harlotries.
Wel koude he stelen corn and tollen thries;

thombe of gold golden thumb (sign of honesty)   *pardee* by God

565   *sowne* sound
therwithal he broghte with it he accompanied
gentil noble   *MAUNCIPLE* purchasing agent*   *temple* Inn of Court*
Of which from whom   *achatours* buyers
byynge buying   *vitaille* victuals, provisions
570   *taille* tally, credit
In any case he was so watchful in his buying
ay biforn always ahead   *staat* position

That such an uneducated man's brain should beat
575   *heep* heap
maistres employers   *mo than thries* more than thrice
curious minutely informed
duszeyne dozen
stywardes stewards   *rente* income
580

propre good his own property
detteless without debt   *but* unless   *wood* mad
Or live as frugally as it might please him to wish
al a shire a whole county
585   *caas* situation
sette hir aller cappe made fools of them all*
REVE reeve, estate manager   *sclendre* thin
ny close
His hair was cropped all round at the level of his ears
590   *dokked* cut short   *biforn* in front

Ylyk like   *ysene* to be seen
He knew how to take care of a granary and a corn-bin
auditour auditor   *on him wynne* get the better of him
595   *wiste* knew
yeldynge yield
neet cattle
His pigs, his horses, his livestock and his poultry

And yet he hadde a thombe of gold, pardee.
A whit cote and a blew hood wered he.
565   A baggepipe wel koude he blowe and sowne,
And therwithal he broghte us out of towne.
     A gentil MAUNCIPLE was ther of a temple,
Of which achatours myghte take exemple
For to be wise in byynge of vitaille;
570   For wheither that he payde or took by taille,
Algate he wayted so in his achaat
That he was ay biforn and in good staat.
Now is nat that of God a ful fair grace
That swich a lewed mannes wit shal pace
575   The wisdom of an heep of lerned men?
Of maistres hadde he mo than thries ten,
That weren of lawe expert and curious,
Of which ther were a duszeyne in that hous
Worthy to been stywardes of rente and lond
580   Of any lord that is in Engelond,
To make hym lyve by his propre good
In honour dettelees (but if he were wood),
Or lyve as scarsly as hym list desire;
And able for to helpen al a shire
585   In any caas that myghte falle or happe.
And yet this Manciple sette hir aller cappe.
     The REVE was a sclendre colerik man.
His berd was shave as ny as ever he kan;
His heer was by his erys ful round yshorn;
590   His top was dokked lyk a preest biforn.
Ful longe were his legges and ful lene,
Ylyk a staf; ther was no calf ysene.
Wel koude he kepe a gerner and a bynne;
Ther was noon auditour koude on him wynne.
595   Wel wiste he by the droghte and by the reyn
The yeldynge of his seed and of his greyn.
His lordes sheep, his neet, his dayerye,
His swyn, his hors, his stoor, and his pultrye

600   *covenant* contract
       Syn since
       arrerage arrears
       There was no farm-manager, herdsman or other servant
       Whose trickery and treachery he did not know
605   *adrad* terrified   *the deeth* the plague
       wonyng dwelling

       koude knew how to   *purchace* buy land
       riche richly   *astored* stocked   *pryvely* secretly
610

       To give and lend him what was his (the lord's) own property*
       cote and hood dress due to a servant
       myster craft (French *métier*)
       wrighte wood-worker
615   *stot* horse
       pomely dapple   *highte* was called
       surcote of pers blue overcoat

       Northfolk Norfolk
620   *clepen* call   *Baldeswelle* Bawdeswell*
       His robe was tucked up about him as a friar's is
       hyndreste hindmost*   *route* party
       SOMONOUR summoner to a church court*
       fyr-reed fire-red   *cherubynnes* cherub's*
625   *saucefleem* pimpled*   *eyen narwe* narrowed eyes
       sparwe sparrow (traditionally lecherous)
       scalled scaly   *piled* scanty*

       lytarge lead monoxide   *brymstoon* sulphur
630   *Boras* borax   *ceruce* white lead   *tartre* tartar
       oynement ointment
       whelkes pustules
       knobbes lumps
       garleek garlic   *lekes* leeks*

Was hoolly in this Reves governynge,
600   And by his covenant yaf the rekenynge,
Syn that his lord was twenty yeer of age.
Ther koude no man brynge hym in arrerage.
Ther nas baillif, ne hierde, nor oother hyne,
That he ne knew his sleighte and his covyne;
605   They were adrad of hym as of the deeth.
His wonyng was ful faire upon an heeth;
With grene trees yshadwed was his place.
He koude bettre than his lord purchace.
Ful riche he was astored pryvely.
610   His lord wel koude he plesen subtilly,
To yeve and lene hym of his owene good,
And have a thank, and yet a cote and hood.
In youthe he hadde lerned a good myster:
He was a wel good wrighte, a carpenter.
615   This Reve sat upon a ful good stot
That was al pomely grey and highte Scot.
A long surcote of pers upon he hade,
And by his syde he baar a rusty blade.
Of Northfolk was this Reve of which I telle,
620   Biside a toun men clepen Baldeswelle.
Tukked he was as is a frere aboute,
And evere he rood the hyndreste of oure route.

   A SOMONOUR was ther with us in that place,
That hadde a fyr-reed cherubynnes face,
625   For saucefleem he was, with eyen narwe.
As hoot he was and lecherous as a sparwe,
With scalled browes blake and piled berd.
Of his visage children were aferd.
Ther nas quyk-silver, lytarge, ne brymstoon,
630   Boras, ceruce, ne oille of tartre noon,
Ne oynement that wolde clense and byte,
That hym myghte helpen of his whelkes white,
Nor of the knobbes sittynge on his chekes.
Wel loved he garleek, oynons, and eek lekes,

635

crie shout   wood mad

termes technical terms
640   decree decretal, text of canon law

clepen 'Watte' call 'Wat' (Walt, Walter)
grope examine further
645

He would always shout 'Questio quid iuris' ('I question which part of
the law [applies here]')· gentil generous   harlot rascal

suffre allow
650

atte fulle at the end (of the year)
He also knew how to pluck a finch quietly*
owher anywhere

655   ercedekenes curs archdeacon's excommunication*
But if unless

lyed lied*
660   him drede be afraid
For excommunication will kill just as absolution saves
And let him also beware of a writ of imprisonment*
In his jurisdiction he had at his own pleasure
girles the young of both sexes
665   conseil secrets   al hir reed adviser to them all
gerland garland
ale-stake sign for an ale-house*
bokeleer buckler   cake loaf*
gentil noble   PARDONER seller of indulgences*
670   Rouncivale Charing Cross hospital*   compeer mate

635 And for to drynken strong wyn, reed as blood;
     Thanne wolde he speke and crie as he were wood.
     And whan that he wel dronken hadde the wyn,
     Thanne wolde he speke no word but Latyn.
     A fewe termes hadde he, two or thre,
640 That he had lerned out of som decree –
     No wonder is, he herde it al the day;
     And eek ye knowen wel how that a jay
     Kan clepen 'Watte' as wel as kan the pope.
     But whoso koude in oother thyng hym grope,
645 Thanne hadde he spent al his philosophie;
     Ay 'Questio quid iuris' wolde he crie.
     He was a gentil harlot and a kynde;
     A bettre felawe sholde men noght fynde.
     He wolde suffre for a quart of wyn
650 A good felawe to have his concubyn
     A twelf month, and excuse hym atte fulle;
     Ful prively a fynch eek koude he pulle.
     And if he foond owher a good fclawe,
     He wolde techen him to have noon awe
655 In swich caas of the ercedekenes curs,
     But if a mannes soule were in his purs;
     For in his purs he sholde ypunysshed be.
     'Purs is the ercedekenes helle,' seyde he.
     But wel I woot he lyed right in dede;
660 Of cursyng oghte ech gilty man him drede,
     For curs wol slee right as assoillyng savith,
     And also war hym of a Significavit.
     In daunger hadde he at his owene gise
     The yonge girles of the diocise,
665 And knew hir conseil, and was al hir reed.
     A gerland hadde he set upon his heed,
     As greet as it were for an ale-stake.
     A bokeleer hadde he maad hym of a cake.
         With hym ther rood a gentil PARDONER
670 Of Rouncivale, his freend and his compeer,

Who had come directly from the Roman Curia

loude loudly   *Com hider* . . . Come hither . . . [a song]

Accompanied him in a strong bass (voice)

trompe trumpet

675   *heer* hair   *wex* wax

smothe smoothly   *heeng* hung   *strike* hank

The (few) locks he had hung separately

And he spread them over his shoulders

by colpons oon and oon in single strands

680   *jolitee* prettiness

walet pouch

It seemed to him that he rode in the latest fashion

Dischevelee with hair unbound   *save* except for

glarynge eyen staring eyes

685   *vernycle* Veronica [medal, with Christ's face]*

lappe large pocket

Bretful brimful   *pardoun* indulgences   *hoot* hot, fresh

smal high   *goot* goat

berd beard

690   *late* recently

geldyng castrated horse   *mare* female horse

craft trade   *fro Berwyk into Ware* in all England*

male mail-bag   *pilwe-beer* pillow-case*

695   *Oure Lady veyl* Our Lady's veil

gobet of the seyl piece of the sail

wente walked ('upon the water', Matthew 14:29)

see sea   *til* until   *hym hente* took him up

croys of latoun brass cross

700

fond found

person parson   *upon lond* in the country*

Upon a in one   *gat hym* got for himself

tweye two

705   *japes* tricks

He made the parson and the people his fools

That streight was comen fro the court of Rome.
Ful loude he soong 'Com hider, love, to me!'
This Somonour bar to hym a stif burdoun;
Was nevere trompe of half so greet a soun.
675   This Pardoner hadde heer as yelow as wex,
But smothe it heeng as dooth a strike of flex;
By ounces henge his lokkes that he hadde,
And therwith he his shuldres overspradde;
But thynne it lay, by colpons oon and oon.
680   But hood, for jolitee, wered he noon,
For it was trussed up in his walet.
Hym thoughte he rood al of the newe jet;
Dischevelee, save his cappe, he rood al bare.
Swiche glarynge eyen hadde he as an hare.
685   A vernycle hadde he sowed upon his cappe.
His walet, biforn hym in his lappe,
Bretful of pardoun comen from Rome al hoot.
A voys he hadde as smal as hath a goot.
No berd hadde he, ne nevere sholde have;
690   As smothe it was as it were late shave.
I trowe he were a geldyng or a mare.
But of his craft, fro Berwyk into Ware
Ne was ther swich another pardoner.
For in his male he hadde a pilwe-beer,
695   Which that he seyde was Oure Lady veyl;
He seyde he hadde a gobet of the seyl
That Seint Peter hadde, whan that he wente
Upon the see, til Jhesu Crist hym hente.
He hadde a croys of latoun ful of stones,
700   And in a glas he hadde pigges bones.
But with thise relikes, whan that he fond
A povre person dwellynge upon lond,
Upon a day he gat hym moore moneye
Than that the person gat in monthes tweye;
705   And thus, with feyned flaterye and japes,
He made the person and the peple his apes.

trewely to tellen to tell the truth, be serious
ecclesiaste ecclesiastic*
lessoun Bible reading   *storie* gospel or saint's life*

710   But best of all he sang an Offertory*
For well he knew that when *that* song was sung
He would have to preach and well smooth his tongue
koude knew how
For that reason he sang the more merrily and loudly

715   *clause* short compass
estaat condition

highte was called   *faste* close   *Belle* Bell, an inn

720

baren us behaved   *ilke* same
alyght arrived
wol will   *viage* journey
remenaunt remainder

725

n'arette do not attribute   *vileynye* rudeness*
Thogh that I if I should
cheere behaviour
hir wordes proprely their words accurately

730   *al so* as

moot must   *reherce* repeat   *ny* closely
Everich a each   *charge* commission
However rudely and freely he (the man of 731) speak

735   *moot* must   *untrewe* untruly
feyne thyng feign things   *newe* other

o one
brode plainly

740   *woot* know
Also Plato says, whoever can read him*
moote must   *cosyn* cousin

But trewely to tellen atte laste,
He was in chirche a noble ecclesiaste.
Wel koude he rede a lessoun or a storie,
710   But alderbest he song an offertorie;
For wel he wiste, whan that song was songe,
He moste preche and wel affile his tonge
To wynne silver, as he ful wel koude;
Therefore he song the murierly and loude.

715   Now have I toold you soothly, in a clause,
Th'estaat, th'array, the nombre, and eek the cause
Why that assembled was this compaignye
In Southwerk at this gentil hostelrye
That highte the Tabard, faste by the Belle.
720   But now is tyme to yow for to telle
How that we baren us that ilke nyght,
Whan we were in that hostelrie alyght;
And after wol I telle of our viage
And al the remenaunt of oure pilgrimage.

725   But first I pray yow, of youre curteisye,
That ye n'arette it nat my vileynye,
Thogh that I pleynly speke in this mateere,
To telle yow hir wordes and hir cheere,
Ne thogh I speke hir wordes proprely.
730   For this ye knowen al so wel as I:
Whoso shal telle a tale after a man,
He moot reherce as ny as evere he kan
Everich a word, if it be in his charge,
Al speke he never so rudeliche and large,
735   Or ellis he moot telle his tale untrewe,
Or feyne thyng, or fynde wordes newe.
He may nat spare, althogh he were his brother;
He moot as wel seye o word as another.
Crist spak hymself ful brode in hooly writ,
740   And wel ye woot no vileynye is it.
Eek Plato seith, whoso kan hym rede,
The wordes moote be cosyn to the dede.

foryeve forgive
Al if   *hir degree* their social rank

745

short insufficient*
Our Host made great cheer for every one of us
soper supper   *sette* seated
vitaille victuals   *at the beste* of the best sort

750   *us leste* it pleased us
semely fit   *HOOSTE* landlord of an inn   *withalle* moreover
marchal marshal, master of ceremonies
stepe prominent, bright
burgeys burgess, citizen   *Chepe* Cheapside*

755   *ytaught* instructed (in his trade)
Not at all did he lack in manly qualities*
Eek therto and in addition
pleyen to play, start a game

760   *maad oure rekenynges* paid our bills
lordynges ladies and gentlemen

trouthe troth   *lye* lie
saugh nat have not seen

765   *Atones* at one time   *herberwe* lodging
I would dearly like to entertain you, if I knew how
bythoght struck by a thought
doon yow ese give you pleasure*
yow speede give you success

770   *blisful* blessed   *quite* give   *meede* reward
woot know   *goon by the weye* go along the road
You propose to tell tales and amuse yourselves
is noon there is no

775   *maken yow disport* devise an entertainment for you
erst first
yow liketh it pleases you   *oon* unanimous
stonden at stand by, accept

Also I prey yow to foryeve it me,
Al have I nat set folk in hir degree
745 Heere in this tale, as that they sholde stonde.
My wit is short, ye may wel understonde.
    Greet chiere made oure Hoost us everichon,
And to the soper sette he us anon.
He served us with vitaille at the beste;
750 Strong was the wyn, and wel to drynke us leste.
A semely man OURE HOOSTE was withalle
For to been a marchal in an halle.
A large man he was with eyen stepe –
A fairer burgeys was ther noon in Chepe –
755 Boold of his speche, and wys, and wel ytaught,
And of manhod hym lakkede right naught.
Eek therto he was right a myrie man;
And after soper pleyen he bigan,
And spak of myrthe amonges othere thynges,
760 Whan that we hadde maad oure rekenynges,
And seyde thus: 'Now, lordynges, trewely,
Ye been to me right welcome, hertely;
For by my trouthe, if that I shal nat lye,
I saugh nat this yeer so myrie a compaignye
765 Atones in this herberwe as is now.
Fayn wolde I doon yow myrthe, wiste I how.
And of a myrthe I am right now bythoght,
To doon yow ese, and it shall coste noght.
    'Ye goon to Caunterbury – God yow speede,
770 The blisful martir quite yow youre meede!
And wel I woot, as ye goon by the weye,
Ye shapen yow to talen and to pleye;
For trewely, confort ne myrthe is noon
To ride by the weye doumb as a stoon;
775 And therfore wol I maken yow disport,
As I seyde erst, and doon yow som confort.
And if yow liketh alle by oon assent
For to stonden at my juggement,

werken do

780

Now, by the soul of my dead father
But ye be if you are not   *yeve* give   *heed* head
Hoold up put up (in sign of agreement)
conseil decision   *for to seche* to discover

785 It did not seem to us to be worth deliberating over
moore avys further consideration
voirdit as hym leste whatever verdict he liked
quod said   *herkneth for the beste* hear the best thing to do

790 *pleyn* plain
to shorte with oure weye so to shorten our road
viage journey   *tweye* two

othere another*
795 *whilom* formerly   *han bifalle* have befallen
which that one   *bereth hym* acquits himself

sentence moral import   *solaas* comfort, pleasure
oure aller of the rest of us

800

agayn back

goodly gladly
cost expense   *gyde* guide
805 *withseye* gainsay*

vouche sauf grant
anon immediately   *mo* more
shape me get ready
810 *othes* oaths   *swore* sworn
preyden (we) prayed
do so i.e. be our guide

reportour reporter

And for to werken as I shal yow seye,
780 Tomorwe, whan ye riden by the weye,
Now, by my fader soule that is deed,
But ye be myrie, I wol yeve yow myn heed!
Hoold up youre hondes, withouten moore speche.'
   Oure conseil was nat longe for to seche.
785 Us thoughte it was noght worth to make it wys,
And graunted hym withouten moore avys,
And bad him seye his voirdit as hym leste.
'Lordynges,' quod he, 'now herkneth for the beste;
But taak it nought, I prey yow, in desdeyn.
790 This is the poynt, to speken short and pleyn,
That ech of yow, to shorte with oure weye,
In this viage shal telle tales tweye
To Caunterbury-ward, I mene it so,
And homward he shal tellen othere two,
795 Of aventures that whilom han bifalle.
And which of yow that bereth hym best of alle –
That is to seyn, that telleth in this caas
Tales of best sentence and moost solaas –
Shal have a soper at oure aller cost
800 Heere in this place, sittynge by this post,
Whan that we come agayn fro Caunterbury.
And for to make yow the moore mury,
I wol myselven goodly with yow ryde,
Right at myn owene cost, and be youre gyde;
805 And whoso wole my juggement withseye
Shal paye al that we spenden by the weye.
And if ye vouche sauf that it be so,
Tel me anon, withouten wordes mo,
And I wol erly shape me therfore.'
810   This thyng was graunted, and oure othes swore
With ful glad herte, and preyden hym also
That he wolde vouche sauf for to do so,
And that he wolde been oure governour,
And of oure tales juge and reportour,

815   *sette* arrange
       reuled been be ruled   *devys* pleasure
       heigh and lough great things and small   *oon assent* unanimously

       therupon at that   *fet* fetched   *anon* straightaway
820   *echon* each one

       Amorwe in the morning
       oure aller cok the cock to all of us*

825   *riden* rode   *paas* walking pace
       Wateryng . . . at the second milestone on the Old Kent Road*
       bigan . . . *areste* pulled up
       leste please
       You know your agreement, and I remind you of it
830   If evening chorus and morning chorus agree*

       As I hope never to drink anything but wine or ale

835   *draweth cut* draw lots*   *ferrer twynne* depart further (from the inn)

       accord decision
       quod said
840   *lat be* leave aside   *shamefastnesse* modesty
       Stop your musing; reach out your hand, every man
       Anon soon   *wight* man

       Whether it was by chance or luck or fate
845   *sothe* truth   *cut* short straw   *fil* fell

       resoun just
       foreward agreement   *composicioun* agreement
       han herd have heard   *mo* further
850

815   And sette a soper at a certeyn pris,
       And we wol reuled been at his devys
       In heigh and lough; and thus by oon assent
       We been acorded to his juggement.
       And therupon the wyn was fet anon;
820   We dronken, and to reste wente echon,
       Withouten any lenger taryynge.
         · Amorwe, whan that day bigan to sprynge,
       Up roos oure Hoost, and was oure aller cok,
       And gadrede us togidre alle in a flok,
825   And forth we riden a litel moore than paas
       Unto the Wateryng of Seint Thomas;
       And there oure Hoost bigan his hors areste
       And seyde, 'Lordynges, herkneth, if yow leste.
       Ye woot youre foreward, and I it yow recorde.
830   If even-song and morwe-song accorde,
       Lat se now who shal telle the firste tale.
       As evere mote I drynke wyn or ale,
       Whoso be rebel to my juggement
       Shal paye for al that by the wey is spent.
835   Now draweth cut, er that we ferrer twynne;
       He which that hath the shorteste shal bigynne.
       Sire Knyght,' quod he, 'my mayster and my lord,
       Now draweth cut, for that is myn accord.
       Cometh neer,' quod he, 'my lady Prioresse.
840   And ye, sire Clerk, lat be youre shamefastnesse,
       Ne studieth noght; ley hond to, every man!'
       Anon to drawen every wight bigan,
       And shortly for to tellen as it was,
       Were it by aventure, or sort, or cas,
845   The sothe is this: the cut fil to the Knyght,
       Of which ful blithe and glad was every wyght,
       And telle he moste his tale, as was resoun,
       By foreward and by composicioun,
       As ye han herd; what nedeth wordes mo?
850   And whan this goode man saugh that it was so,

As he that as a man who

Syn since
a in
855   *herkneth* hearken to

cheere expression

As he that wys was and obedient
To kepe his foreward by his free assent,
He seyde, 'Syn I shal bigynne the game,
What, welcome be the cut, a Goddes name!
855 Now lat us ryde, and herkneth what I seye.'
And with that word we ryden forth oure weye,
And he bigan with right a myrie cheere
His tale anon, and seyde as ye may heere.

Iamque domos etc And now to his native land, after fierce battles with
the people of Scythia, in his triumphal chariot (Theseus . . .)
An MS gloss, quoted from the *Thebaid* of Statius.
Whilom once   *olde stories*
860   *duc* duke*   *highte* was called

865

regne of Femenye land of the Amazons*
ycleped called
Ypolita Hippolita

870   *solempnytee* ceremony
eek also   *suster* sister

Lete I I leave
hoost army
875   *certes* certainly   *nere* were not   *heere* hear

chivalrye mounted knights (or knightly deeds)
for the nones on the occasion
880   Between Athens and the Amazons

THE KNIGHT'S TALE

Iamque domos patrias, Scithice post aspera gentis
Prelia, laurigero, &c.

    Whilom, as olde stories tellen us,
860 Ther was a duc that highte Theseus;
Of Atthenes he was lord and governour,
And in his tyme swich a conquerour
That gretter was ther noon under the sonne.
Ful many a riche contree hadde he wonne;
865 What with his wysdom and his chivalrie,
He conquered al the regne of Femenye,
That whilom was ycleped Scithia,
And weddede the queene Ypolita,
And broghte hire hoom with hym in his contree
870 With muchel glorie and greet solempnytee,
And eek hir yonge suster Emelye.
And thus with victorie and with melodye
Lete I this noble duc to Atthenes ryde,
And al his hoost in armes hym bisyde.
875   And certes, if it nere to long to heere,
I wolde have toold yow fully the manere
How wonnen was the regne of Femenye
By Theseus and by his chivalrye;
And of the grete bataille for the nones
880 Bitwixen Atthenes and Amazones;

asseged besieged
hardy brave
feste festivities
tempest storm*

885   But all that matter I must now forbear (to treat)
woot knows   *ere* sow*
wayke weak

Also, I do not wish to hold up anyone in this company
890   *aboute* in turn
lat se let's see
ther where   *lefte* left off   *ayeyn* again

the toun the town of Athens
895   *wele* prosperity   *mooste* greatest
was war noticed
heighe weye highway
tweye and tweye two by two
Ech after oother each of them after the other
900   *swich a wo* such a lament
nys is not
waymentynge lamentation
nolde nevere stenten would never stop
Until they had caught hold of the reins of his bridle
905   *folk been ye* people might you be
Perturben disturb   *feste* celebration
envye envy

mysboden threatened   *offended* mistreated
910   *telleth* tell (imperative plural)

swowned swooned   *deedly cheere* deathly look
routhe a pity
915   *yiven* granted
lyven live

And how asseged was Ypolita,
The faire, hardy queene of Scithia;
And of the feste that was at hir weddynge,
And of the tempest at hir hoom-comynge;
885 But al that thyng I moot as now forbere.
I have, God woot, a large feeld to ere,
And wayke been the oxen in my plough.
The remenant of the tale is long ynough.
I wol nat letten eek noon of this route;
890 Lat every felawe telle his tale aboute,
And lat se now who shal the soper wynne;
And ther I lefte, I wol ayeyn bigynne.

     This duc, of whom I make mencioun,
Whan he was come almoost unto the toun,
895 In al his wele and in his mooste pride,
He was war, as he caste his eye aside,
Where that ther kneled in the heighe weye
A compaignye of ladyes, tweye and tweye,
Ech after oother clad in clothes blake;
900 But swich a cry and swich a wo they make
That in this world nys creature lyvynge
That herde swich another waymentynge;
And of this cry they nolde nevere stenten
Til they the reynes of his brydel henten.
905   'What folk been ye, that at myn hom-comynge
Perturben so my feste with criynge?'
Quod Theseus. 'Have ye so greet envye
Of myn honour, that thus compleyne and crye?
Or who hath yow mysboden or offended?
910 And telleth me if it may been amended,
And why that ye been clothed thus in blak.'
     The eldeste lady of hem alle spak,
Whan she hadde swowned with a deedly cheere,
That it was routhe for to seen and heere;
915 She seyde, 'Lord, to whom Fortune hath yiven
Victorie, and as a conqueror to lyven,

Nat greveth us grieves us not at all
biseken biseech

920   *thurgh* by reason of   *gentillesse* nobility
lat thou falle will you please allow to fall

caytyves lowest of the low
925   *Fortune* the Roman goddess*   *false* treacherous
estaat condition   *weel* well
certes indeed   *abyden* wait   *presence* arrival
Clemence   Clemency*
fourtenyght fortnight
930   *sith* since   *myght* power
wrecche wretch
whilom once   *Cappaneus* Capaneus, one of the Seven Against Thebes*
starf died
array state
935

seege siege
yet even   *Creon**   *weylaway* alas

940
despit spite
vileynye dishonour
been yslawe had been slain
ydrawe dragged
945   *suffren hem* allow them   *assent* agreement
yburyed nor ybrent buried nor cremated
But makes dogs eat them, in contempt
respit respite, delay
fillen gruf prostrated themselves   *pitously* pitiably
950
sorwe sorrow*
This noble duke leapt down from his war-horse

Nat greveth us youre glorie and youre honour,
But we biseken mercy and socour.
Have mercy on oure wo and oure distresse!
920 Som drope of pitee, thurgh thy gentillesse,
Upon us wrecched wommen lat thou falle,
For, certes, lord, ther is noon of us alle
That she ne hath been a duchesse or a queene.
Now be we caytyves, as it is wel seene,
925 Thanked be Fortune and hire false wheel,
That noon estaat assureth to be weel.
And certes, lord, to abyden youre presence,
Heere in this temple of the goddesse Clemence
We han ben waitynge al this fourtenyght.
930 Now help us, lord, sith it is in thy myght.
    'I, wrecche, which that wepe and wayle thus,
Was whilom wyf to kyng Cappaneus,
That starf at Thebes – cursed be that day! –
And alle we that been in this array
935 And maken al this lamentacioun,
We losten alle oure housbondes at that toun,
Whil that the seege theraboute lay.
And yet now the olde Creon – weylaway! –
That lord is now of Thebes the citee,
940 Fulfild of ire and of iniquitee,
He, for despit and for his tirannye,
To do the dede bodyes vileynye
Of alle oure lordes whiche that been yslawe,
Hath alle the bodyes on an heep ydrawe,
945 And wol nat suffren hem, by noon assent,
Neither to been yburyed nor ybrent,
But maketh houndes ete hem in despit.'
    And with that word, withouten moore respit,
They fillen gruf and criden pitously,
950 'Have on us wrecched wommen som mercy,
And lat oure sorwe synken in thyn herte.'
    This gentil duc doun from his courser sterte

pitous pitying

955   *pitous* pitiable   *maat* downcast

hente took
in ful good entente most kindly

960   That he would so thoroughly exert his strength
hem to wreke to avenge them

of by   *yserved* dealt with
As he that as one who
965   *right* right away   *abood* delay
desplayeth displays (in declaration of war)
biside with him
neer nearer   *go* walk
ese ease   *fully* (for) even
970   *lay* slept

sheene beautiful

rit rideth, rides
975   *rede* red   *statue* figure   *targe* shield

feeldes fields
penoun pennon, personal ensign
ybete embroidered
980   *Mynotaur* Minotaur*   *wan* conquered
rit rideth, rides
flour flower
alighte alighted
thoughte planned
985

slough slew   *manly* manfully
pleyn open

With herte pitous, whan he herde hem speke.
Hym thoughte that his herte wolde breke,
955 Whan he saugh hem so pitous and so maat,
That whilom weren of so greet estaat;
And in his armes he hem alle up hente,
And hem conforteth in ful good entente,
And swoor his ooth, as he was trewe knyght,
960 He wolde doon so ferforthly his myght
Upon the tiraunt Creon hem to wreke
That al the peple of Grece sholde speke
How Creon was of Theseus yserved
As he that hadde his deeth ful wel deserved.
965 And right anoon, withouten moore abood,
His baner he desplayeth, and forth rood
To Thebes-ward, and al his hoost biside.
No neer Atthenes wolde he go ne ride,
Ne take his ese fully half a day,
970 But onward on his wey that nyght he lay,
And sente anon Ypolita the queene,
And Emelye, hir yonge suster sheene,
Unto the toun of Atthenes to dwelle,
And forth he rit; ther is namoore to telle.
975   The rede statue of Mars, with spere and targe,
So shyneth in his white baner large
That alle the feeldes glyteren up and doun;
And by his baner born is his penoun
Of gold ful riche, in which ther was ybete
980 The Mynotaur, which that he wan in Crete.
Thus rit this duc, thus rit this conquerour,
And in his hoost of chivalrie the flour,
Til that he cam to Thebes and alighte
Faire in a feeld, ther as he thoughte to fighte.
985 But shortly for to speken of this thyng,
With Creon, which that was of Thebes kyng,
He faught, and slough hym manly as a knyght
In pleyn bataille, and putte the folk to flyght;

assaut assault
990   *rente* tore   *sparre* beam

tho the gyse then the custom
But it would be much too long to describe*
995   *waymentynge* lamentation

Dooth does
1000   *entente* intention

Stille in that feeld in that same field
hym leste it pleased him
1005   *taas* heap
strepe strip   *harneys* armour   *wede* clothes
The pillagers worked hard and carefully*
disconfiture defeat
so bifil it so happened
1010   *Thurgh-girt* pierced through
liggynge by and by lying side by side
oon armes the same heraldic device
Of these two knights, one was called Arcite

1015   *quyke* alive
cote-armures heraldic over-tunic   *gere* gear
heraudes heralds   *special* particular
they that weren those who were
sustren sisters
1020   *taas* heap   *pilours* pillagers
softe gently

nolde no raunsoun would accept no ransom*

And by assault he wan the citee after,
990 And rente adoun bothe wall and sparre and rafter;
And to the ladyes he restored agayn
The bones of hir freendes that were slayn,
To doon obsequies, as was tho the gyse.
But it were al to longe for to devyse
995 The grete clamour and the waymentynge
That the ladyes made at the brennynge
Of the bodies, and the grete honour
That Theseus, the noble conquerour,
Dooth to the ladyes, whan they from hym wente;
1000 But shortly for to telle is myn entente.

Whan that this worthy duc, this Theseus,
Hath Creon slayn and wonne Thebes thus,
Stille in that feeld he took al nyght his reste,
And dide with al the contree as hym leste.
1005 To ransake in the taas of bodyes dede,
Hem for to strepe of harneys and of wede,
The pilours diden bisynesse and cure
After the bataille and disconfiture.
And so bifel that in the taas they founde,
1010 Thurgh-girt with many a grevous blody wounde,
Two yonge knyghtes liggynge by and by,
Bothe in oon armes, wroght ful richely,
Of whiche two Arcita highte that oon,
And that oother knyght highte Palamon.
1015 Nat fully quyke, ne fully dede they were,
But by hir cote-armures and by hir gere
The heraudes knewe hem best in special
As they that weren of the blood roial
Of Thebes, and of sustren two yborn.
1020 Out of the taas the pilours han hem torn,
And han hem caried softe unto the tente
Of Theseus; and he ful soone hem sente
To Atthenes, to dwellen in prisoun
Perpetuelly – he nolde no raunsoun.

1025

rit rideth, rides
laurer laurel (triumphal wreath)

Terme for the duration   *mo* more
1030   *tour* tower

quite ransom

fil happened   *ones* once   *in a morwe* on a morning
1035   *to sene* to behold
his its
with floures newe with its new flowers
For her hue vied with the colour of the rose
noot do not know
1040   *Er* before   *wone* custom
dight dressed
slogardie sluggardliness   *anyght* at night

his its   *sterte* start
1045

To describe her, she was dressed in bright colours
broyded braided
1050

sonne upriste rising of the sun
hire liste it pleased her
party divided between
subtil finely woven   *gerland* garland
1055   *aungel* angel   *hevenysshly* in a heavenly way

dongeoun tower, keep

which whom
1060   *evene joynant* immediately adjoining

1025 And whan this worthy duc hath thus ydon,
He took his hoost, and hoom he rit anon
With laurer crowned as a conquerour;
And ther he lyveth in joye and in honour
Terme of his lyf; what nedeth wordes mo?
1030 And in a tour, in angwissh and in wo,
This Palamon and his felawe Arcite
For everemoore; ther may no gold hem quite.
This passeth yeer by yeer and day by day,
Till it fil ones, in a morwe of May,
1035 That Emelye, that fairer was to sene
Than is the lylie upon his stalke grene,
And fressher than the May with floures newe –
For with the rose colour stroof hire hewe,
I noot which was the fyner of hem two –
1040 Er it were day, as was hir wone to do,
She was arisen and al redy dight,
For May wole have no slogardie anyght.
The sesoun priketh every gentil herte,
And maketh it out of his slep to sterte,
1045 And seith 'Arys, and do thyn observaunce.'
This maked Emelye have remembraunce
To doon honour to May, and for to ryse.
Yclothed was she fressh, for to devyse:
Hir yelow heer was broyded in a tresse
1050 Bihynde hir bak, a yerde long, I gesse.
And in the gardyn, at the sonne upriste,
She walketh up and doun, and as hire liste
She gadereth floures, party white and rede,
To make a subtil gerland for hire hede;
1055 And as an aungel hevenysshly she soong.
The grete tour, that was so thikke and stroong,
Which of the castel was the chief dongeoun
(Ther as the knyghtes weren in prisoun
Of which I tolde yow and tellen shal),
1060 Was evene joynant to the gardyn wal

pleyynge recreation

wone habit   *leve* leave   *gayler* jailer
1065   *romed* he paced about   *an heigh* on high
In from   *seigh* saw

shene beautiful

1070

And it so happened, by chance or accident*
1075   *thikke of* thick with
greet massive   *sparre* beam

bleynte blanched, turned pale

1080   *sterte* leapt up
eyleth ails
deedly deathly
cridestow didst thou cry   *offence* injury

1085   *noon other* not otherwise
yeven given
wikke wicked   *aspect* (planetary) aspect*
Saturne the planet and god Saturn
it sworn sworn the contrary
1090   *hevene* heavens

agayn in answer
of in
veyn ymaginacioun wrong idea
1095

thurghout through

Ther as this Emelye hadde hir pleyynge.
Bright was the sonne and cleer that morwenynge,
And Palamoun, this woful prisoner,
As was his wone, by leve of his gayler,
1065 Was risen and romed in a chambre an heigh,
In which he al the noble citee seigh,
And eek the gardyn, ful of braunches grene,
Ther as this fresshe Emelye the shene
Was in hire walk, and romed up and doun.
1070 This sorweful prisoner, this Palamoun,
Goth in the chambre romynge to and fro
And to hymself compleynynge of his wo.
That he was born, ful ofte he seyde, 'allas!'
And so bifel, by aventure or cas,
1075 That thurgh a wyndow, thikke of many a barre
Of iren greet and square as any sparre,
He cast his eye upon Emelya,
And therwithal he bleynte and cride, 'A!'
As though he stongen werc unto the herte.
1080 And with that cry Arcite anon up sterte
And seyde, 'Cosyn myn, what eyleth thee,
That art so pale and deedly on to see?
Why cridestow? Who hath thee doon offence?
For Goddes love, taak al in pacience
1085 Oure prisoun, for it may noon oother be.
Fortune hath yeven us this adversitee.
Som wikke aspect or disposicioun
Of Saturne, by som constellacioun,
Hath yeven us this, although we hadde it sworn;
1090 So stood the hevene whan that we were born.
We moste endure it; this is the short and playn.'
     This Palamon answerde and seyde agayn,
'Cosyn, for sothe, of this opinioun
Thow hast a veyn ymaginacioun.
1095 This prison caused me nat for to crye,
But I was hurt right now thurghout myn ye

bane killer

romen to roam, pace

1100

noot wher do not know whether

1105   *Yow . . . transfigure* transfigure yourself

scapen escape
shapen determined
eterne word eternal decree
1110   *lynage* lineage, family

gan espye saw

1115   *sore* painfully

sleeth kills

1120   *but* unless
So that I can at least see her
nam but deed am as good as dead
tho those
Dispitously contemptuously
1125   Do you say this seriously or in jest?
fey faith
me list ful yvele pleye it pleases me very ill to jest
gan knytte his browes tweye knitted his brow
nere would not be

1130

Ysworn ful depe very deeply sworn*   *til* to

Into myn herte, that wol my bane be.
The fairnesse of that lady that I see
Yond in the gardyn romen to and fro
1100   Is cause of al my criyng and my wo.
I noot wher she be womman or goddesse,
But Venus is it soothly, as I gesse.'
And therwithal on knees doun he fil,
And seyde, 'Venus, if it be thy wil
1105   Yow in this gardyn thus to transfigure
Bifore me, sorweful, wrecched creature,
Out of this prisoun help that we may scapen.
And if so be my destynee be shapen
By eterne word to dyen in prisoun,
1110   Of oure lynage have som compassioun,
That is so lowe ybroght by tirannye.'
And with that word Arcite gan espye
Wher as this lady romed to and fro,
And with that sighte hir beautee hurte hym so,
1115   That, if that Palamon was wounded sore,
Arcite is hurt as muche as he, or moore.
And with a sigh he seyde pitously,
'The fresshe beautee sleeth me sodeynly
Of hire that rometh in the yonder place;
1120   And but I have hir mercy and hir grace,
That I may seen hire atte leeste weye,
I nam but deed; ther nis namoore to seye.'
    This Palamon, whan he tho wordes herde,
Dispitously he looked and answerde,
1125   'Wheither seistow this in ernest or in pley?'
    'Nay,' quod Arcite, 'in ernest, by my fey!
God helpe me so, me list ful yvele pleye.'
    This Palamon gan knytte his browes tweye.
'It nere,' quod he, 'to thee no greet honour
1130   For to be fals, ne for to be traitour
To me, that am thy cosyn and thy brother
Ysworn ful depe, and ech of us til oother,

That never, though we had to die by torture
Till death shall part the two of us

1135

leeve dear
forthren further, aid

1140   *woot* know   *withseyn* deny
        artow of my conseil you are party to my secret (I have confided my
            love to you)   *out of doute* clearly

        sterve die
1145   *certes* indeed

        conseil trusted adviser

1150

        ageyn in answer

        outrely flatly
1155   *paramour* par amour, with a man's love for a woman
        Thou woost nat yet now Even now you still do not know

        affeccioun of hoolynesse religious devotion

1160   *myn aventure* what befell me

        pose posit, suppose for argument's sake
        Wostow don't you know   *sawe* saw, saying
        yeve give
1165   Love . . . *lawe**   *pan* head

        positif formally enacted (*i.e.* human)*
        degree rank of life

That nevere, for to dyen in the peyne,
Til that the deeth departe shal us tweyne,
1135   Neither of us in love to hyndre oother,
Ne in noon oother cas, my leeve brother,
But that thou sholdest trewely forthren me
In every cas, as I shal forthren thee –
This was thyn ooth, and myn also, certeyn;
1140   I woot right wel, thou darst it nat withseyn.
Thus artow of my conseil, out of doute,
And now thow woldest falsly been aboute
To love my lady, whom I love and serve,
And evere shal til that myn herte sterve.
1145   Nay, certes, false Arcite, thow shalt nat so.
I loved hire first, and tolde thee my wo
As to my conseil and my brother sworn
To forthre me, as I have toold biforn.
For which thou art ybounden as a knyght
1150   To helpen me, if it lay in thy myght,
Or elles artow fals, I dar wel seyn.'
    This Arcite ful proudly spak ageyn:
'Thow shalt,' quod he, 'be rather fals than I;
And thou art fals, I telle thee outrely,
1155   For paramour I loved hire first er thow.
What wiltow seyen? Thou woost nat yet now
Wheither she be a womman or goddesse!
Thyn is affeccioun of hoolynesse,
And myn is love as to a creature;
1160   For which I tolde thee myn aventure
As to my cosyn and my brother sworn.
I pose that thow lovedest hire biforn;
Wostow nat wel the olde clerkes sawe,
That "who shal yeve a lovere any lawe?"
1165   Love is a gretter lawe, by my pan,
Than may be yeve to any erthely man;
And therfore positif lawe and swich decree
Is broken al day for love in ech degree.

1170   A man must needs love, in spite of his intention
        fleen escape

        stonden in hir grace be in her favour
        woost knowest   *verraily* truly
1175   *dampned* condemned
        us gayneth avails us
        houndes dogs   *boon* bone*

        wrothe angry
1180   *baar* carried

        noon oother no other way
        thee list it please you   *ay* ever

1185

        aventure chance

        leyser leisure

1190

        duc duke   *highte* was called   *Perotheus* Pirithous*
        felawe comrade
        Syn since   *thilke* that   *lite* little

1195   *pleye* enjoy himself

        that oon the one
1200
        list me it pleases me   *write**

        preyere prayer

A man moot nedes love, maugree his heed;
1170 He may nat fleen it, thogh he sholde be deed,
Al be she mayde, or wydwe, or elles wyf.
And eek it is nat likly al thy lyf
To stonden in hir grace; namoore shal I;
For wel thou woost thyselven, verraily,
1175 That thou and I be dampned to prisoun
Perpetuelly; us gayneth no raunsoun.
We stryve as dide the houndes for the boon;
They foughte al day, and yet hir part was noon.
Ther cam a kyte, whil that they were so wrothe,
1180 And baar awey the boon bitwixe hem bothe.
And therfore, at the kynges court, my brother,
Ech man for hymself, ther is noon oother.
Love, if thee list, for I love and ay shal;
And soothly, leeve brother, this is al.
1185 Heere in this prisoun moote we endure,
And everich of us take his aventure.'
      Greet was the strif and long bitwix hem tweye,
If that I hadde leyser for to seye;
But to th'effect. It happed on a day,
1190 To telle it yow as shortly as I may,
A worthy duc that highte Perotheus,
That felawe was unto duc Theseus
Syn thilke day that they were children lite,
Was come to Atthenes his felawe to visite,
1195 And for to pleye as he was wont to do;
For in this world he loved no man so,
And he loved hym als tendrely agayn.
So wel they lovede, as olde bookes sayn,
That whan that oon was deed, soothly to telle,
1200 His felawe wente and soughte hym doun in helle —
But of that storie list me nat to write.
Duc Perotheus loved wel Arcite,
And hadde hym knowe at Thebes yeer by yere,
And finally at requeste and preyere

1205

gyse manner
forward agreement   *endite* write*

1210   *hym* this

oo stounde for one moment
of belonging to

1215   *lese* lose
reed course of action
homward he him spedde he (Arcite) hastened home
lith to wedde lies in pawn, is pledged as a forfeit

1220

He watches for a chance to kill himself secretly

1225   *me shape* ordained to me
*purgatorie**

Yfetered fettered
1230
Oonly the sighte the sight alone

1235

maistow dure may you stay

yturned thee the dys thrown the dice for you

1240   *syn* since

1205 Of Perotheus, withouten any raunsoun,
Duc Theseus hym leet out of prisoun
Frely to goon wher that hym liste over al,
In swich a gyse as I you tellen shal.
    This was the forward, pleynly for t'endite,
1210 Bitwixen Theseus and hym Arcite:
That if so were that Arcite were yfounde
Evere in his lif, by day or nyght, oo stounde
In any contree of this Theseus,
And he were caught, it was acorded thus,
1215 That with a swerd he sholde lese his heed.
Ther nas noon oother remedie ne reed;
But taketh his leve, and homward he him spedde.
Lat hym be war! His nekke lith to wedde.
    How greet a sorwe suffreth now Arcite!
1220 The deeth he feeleth thurgh his herte smyte;
He wepeth, wayleth, crieth pitously;
To sleen hymself he waiteth prively.
He seyde, 'Allas that day that I was born!
Now is my prisoun worse than biforn;
1225 Now is me shape eternally to dwelle
Noght in purgatorie, but in helle.
Allas, that evere knew I Perotheus!
For elles hadde I dwelled with Theseus,
Yfetered in his prisoun everemo.
1230 Thanne hadde I been in blisse and nat in wo.
Oonly the sighte of hire whom that I serve,
Though that I nevere hir grace may deserve,
Wolde han suffised right ynough for me.
O deere cosyn Palamon,' quod he,
1235 'Thyn is the victorie of this aventure.
Ful blisfully in prison maistow dure –
In prison? Certes nay, but in paradys!
Wel hath Fortune yturned thee the dys,
That hast the sighte of hire, and I th'absence.
1240 For possible is, syn thou hast hire presence,

atteyne attain
bareyne barren

1245

nys (*ne is*) is not
hem them (the elements)

sterve die   *wanhope* despair

1250   *lust* delight
pleynen complain*   *in commune* generally
On purveiaunce of the providence*
yeveth gives   *gyse* way
devyse imagine

1255

mordre murder
wolde . . . fayn dearly wishes
of his meynee by his retainers

1260   *witen* know   *preyen* pray for*
faren proceed
woot knows
noot knows not   *thider* thither
slider slippery

1265

faste eagerly

We may all say as much, and I especially
wende thought

1270

heele well-being
Ther whereas   *wele* happiness

I nam but deed I am as good as dead*

1275   *that oother syde* the other hand
wiste knew   *agon* gone

And art a knyght, a worthy and an able,
That by som cas, syn Fortune is chaungeable,
Thow maist to thy desir somtyme atteyne.
But I, that am exiled and bareyne
1245 Of alle grace, and in so greet dispeir
That ther nys erthe, water, fir, ne eir,
Ne creature that of hem maked is,
That may me helpe or doon confort in this,
Wel oughte I sterve in wanhope and distresse.
1250 Farewel my lif, my lust, and my gladnesse!
      'Allas, why pleynen folk so in commune
On purveiaunce of God, or of Fortune,
That yeveth hem ful ofte in many a gyse
Wel bettre than they kan hemself devyse?
1255 Som man desireth for to han richesse,
That cause is of his mordre or greet siknesse;
And som man wolde out of his prisoun fayn,
That in his hous is of his meynee slayn.
Infinite harmes been in this mateere.
1260 We witen nat what thing we preyen heere;
We faren as he that dronke is as a mous.
A dronke man woot wel he hath an hous,
But he noot which the righte wey is thider,
And to a dronke man the wey is slider.
1265 And certes, in this world so faren we;
We seken faste after felicitee,
But we goon wrong ful often, trewely.
Thus may we seyen alle, and namely I,
That wende and hadde a greet opinioun
1270 That if I myghte escapen from prisoun,
Thanne hadde I been in joye and parfit heele,
Ther now I am exiled fro my wele.
Syn that I may nat seen you, Emelye,
I nam but deed; ther nys no remedye.'
1275   Upon that oother syde Palamon,
Whan that he wiste Arcite was agon,

Resouneth of resounds with   *youlyng* wailing
pure fettres very fetters   *grete* massive*

1280

woot knows   *fruyt* fruit
at thy large in freedom
And little care do you expend upon my sorrow
1285 *manhede* manhood
kynrede kindred
werre war
tretee treaty

1290 *moste nedes lese* must needs lose

Sith since

sterve die
1295 *moot* must

sterte leapt
1300

So madly, that to look at he was like
The boxtree box-wood*   *asshen* ashes
*O crueel goddes**
bynding the binding power   *eterne* eternal
1305 And engrave in the tablet of adamant
parlement decree   *graunt* allocation
What how   *holde* beholden, obliged
rouketh cowers*

1310 *arreest* restraint

pardee by God, indeed

Swich sorwe he maketh that the grete tour
Resouneth of his youlyng and clamour.
The pure fettres on his shynes grete
1280   Weren of his bittre, salte teeres wete.
'Allas,' quod he, 'Arcita, cosyn myn,
Of al oure strif, God woot, the fruyt is thyn.
Thow walkest now in Thebes at thy large,
And of my wo thow yevest litel charge.
1285   Thou mayst, syn thou hast wisdom and manhede,
Assemblen alle the folk of oure kynrede,
And make a werre so sharp on this citee
That by som aventure or some tretee
Thow mayst have hire to lady and to wyf
1290   For whom that I moste nedes lese my lyf.
For, as by wey of possibilitee,
Sith thou art at thy large, of prisoun free,
And art a lord, greet is thyn avauntage
Moore than is myn, that sterve here in a cage.
1295   For I moot wepe and wayle, whil I lyve,
With al the wo that prison may me yive,
And eek with peyne that love me yeveth also,
That doubleth al my torment and my wo.'
Therwith the fyr of jalousie up sterte
1300   Withinne his brest, and hente him by the herte
So woodly that he lyk was to biholde
The boxtree or the asshen dede and colde.
      Thanne seyde he, 'O crueel goddes that governe
This world with byndyng of youre word eterne,
1305   And writen in the table of atthamaunt
Youre parlement and youre eterne graunt,
What is mankynde moore unto you holde
Than is the sheep that rouketh in the folde?
For slayn is man right as another beest,
1310   And dwelleth eek in prison and arreest,
And hath siknesse and greet adversitee,
And ofte tymes giltelees, pardee.

prescience foreknowledge
That torments guiltless innocence
1315   *encresseth this* this increases   *penaunce* pain
bounden bound   *observaunce* duty
letten of his wille refrain from his desire
Ther as whereas   *beest* beast   *lust* desire

1320   *moot* must   *pleyne* complain

stonden so turn out to be so
lete leave   *dyvynys* divines, theologians
woot know   *pyne ys* pain is
1325

That who many to many   *mescheef* injury
Go free, able to go where it please him
moot must
jalous* *wood* mad
1330   *wel ny* well nigh   *blood* noble families
Of Thebes, with her wide walls laid waste
sleeth slayeth
fere of hym Arcite fear of Arcite
stynte of leave off   *a lite* for a little time
1335   *stille* meanwhile, ever

Encressen double wise increase to double

1340   *wofuller mester* more miserable occupation

upon his heed on pain of losing his head
1345   From that country for ever

axe ask   *this questioun**

'What governance is in this prescience,
That giltelees tormenteth innocence?
1315 And yet encresseth this al my penaunce,
That man is bounden to his observaunce,
For Goddes sake, to letten of his wille,
Ther as a beest may al his lust fulfille.
And whan a beest is deed he hath no peyne;
1320 But man after his deeth moot wepe and pleyne,
Though in this world he have care and wo.
Withouten doute it may stonden so.
The answere of this lete I to dyvynys,
But wel I woot that in this world greet pyne ys.
1325 Allas, I se a serpent or a theef,
That many a trewe man hath doon mescheef,
Goon at his large, and where hym list may turne.
But I moot been in prisoun thurgh Saturne,
And eek thurgh Juno, jalous and eek wood,
1330 That hath destroyed wel ny al the blood
Of Thebes with his waste walles wyde;
And Venus sleeth me on that oother syde
For jalousie and fere of hym Arcite.'
      Now wol I stynte of Palamon a lite,
1335 And lete hym in his prisoun stille dwelle,
And of Arcita forth I wol yow telle.

      The somer passeth, and the nyghtes longe
Encressen double wise the peynes stronge
Bothe of the lovere and the prisoner.
1340 I noot which hath the wofuller mester.
For, shortly for to seyn, this Palamoun
Perpetuelly is dampned to prisoun,
In cheynes and in fettres to been deed;
And Arcite is exiled upon his heed
1345 For everemo, as out of that contree,
Ne nevere mo ne shal his lady see.
      Yow loveres axe I now this questioun:
Who hath the worse, Arcite or Palamoun?

1350   *moot* must
      hym list it pleases him   *go* walk

      demeth judge (imperative plural)   *liste* pleases   *kan* know how

      Explicit prima pars Here ends the first part

      Sequitur pars secunda Here follows the second part*

1355
      Ful ofte many times   *swelte* swooned
      seen see
      concluden sum up
      sorwe sorrow (object of *hadde*)*
1360   *dure* endure, last
      mete food   *biraft* taken away from
      lene thin   *wex* grew   *shaft* stick

      hewe hue   *falow* fallow, pale yellow
1365
      mone moan

      myghte could   *stent* stopped

1370   *knowe* recognize

      geere manner   *ferde* behaved
      loveris lover's
      Hereos Eros   *manye* mania*
1375   *humour malencolik* the melancholy humour
      In the frontal, imaginative, lobe of the brain
      up so doun upside down
      habit bodily condition   *disposicioun* temperament

That oon may seen his lady day by day,
1350   But in prison he moot dwelle alway;
That oother wher hym list may ride or go,
But seen his lady shal he nevere mo.
Now demeth as yow liste, ye that kan,
For I wol telle forth as I bigan.

Explicit prima pars

Sequitur pars secunda

1355   Whan that Arcite to Thebes comen was,
Ful ofte a day he swelte and seyde 'Allas!'
For seen his lady shal he nevere mo.
And shortly to concluden al his wo,
So muche sorwe hadde nevere creature
1360   That is, or shal, whil that the world may dure.
His slep, his mete, his drynke, is hym biraft,
That lene he wex and drye as is a shaft;
His eyen holwe and grisly to biholde,
His hewe falow and pale as asshen colde,
1365   And solitarie he was and evere allone,
And waillynge al the nyght, makynge his mone;
And if he herde song or instrument,
Thanne wolde he wepe, he myghte nat be stent.
So feble eek were his spiritz, and so lowe,
1370   And chaunged so, that no man koude knowe
His speche nor his voys, though men it herde.
And in his geere for al the world he ferde
Nat oonly lik the loveris maladye
Of Hereos, but rather lyk manye,
1375   Engendred of humour malencolik
Biforen, in his celle fantastik.
And shortly, turned was al up so doun
Bothe habit and eek disposicioun

1380   *daun* Don, lord
        Why should I write about his sorrow all day?

1385   *Hym thoughte* it seemed to him   *Mercurie* Mercury*

        slepy yerde sleep-inducing wand
        heris hair
        as he took keep as he (Arcite) noticed
1390   *Argus* the hundred-eyed guardian of the nymph Io*
        wende go
        shapen ordained
        wook awoke   *sterte* started
        hou soore that me smerte however much it hurts me
1395   *fare* go
        Nor for the fear of death shall I refrain
        that whom
        I recche nat to sterve I care not if I die

1400

        al in another kynde (looked) quite different
        ran hym occurred to him

        Of maladye by the illness
1405   *bar hym lowe* acted humbly
        unknowe unknown
        ny nigh
        right anon at once

1410

        privetee private affairs   *cas* situation
        povrely poorly
        nexte nearest

Of hym, this woful lovere daun Arcite.
1380   What sholde I al day of his wo endite?
Whan he endured hadde a yeer or two
This crueel torment and this peyne and wo,
At Thebes, in his contree, as I seyde,
Upon a nyght in sleep as he hym leyde,
1385 Hym thoughte how that the wynged god Mercurie
Biforn hym stood and bad hym to be murie.
His slepy yerde in hond he bar uprighte;
An hat he werede upon his heris brighte.
Arrayed was this god, as he took keep,
1390 As he was whan that Argus took his sleep;
And seyde hym thus: 'To Atthenes shaltou wende,
Ther is thee shapen of thy wo an ende.'
And with that word Arcite wook and sterte.
'Now trewely, hou soore that me smerte,'
1395 Quod he, 'to Atthenes right now wol I fare,
Ne for the drede of deeth shal I nat spare
To se my lady, that I love and serve.
In hire presence I recche nat to sterve.'
    And with that word he caughte a greet mirour,
1400 And saugh that chaunged was al his colour,
And saugh his visage al in another kynde.
And right anon it ran hym in his mynde,
That, sith his face was so disfigured
Of maladye the which he hadde endured,
1405 He myghte wel, if that he bar hym lowe,
Lyve in Atthenes everemoore unknowe,
And seen his lady wel ny day by day.
And right anon he chaunged his array,
And cladde hym as a povre laborer,
1410 And al allone, save oonly a squier
That knew his privetee and al his cas,
Which was disgised povrely as he was,
To Atthenes is he goon the nexte way.
And to the court he wente upon a day,

1415   *profreth* offers
        To drudge and draw (water), whatever is asked

        He found a position with a household officer

1420   For he was acute and kept a sharp eye
        Of on   *here* her
        He was well able to hew wood and carry water
        myghty for the nones very strong
        therto also   *long* tall   *big* strong
1425   *wight* person   *devyse* require

        Page of the chambre personal servant
        *Philostrate** *highte* was called

1430   *degree* rank
        gentil of condicioun noble of nature

        degree rank
1435   *worshipful* honourable
        vertu quality

        goode tonge courteous speech
        taken brought   *neer* close
1440

        pryvely secretly   *rente* revenue
        slyly discreetly
1445

        ladde led
        bar conducted
        hath derre holds more dear
        lete leave
1450

1415 And at the gate he profreth his servyse
To drugge and drawe, what so men wol devyse.
And shortly of this matere for to seyn,
He fil in office with a chamberleyn
The which that dwellynge was with Emelye,
1420 For he was wys and koude soone espye,
Of every servaunt, which that serveth here.
Wel koude he hewen wode, and water bere,
For he was yong and myghty for the nones,
And therto he was long and big of bones
1425 To doon that any wight kan hym devyse.
A yeer or two he was in this servyse,
Page of the chambre of Emelye the brighte,
And Philostrate he seyde that he highte.
But half so wel biloved a man as he
1430 Ne was ther nevere in court of his degree;
He was so gentil of condicioun
That thurghout al the court was his renoun.
They seyden that it were a charitee
That Theseus wolde enhauncen his degree,
1435 And putten hym in worshipful servyse,
Ther as he myghte his vertu excercise.
And thus withinne a while his name is spronge,
Bothe of his dedes and his goode tonge,
That Theseus hath taken hym so neer
1440 That of his chambre he made hym a squier,
And gaf hym gold to mayntene his degree.
And eek men broghte hym out of his contree,
From yeer to yeer, ful pryvely his rente;
But honestly and slyly he it spente,
1445 That no man wondred how that he it hadde.
And thre yeer in this wise his lif he ladde,
And bar hym so, in pees and eek in werre,
Ther was no man that Theseus hath derre.
And in this blisse lete I now Arcite,
1450 And speke I wole of Palamon a lite.

seten sat
Forpyned tormented
soor pain   hevynesse grief
1455   destreyneth afflicts
wood mad
therto in addition

ryme rhyme
1460

1465   aventure chance
shapen determined

brak broke out of

1470   yeve given   gayler jailer
clarree sweet liqueur
opie . . . fyn a fine opiate   Thebes*

sleep slept
1475

faste by near
nedes cost of necessity   moot must
til to   faste close
dredeful fearful   stalketh steals
1480

preye ask
werreye make war
1485   outher either   lese lose

In derknesse and horrible and strong prisoun
Thise seven yeer hath seten Palamoun
Forpyned, what for wo and for distresse.
Who feeleth double soor and hevynesse
1455 But Palamon, that love destreyneth so
That wood out of his wit he goth for wo?
And eek therto he is a prisoner
Perpetuelly, noght oonly for a yer.

Who koude ryme in Englyssh proprely
1460 His martirdom? For sothe it am nat I;
Therfore I passe as lightly as I may.

It fel that in the seventhe yer, of May
The thridde nyght (as olde bookes seyn,
That al this storie tellen moore pleyn),
1465 Were it by aventure or destynee –
As, whan a thyng is shapen, it shal be –
That soone after the mydnyght Palamoun,
By helpyng of a freend, brak his prisoun
And fleeth the citee faste as he may go.
1470 For he hadde yeve his gayler drynke so
Of a clarree maad of a certeyn wyn,
With nercotikes and opie of Thebes fyn,
That al that nyght, thogh that men wolde him shake,
The gayler sleep; he myghte nat awake.
1475 And thus he fleeth as faste as evere he may.
The nyght was short and faste by the day
That nedes cost he moot hymselven hyde,
And til a grove faste ther bisyde
With dredeful foot thanne stalketh Palamon.
1480 For, shortly, this was his opinion:
That in that grove he wolde hym hyde al day,
And in the nyght thanne wolde he take his way
To Thebes-ward, his freendes for to preye
On Theseus to helpe him to werreye;
1485 And shortly, outher he wolde lese his lif
Or wynnen Emelye unto his wyf.

effect purpose   *entente pleyn* full intention

Who little knew how near his trouble was
1490   *broght him in* led him into
messager messenger
Salueth salutes   *morwe gray* grey morning
Phebus Phoebus (god of the sun)
orient east*   *of* with
1495   *stremes* beams   *greves* groves

1500

poynt goal (*i.e.* Emily)
courser hunter   *startlynge* prancing   *fir* fire

were it it might be
1505

gan to holde took
greves groves
wodebynde woodbine
ayeyn in   *shene* bright
1510

some grene some greenery
lusty joyful
sterte sprang
1515   *rometh* paces

that where
soore afered sorely afraid

1520   *trowed* believed
It has been truly said, this many years hast
feeld hath eyen the field has eyes

This is th'effect and his entente pleyn.
　　Now wol I turne to Arcite ageyn,
That litel wiste how ny that was his care,
1490　Til that Fortune had broght him in the snare.
　　The bisy larke, messager of day,
Salueth in hir song the morwe gray,
And firy Phebus riseth up so bright
That al the orient laugheth of the light,
1495　And with his stremes dryeth in the greves
The silver dropes hangynge on the leves.
And Arcita, that in the court roial
With Theseus is squier principal,
Is risen and looketh on the myrie day.
1500　And for to doon his observaunce to May,
Remembrynge on the poynt of his desir,
He on a courser, startlynge as the fir,
Is riden into the feeldes hym to pleye,
Out of the court, were it a myle or tweye.
1505　And to the grove of which that I yow tolde
By aventure his wey he gan to holde
To maken hym a gerland of the greves,
Were it of wodebynde or hawethorn leves,
And loude he song ayeyn the sonne shene:
1510　'May, with alle thy floures and thy grene,
Welcome be thou, faire, fresshe May,
In hope that I som grene gete may.'
And from his courser, with a lusty herte,
Into the grove ful hastily he sterte,
1515　And in a path he rometh up and doun,
Ther as by aventure this Palamoun
Was in a bussh, that no man myghte hym se,
For soore afered of his deeth was he.
No thyng ne knew he that it was Arcite;
1520　God woot he wolde have trowed it ful lite.
But sooth is seyd, go sithen many yeres,
That 'feeld hath eyen and the wode hath eres.'

It is good for a man to behave with discipline
For every day one meets with an unexpected hour
1525   *woot* knows
so ny near enough   *al his sawe* all he said
stille motionless

roundel a song to accompany a round dance*
1530   *studie* study, reverie
thise these   *queynte geres* strange ways
crope tree-top   *breres* briars

1535

geery changeable   *overcaste* overthrow
hir day her day, Friday*
gereful variable   *array* dress, aspect
Seldom is Friday like the rest of the week
1540   *sike* sigh

bore born
*crueltee**
Woltow werreyen wilt thou make war on
1545

Cadme Cadmus   *Amphioun* Amphion*

bulte built   *bigan* founded

1550   *lynage* lineage
verray ligne direct line of descent
caytyf wretched   *thral* enslaved

povrely in poverty
1555   *wel* much
biknowe acknowledge
highte be called
myte a very small coin

It is ful fair a man to bere hym evene,
For al day meeteth men at unset stevene.
1525 Ful litel woot Arcite of his felawe,
That was so ny to herknen al his sawe,
For in the bussh he sitteth now ful stille.
    Whan that Arcite hadde romed al his fille,
And songen al the roundel lustily,
1530 Into a studie he fil sodeynly,
As doon thise loveres in hir queynte geres,
Now in the crope, now doun in the breres,
Now up, now doun, as boket in a welle.
Right as the Friday, soothly for to telle,
1535 Now it shyneth, now it reyneth faste,
Right so kan geery Venus overcaste
The hertes of hir folk; right as hir day
Is gereful, right so chaungeth she array.
Selde is the Friday al the wowke ylike.
1540   Whan that Arcite had songe, he gan to sike
And sette hym doun withouten any moore.
'Allas,' quod he, 'that day that I was bore!
How longe, Juno, thurgh thy crueltee,
Woltow werreyen Thebes the citee?
1545 Allas, ybroght is to confusioun
The blood roial of Cadme and Amphioun –
Of Cadmus, which that was the firste man
That Thebes bulte, or first the toun bigan,
And of the citee first was crouned kyng.
1550 Of his lynage am I and his ofspryng
By verray ligne, as of the stok roial,
And now I am so caytyf and so thral,
That he that is my mortal enemy,
I serve hym as his squier povrely.
1555 And yet dooth Juno me wel moore shame,
For I dar noght biknowe myn owene name;
But ther as I was wont to highte Arcite,
Now highte I Philostrate, noght worth a myte.

felle fierce*
1560   *fordo* destroyed

martireth persecutes
sleen slay   *outrely* utterly

1565   *careful* sorrowful
That my death was destined before my (first) shirt (was made)

care sorrow
1570   I would not give the value of a weed (*i.e.* anything)
to youre plesaunce to give you pleasure

1575

quook trembled   *byde* wait

wood mad
stirte hym jumped   *buskes* bushes
1580   *wikke* wicked
hent caught

to my conseil to respect my confidence

1585   *byjaped* tricked

namo no others
1590

astert escaped*
drede doubt   *outher* either

Allas, thou felle Mars! Allas, Juno!
1560 Thus hath youre ire oure lynage al fordo,
Save oonly me and wrecched Palamoun,
That Theseus martireth in prisoun.
And over al this, to sleen me outrely
Love hath his firy dart so brennyngly
1565 Ystiked thurgh my trewe, careful herte
That shapen was my deeth erst than my sherte.
Ye sleen me with youre eyen, Emelye!
Ye been the cause wherfore that I dye.
Of al the remenant of myn oother care
1570 Ne sette I nat the montance of a tare,
So that I koude doon aught to youre plesaunce.'
And with that word he fil doun in a traunce
A longe tyme, and after he up sterte.
    This Palamoun, that thoughte that thurgh his herte
1575 He felte a coold swerd sodeynliche glyde,
For ire he quook; no lenger wolde he byde.
And whan that he had herd Arcites tale,
As he were wood, with face deed and pale,
He stirte hym up out of the buskes thikke
1580 And seide: 'Arcite, false traytour wikke,
Now artow hent, that lovest my lady so,
For whom that I have al this peyne and wo,
And art my blood, and to my conseil sworn,
As I ful ofte have told thee heerbiforn,
1585 And hast byjaped heere duc Theseus,
And falsly chaunged hast thy name thus!
I wol be deed, or elles thou shalt dye.
Thou shalt nat love my lady Emelye,
But I wol love hire oonly and namo;
1590 For I am Palamon, thy mortal foo.
And though that I no wepene have in this place,
But out of prison am astert by grace,
I drede noght that outher thow shalt dye,
Or thow ne shalt nat loven Emelye.

1595   *Chees* choose   *asterte* escape
        despitous scornful

        sit sitteth, sits
1600   *Nere it* were it not   *wood* mad

        ne sholdest shouldst not (first)
        defye the seurete repudiate the undertaking
1605   *seist* sayest
        thynk wel understand
        maugree in spite of

        wilnest desire   *darreyne* decide your right to
1610   *Have heer my trouthe* take my troth
        wityng knowledge

        harneys armour
        leef leave
1615   *mete* food

        ther which

1620

        amorwe morning
        leyd his feith to borwe given his faith in pledge
        out of without
        regne reign   *felawe* partner
1625
        his thankes willingly   *felaweshipe* partnership
        fynden experience

1630   *harneys* sets of armour   *dight* prepared

1595 Chees which thou wolt, or thou shalt nat asterte!'
     This Arcite, with ful despitous herte,
     Whan he hym knew, and hadde his tale herd,
     As fiers as leon pulled out his swerd,
     And seyde thus: 'By God that sit above,
1600 Nere it that thou art sik and wood for love,
     And eek that thow no wepne hast in this place,
     Thou sholdest nevere out of this grove pace,
     That thou ne sholdest dyen of myn hond.
     For I defye the seurete and the bond
1605 Which that thou seist that I have maad to thee.
     What! Verray fool, thynk wel that love is free,
     And I wol love hire maugree al thy myght!
     But for as muche thou art a worthy knyght
     And wilnest to darreyne hire by bataille,
1610 Have heer my trouthe; tomorwe I wol nat faille,
     Withoute wityng of any oother wight,
     That heere I wol be founden as a knyght,
     And bryngen harneys right ynough for thee;
     And ches the beste, and leef the worste for me.
1615 And mete and drynke this nyght wol I brynge
     Ynough for thee, and clothes for thy beddynge.
     And if so be that thou my lady wynne,
     And sle me in this wode ther I am inne,
     Thow mayst wel have thy lady as for me.'
1620   This Palamon answerde, 'I graunte it thee.'
     And thus they been departed til amorwe,
     Whan ech of hem had leyd his feith to borwe.
        O Cupide, out of alle charitee!
     O regne, that wolt no felawe have with thee!
1625 Ful sooth is seyd that love ne lordshipe
     Wol noght, his thankes, have no felaweshipe.
     Wel fynden that Arcite and Palamoun.
     Arcite is riden anon unto the toun,
     And on the morwe, er it were dayes light,
1630 Ful prively two harneys hath he dight,

mete fitting   *darreyne* decide rightly

1635

regne of Trace kingdom of Thrace
stondeth stand (plural)   *gappe* gap

1640

greves groves
breketh (singular)   *bowes* boughs
thynketh (plural)
moot must

1645

if that me myshappe if it goes wrong for me
ferden they they behaved   *hewe* hue
As far as each of them acknowledged the other
saluyng greeting

1650   *rehersyng* repetition (of their agreement)

foynen thrust   *wonder* wonderfully
1655   *wene* think
wood mad

bores boars   *gonne* began   *smyte* strike, clash
Which, mad with rage, froth as white as foam
1660   *ancle* ankle*   *hir* their
lete hem fightyng dwelle leave them still fighting

The destinee Destiny*
executeth carries out
1665   *purveiaunce* providence   *seyn* seen
it (i.e. Destiny)

Bothe suffisaunt and mete to darreyne
The bataille in the feeld bitwix hem tweyne;
And on his hors, allone as he was born,
He carieth al the harneys hym biforn.
1635 And in the grove, at tyme and place yset,
This Arcite and this Palamon ben met.
To chaungen gan the colour in hir face;
Right as the hunters in the regne of Trace,
That stondeth at the gappe with a spere,
1640 Whan hunted is the leon or the bere,
And hereth hym come russhyng in the greves,
And breketh bothe bowes and the leves,
And thynketh, 'Heere cometh my mortal enemy!
Withoute faille, he moot be deed, or I,
1645 For outher I moot sleen hym at the gappe,
Or he moot sleen me, if that me myshappe.'
So ferden they in chaungyng of hir hewe,
As fer as everich of hem oother knewe.

          Ther nas no good day, ne no saluyng,
1650 But streight, withouten word or rehersyng,
Everich of hem heelp for to armen oother
As freendly as he were his owene brother;
And after that, with sharpe speres stronge
They foynen ech at oother wonder longe.
1655 Thou myghtest wene that this Palamon
In his fightyng were a wood leon,
And as a crueel tigre was Arcite;
As wilde bores gonne they to smyte,
That frothen whit as foom for ire wood.
1660 Up to the ancle foghte they in hir blood.
And in this wise I lete hem fightyng dwelle,
And forth I wole of Theseus yow telle.

          The destinee, ministre general,
That executeth in the world over al
1665 The purveiaunce that God hath seyn biforn,
So strong it is that, though the world had sworn

by ye or nay absolutely

That falleth nat eft what will not happen again

1670

Be it whether
sighte foresight
by with reference to

1675   *namely* especially   *at after*   *hert* hart
daweth hym dawns for him
That he nys clad on which he is not dressed
hunte huntsman

1680

bane killer
Mars god of war   *Dyane* goddess of the hunt

1685

faste near

1690

launde glade
For thither the hart was wont to fly
his the hart's
cours course
1695   *hym list* pleased him

Under shading his eyes from

breme fiercely   *bores* boars
1700

The contrarie of a thyng by ye or nay,
Yet somtyme it shal fallen on a day
That falleth nat eft withinne a thousand yeer.
1670 For certeinly, oure appetites heer,
Be it of werre, or pees, or hate, or love,
Al is this reuled by the sighte above.
    This mene I now by myghty Theseus,
That for to hunten is so desirus,
1675 And namely at the grete hert in May,
That in his bed ther daweth hym no day
That he nys clad, and redy for to ryde
With hunte and horn and houndes hym bisyde.
For in his huntyng hath he swich delit
1680 That it is al his joye and appetit
To been hymself the grete hertes bane,
For after Mars he serveth now Dyane.
    Cleer was the day, as I have toold er this,
And Theseus with alle joye and blis,
1685 With his Ypolita, the faire queene,
And Emelye, clothed al in grene,
On huntyng be they riden roially.
And to the grove that stood ful faste by,
In which ther was an hert, as men hym tolde,
1690 Duc Theseus the streighte wey hath holde.
And to the launde he rideth hym ful right,
For thider was the hert wont have his flight,
And over a brook, and so forth on his weye.
This duc wol han a cours at hym or tweye
1695 With houndes swiche as that hym list comaunde.
    And whan this duc was come unto the launde,
Under the sonne he looketh, and anon
He was war of Arcite and Palamon,
That foughten breme as it were bores two.
1700 The brighte swerdes wenten to and fro
So hidously that with the leeste strook
It semed as it wolde felle an ook.

But who they were, he had no idea
courser hunter   *spores* spurs   *smoot* struck
1705   *at a stert* in one movement
Hoo stop
up peyne of lesynge on pain of losing

1710   *myster* kind of
hardy foolhardy
juge judge*
lystes roially lists, under the appointed form

1715

encombred of encumbered by

1720   *Ne yif* do not give

1725

highte was called
japed tricked
1730

sith since

thilke that same
1735

hoote hotly

But what they were, no thyng he ne woot.
This duc his courser with his spores smoot,
1705 And at a stert he was bitwix hem two,
And pulled out a swerd and cride, 'Hoo!
Namoore, up peyne of lesynge of youre heed!
By myghty Mars, he shal anon be deed
That smyteth any strook that I may seen.
1710 But telleth me what myster men ye been,
That been so hardy for to fighten heere
Withouten juge or oother officere,
As it were in a lystes roially.'
    This Palamon answerde hastily
1715 And seyde, 'Sire, what nedeth wordes mo?
We have the deeth disserved bothe two.
Two woful wrecches been we, two caytyves,
That been encombred of oure owene lyves;
And as thou art a rightful lord and juge,
1720 Ne yif us neither mercy ne refuge,
But sle me first, for seinte charitee!
But sle my felawe eek as wel as me;
Or sle hym first, for though thow knowest it lite,
This is thy mortal foo, this is Arcite,
1725 That fro thy lond is banysshed on his heed,
For which he hath deserved to be deed.
For this is he that cam unto thy gate
And seyde that he highte Philostrate.
Thus hath he japed thee ful many a yer,
1730 And thou hast maked hym thy chief squier;
And this is he that loveth Emelye.
For sith the day is come that I shal dye,
I make pleynly my confessioun
That I am thilke woful Palamoun
1735 That hath thy prisoun broken wikkedly.
I am thy mortal foo, and it am I
That loveth so hoote Emelye the brighte
That I wol dye present in hir sighte.

axe ask for   *juwise* sentence

1740

1745   *recorde* pronounce
      pyne torture
      rede red
      wommanhede womanliness, womanly nature

1750

      thoughte hem seemed to

      gentil noble   *estaat* birth

1755   *saugh hir* saw their

1760   *aslaked* abated
      For in a noble heart pity quickly flows*
      quook shook   *sterte* trembled
      in a clause briefly
      trespas offence

1765

1770

      wepen evere in oon wept continually

      Fy fie, shame

Wherfore I axe deeth and my juwise;
1740 But sle my felawe in the same wise,
For bothe han we deserved to be slayn.'
    This worthy duc answerde anon agayn,
And seyde, 'This is a short conclusioun.
Youre owene mouth, by youre confessioun,
1745 Hath dampned yow, and I wol it recorde;
It nedeth noght to pyne yow with the corde.
Ye shal be deed, by myghty Mars the rede!'
    The queene anon, for verray wommanhede,
Gan for to wepe, and so dide Emelye,
1750 And alle the ladyes in the compaignye.
Greet pitee was it, as it thoughte hem alle,
That evere swich a chaunce sholde falle,
For gentil men they were of greet estaat,
And no thyng but for love was this debaat;
1755 And saugh hir blody woundes wyde and soore,
And alle crieden, bothe lasse and moore,
'Have mercy, Lord, upon us wommen alle!'
And on hir bare knees adoun they falle
And wolde have kist his feet ther as he stood;
1760 Til at the laste aslaked was his mood,
For pitee renneth soone in gentil herte.
And though he first for ire quook and sterte,
He hath considered shortly, in a clause,
The trespas of hem bothe, and eek the cause,
1765 And although that his ire hir gilt accused,
Yet in his resoun he hem bothe excused,
As thus: he thoghte wel that every man
Wol helpe hymself in love, if that he kan,
And eek delivere hymself out of prisoun.
1770 And eek his herte hadde compassioun
Of wommen, for they wepen evere in oon,
And in his gentil herte he thoughte anon,
And softe unto hymself he seyde, 'Fy
Upon a lord that wol have no mercy,

1775

As wel as just as much as   despitous scornful
mayntene persist in

1780   kan knows   divisioun distinction
weyeth weighs   after oon as the same
agoon gone

on highte aloud
1785   a benedicite ah, bless you*

Against his power no obstacles avail
may be cleped may well be called
at his owene gyse in his own way
1790   as that hym list divyse as it pleases him to ordain

quitly completely

witen know
1795   lith lies
maugree in spite of   eyen eyes*
hyder hither
an heigh folye the height of folly
but if unless
1800   sit sitteth, sits
Se see   arrayed turned out
hir their   ypayed paid

wenen for to been think themselves
1805   for aught that may bifalle whatever happens
game joke
jolitee sport
Can no more thank them for it than she can thank me
woot knows*   hoote fare warm work
1810   cokkow cuckoo*

1775 But been a leon, bothe in word and dede,
To hem that been in repentaunce and drede,
As wel as to a proud despitous man
That wol mayntene that he first bigan.
That lord hath litel of discrecioun,
1780 That in swich cas kan no divisioun
But weyeth pride and humblesse after oon.'
And shortly, whan his ire is thus agoon,
He gan to looken up with eyen lighte
And spak thise same wordes al on highte:
1785   'The god of love, a benedicite!
How myghty and how greet a lord is he!
Ayeyns his myght ther gayneth none obstacles.
He may be cleped a god for his myracles,
For he kan maken, at his owene gyse,
1790 Of everich herte as that hym list divyse.
Lo heere this Arcite and this Palamoun,
That quitly weren out of my prisoun,
And myghte han lyved in Thebes roially,
And witen I am hir mortal enemy,
1795 And that hir deth lith in my myght also,
And yet hath love, maugree hir eyen two,
Broght hem hyder bothe for to dye.
Now looketh, is nat that an heigh folye?
Who may been a fool but if he love?
1800 Bihoold, for Goddes sake that sit above,
Se how they blede! Be they noght wel arrayed?
Thus hath hir lord, the god of love, ypayed
Hir wages and hir fees for hir servyse!
And yet they wenen for to been ful wyse
1805 That serven love, for aught that may bifalle.
But this is yet the beste game of alle,
That she for whom they han this jolitee
Kan hem therfore as muche thank as me.
She woot namoore of al this hoote fare,
1810 By God, than woot a cokkow or an hare!

all moot ben assayed everything has to be tried
moot ben has to be   *or . . . or* either . . . or
I experienced it for myself very long ago*
servant servant of Love*   *oon* one

1815

distreyne afflict
ofte in his laas often in his snare

1820   *suster* sister (in law)

dere harm

1825   *every deel* every bit, completely
his axyng what he asked
of lordshipe for protection   *preyde* begged

1830

tyme is the time comes

1835

Atones at once
al be hym looth or lief whether he like it or not
moot go pipen may as well go whistle*

1840   *wrothe* angry
forthy therefore   *degree* (equal) position

herkneth hearken   *wyse* way
heere here is   *devyse* arrange
1845   *plat* flat
repplicacioun reply

But all moot ben assayed, hoot and coold;
A man moot ben a fool, or yong or oold –
I woot it by myself ful yore agon,
For in my tyme a servant was I oon.

1815 And therfore, syn I knowe of loves peyne
And woot hou soore it kan a man distreyne,
As he that hath ben caught ofte in his laas,
I yow foryeve al hoolly this trespaas,
At requeste of the queene, that kneleth heere,

1820 And eek of Emelye, my suster deere.
And ye shul bothe anon unto me swere
That nevere mo ye shal my contree dere,
Ne make werre upon me nyght ne day,
But been my freendes in all that ye may.

1825 I yow foryeve this trespas every deel.'
And they hym sworen his axyng faire and weel,
And hym of lordshipe and of mercy preyde,
And he hem graunteth grace, and thus he seyde:
    'To speke of roial lynage and richesse,

1830 Though that she were a queene or a princesse,
Ech of you bothe is worthy, doutelees,
To wedden whan tyme is; but nathelees –
I speke as for my suster Emelye,
For whom ye have this strif and jalousye –

1835 Ye woot yourself she may nat wedden two
Atones, though ye fighten everemo,
That oon of you, al be hym looth or lief,
He moot go pipen in an yvy leef;
This is to seyn, she may nat now han bothe,

1840 Al be ye never so jalouse ne so wrothe.
And forthy I yow putte in this degree,
That ech of yow shal have his destynee
As hym is shape, and herkneth in what wyse;
Lo, heere youre ende of that I shal devyse.

1845   'My wyl is this, for plat conclusioun,
Withouten any repplicacioun –

If it please you, make the best of it

daunger difficulty
1850 *fer ne ner* more or less

up at alle rightes in all respects
darreyne decide the right to
bihote promise
1855

wheither whichever

contrarie opponent
1860 *to wyve* as a wife

so wisly as surely   *rewe* have mercy
evene fair
1865 *ende* conclusion

yow thynketh it seems to you
avys opinion   *apayd* satisfied

1870 *lightly* cheerfully

kouthe could   *endite* write

1875 *maner wight* kind of person

namely especially   *often sithe* many a time

1880 *his* its   *wyde* wide*

Explicit secunda pars Here ends the second part

If that you liketh, take it for the beste:
That everich of you shal goon where hym leste
Frely, withouten raunson or daunger,
1850 And this day fifty wykes, fer ne ner,
Everich of you shal brynge an hundred knyghtes
Armed for lystes up at alle rightes,
Al redy to darreyne hire by bataille.
And this bihote I yow withouten faille,
1855 Upon my trouthe, and as I am a knyght,
That wheither of yow bothe that hath myght –
This is to seyn, that wheither he or thow
May with his hundred, as I spak of now,
Sleen his contrarie, or out of lystes dryve,
1860 Thanne shal I yeve Emelya to wyve
To whom that Fortune yeveth so fair a grace.
The lystes shal I maken in this place,
And God so wisly on my soule rewe
As I shal evene juge been and trewe.
1865 Ye shul noon oother ende with me maken.
That oon of yow ne shal be deed or taken.
And if yow thynketh this is weel ysayd,
Seyeth youre avys, and holdeth you apayd.
This is youre ende and youre conclusioun.'
1870   Who looketh lightly now but Palamoun?
Who spryngeth up for joye but Arcite?
Who kouthe telle, or who kouthe it endite,
The joye that is maked in the place
Whan Theseus hath doon so fair a grace?
1875 But doun on knees wente every maner wight,
And thonked hym with al hir herte and myght,
And namely the Thebans often sithe.
And thus with good hope and with herte blithe
They taken hir leve, and homward gonne they ride
1880 To Thebes with his olde walles wyde.

Explicit secunda pars

Sequitur pars tercia Here follows the third part*

trowe believe
dispence expenditure

1885   *theatre* amphitheatre*

dyched al withoute surrounded by a ditch
compas a circle
1890   *degrees* steps, tiers   *pas* paces, yards
o one
letted prevented

1895

space space of time
crafty skilful
ars-metrike the art of measurement, arithmetic   *kan* knows
portreyour painter   *kervere* carver in stone
1900   *mete* food
devyse contrive
ryte rite

1905   *Doon make* had made   *auter* altar   *oratorie* shrine, chapel
memorie commemoration

fother cartload
touret turret
1910

Dyane of chastitee Diana, goddess of chastity

Sequitur pars tercia

       I trowe men wolde deme it necligence
       If I foryete to tellen the dispence
       Of Theseus, that gooth so bisily
       To maken up the lystes roially,
1885   That swich a noble theatre as it was
       I dar wel seyen in this world ther nas.
       The circuit a myle was aboute,
       Walled of stoon, and dyched al withoute.
       Round was the shap, in manere of compas,
1890   Ful of degrees, the heighte of sixty pas;
       That whan a man was set on o degree,
       He letted nat his felawe for to see.
            Estward ther stood a gate of marbul whit,
       Westward right swich another in the opposit.
1895   And shortly to concluden, swich a place
       Was noon in erthe, as in so litel space;
       For in the lond ther was no crafty man
       That geometrie or ars-metrike kan,
       Ne portreyour, ne kervere of ymages,
1900   That Theseus ne yaf him mete and wages
       The theatre for to maken and devyse.
       And for to doon his ryte and sacrifise,
       He estward hath, upon the gate above,
       In worshipe of Venus, goddesse of love,
1905   Doon make an auter and an oratorie;
       And on the gate westward, in memorie
       Of Mars, he maked hath right swich another,
       That coste largely of gold a fother.
       And northward, in a touret on the wal,
1910   Of alabastre whit and reed coral,
       An oratorie, riche for to see,
       In worshipe of Dyane of chastitee,

Hath . . . doon wroght has had made   *wyse* manner
devyse describe
1915   *portreitures* paintings
contenaunce appearance

*the temple of Venus**
pitous pitiful
1920   *sikes* sighs
waymentynge lamentation

The oaths that confirm their vows
1925   *Plesaunce* Pleasure*
Bauderie Jollity
Charmes Tricks   *Lesynges* Lies
Despense Expense   *Bisynesse* Attentiveness
Who wore a garland of yellow marigolds*
1930   *cokkow* cuckoo*
caroles songs for ring-dances
Lust pleasure of the senses   *array* display
rekned have mentioned
By ordre in order
1935
Citheroun Cithaeron (a mistake for Cythera)*

lustynesse delight
1940   *Ydelnesse**
Nor the beautiful Narcissus of long ago*
folye folly   *Salomon* Solomon*
Ercules Hercules*
Circes Circe*
1945   *Turnus**   *hardy* brave
Cresus Croesus*   *kaytyf in servage* wretched in captivity

sleighte trickery   *hardynesse* courage

Hath Theseus doon wroght in noble wyse.
   But yet hadde I foryeten to devyse
1915 The noble kervyng and the portreitures,
   The shap, the contenaunce, and the figures
   That weren in thise oratories thre.
      First in the temple of Venus maystow se
   Wroght on the wal, ful pitous to biholde,
1920 The broken slepes, and the sikes colde,
   The sacred teeris, and the waymentynge,
   The firy strokes of the desirynge
   That loves servantz in this lyf enduren;
   The othes that hir covenantz assuren;
1925 Plesaunce and Hope, Desir, Foolhardynesse,
   Beautee and Youthe, Bauderie, Richesse,
   Charmes and Force, Lesynges, Flaterye,
   Despense, Bisynesse, and Jalousye,
   That wered of yelewe goolde a gerland,
1930 And a cokkow sittynge on hir hand;
   Festes, instrumentz, caroles, daunces,
   Lust and array, and alle the circumstaunces
   Of love, which that I rekned and rekne shal,
   By ordre weren peynted on the wal,
1935 And mo than I kan make of mencioun.
   For soothly al the mount of Citheroun,
   Ther Venus hath hir principal dwellynge,
   Was shewed on the wal in portreyynge,
   With al the gardyn and the lustynesse.
1940 Nat was foryeten the porter, Ydelnesse,
   Ne Narcisus the faire of yore agon,
   Ne yet the folye of kyng Salomon,
   Ne yet the grete strengthe of Ercules –
   Th'enchauntementz of Medea and Circes –
1945 Ne of Turnus, with the hardy fiers corage,
   The riche Cresus, kaytyf in servage.
   Thus may ye seen that wysdom ne richesse,
   Beautee ne sleighte, strengthe ne hardynesse,

champartie share in power

1950   *hir list* it pleases her   *than* then   *gye* guide

las snare

And though although   *rekene* mention   *mo* more

1955   *The statue of Venus** *se* see

fletynge floating   *large* wide

wawes waves

citole stringed instrument like a zither

1960   *semely* lovely   *se* see

gerland garland

dowves doves   *flikerynge* fluttering

Biforn in front of   *sone Cupido* son Cupid*

shuldres shoulders

1965   *seene* represented

bar carried

noght not   *eek* also

Mars* *rede* red

1970   *brede* breadth

estres interior

highte is called   *Trace* Thrace

thilke that

Ther as where   *sovereyn* principal

1975

best beast

knarry gnarled   *bareyne* barren

stubbes stub-like branches   *hidouse* hideous

In through   *rumbel* rumbling   *swough* rushing

1980   *bresten* break

under below   *bente* grassy slope

armypotente powerful in arms

Wroght built   *burned* burnished   *entree* entrance

streit narrow   *gastly* terrifying

Ne may with Venus holde champartie,
1950 For as hir list the world than may she gye.
Lo, alle thise folk so caught were in hir las,
Til they for wo ful ofte seyde 'allas!'
Suffiseth heere ensamples oon or two,
And though I koude rekene a thousand mo.

1955   The statue of Venus, glorious for to se,
Was naked, fletynge in the large see,
And fro the navele doun al covered was
With wawes grene, and brighte as any glas.
A citole in hir right hand hadde she,
1960 And on hir heed, ful semely for to se,
A rose gerland, fressh and wel smellynge;
Above hir heed hir dowves flikerynge.
Biforn hire stood hir sone Cupido;
Upon his shuldres wynges hadde he two,
1965 And blynd he was, as it is often seene;
A bowe he bar and arwes brighte and kene.

Why sholde I noght as wel eek telle yow al
The portreiture that was upon the wal
Withinne the temple of myghty Mars the rede?
1970 Al peynted was the wal, in lengthe and brede,
Lyk to the estres of the grisly place
That highte the grete temple of Mars in Trace,
In thilke colde, frosty regioun
Ther as Mars hath his sovereyn mansioun.

1975   First on the wal was peynted a forest,
In which ther dwelleth neither man ne best,
With knotty, knarry, bareyne trees olde,
Of stubbes sharpe and hidouse to biholde,
In which ther ran a rumbel in a swough,
1980 As though a storm sholde bresten every bough.
And dounward from an hille, under a bente,
Ther stood the temple of Mars armypotente,
Wroght al of burned steel, of which the entree
Was long and streit, and gastly for to see.

1985   *rage* roar   *veze* blast
         rese shake
         northren northern*   *shoon* shone

1990   *adamant**   *eterne* eternal
         Braced crosswise and lengthwise

         pyler pillar   *sustene* support
         tonne-greet as thick as a barrel   *shene* shining
1995   *saugh* saw   *ymaginyng* plotting
         Felonye Crime, Treachery   *compassyng* scheming
         Ire Anger   *reed* red   *gleede* coal
         pykepurs pick-purse   *eek* also   *Drede* Terror
         smylere smiling man   *cloke* cloak
2000   *shepne* stable   *brennynge* burning
         mordrynge murder
         Open War, all covered with blood from wounds
         Contek strife   *manace* threat
         chirkyng grating noises   *sory* sorry
2005   *sleere* slayer   *yet* further   *saugh* saw
         heer hair
         The nail driven into the crown of the head at night
         upright upwards
         Amyddes amid   *Meschaunce* Misfortune
2010   *disconfort* discouragement
         Yet furthermore   *Woodnesse* Madness
         Compleint Grievance   *Outhees* Outcry
         careyne corpse   *busk* bush   *ycorve* cut
         qualm plague   *ystorve* dead
2015   *tiraunt* tyrant   *pray* prey   *yraft* seized

         brent burnt   *hoppesteres* dancers*
         hunte hunter   *strangled with* killed by   *beres* bears
         sowe sow   *freten* eating
2020   *for al* despite

1985   And therout came a rage and swich a veze
      That it made al the gate for to rese.
      The northren lyght in at the dores shoon,
      For wyndowe on the wal ne was ther noon,
      Thurgh which men myghten any light discerne.
1990   The dore was al of adamant eterne,
      Yclenched overthwart and endelong
      With iren tough; and for to make it strong,
      Every pyler, the temple to sustene,
      Was tonne-greet, of iren bright and shene.
1995   Ther saugh I first the derke ymaginyng
      Of Felonye, and al the compassyng;
      The crueel Ire, reed as any gleede;
      The pykepurs, and eek the pale Drede;
      The smylere with the knyf under the cloke;
2000   The shepne brennynge with the blake smoke;
      The tresoun of the mordrynge in the bedde;
      The open werre, with woundes al bibledde;
      Contek, with blody knyf and sharp manace.
      Al ful of chirkyng was that sory place.
2005   The sleere of hymself yet saugh I ther –
      His herte-blood hath bathed al his heer –
      The nayl ydryven in the shode anyght;
      The colde deeth, with mouth gapyng upright.
      Amyddes of the temple sat Meschaunce,
2010   With disconfort and sory contenaunce.
      Yet saugh I Woodnesse, laughynge in his rage,
      Armed Compleint, Outhees, and fiers Outrage;
      The careyne in the busk, with throte ycorve;
      A thousand slayn, and nat of qualm ystorve;
2015   The tiraunt, with the pray by force yraft;
      The toun destroyed, ther was no thyng laft.
      Yet saugh I brent the shippes hoppesteres;
      The hunte strangled with the wilde beres;
      The sowe freten the child right in the cradel;
2020   The cook yscalded, for al his longe ladel.

Nothing of the evil influence of Mars was forgotten
cartere charioteer   *overryden with* run over by

divisioun region of influence
2025   *barbour* barber   *bocher* butcher
styth anvil
al above above all   *depeynted* depicted   *tour* tower

2030   *soutil* slender   *twynes threed* thread of twine*
Julius Julius Caesar*
Nero *   *Antonius* Antony*
Al be that although   *thilke* that
ther-biforn beforehand
2035   *manasynge* menace   *figure* configuration of stars
portreiture painting

deed dead
ensample example   *in* from
2040   I could not mention them all, if I wished to
carte chariot
wood mad
shynen shine
cleped called   *scriptures* astrological writings
2045   *Puella* the Girl   *Rubeus* the Ruddy One*

eyen eyes   *eet* ate*
soutil subtle   *pencel* pencil, brush
2050   *redoutynge* awful reverence
Dyane *
me haste hurry myself

2055   *shamefast* modest
Calistopee Callisto*

Noght was foryeten by the infortune of Marte.
The cartere overryden with his carte –
Under the wheel ful lowe he lay adoun.
Ther were also, of Martes divisioun,
2025 The barbour, and the bocher, and the smyth,
That forgeth sharpe swerdes on his styth.
And al above, depeynted in a tour,
Saugh I Conquest, sittynge in greet honour,
With the sharpe swerd over his heed
2030 Hangynge by a soutil twynes threed.
Depeynted was the slaughtre of Julius,
Of grete Nero, and of Antonius;
Al be that thilke tyme they were unborn,
Yet was hir deth depeynted ther-biforn
2035 By manasynge of Mars, right by figure;
So was it shewed in that portreiture,
As is depeynted in the sterres above
Who shal be slayn or elles deed for love.
Suffiseth oon ensample in stories olde;
2040 I may nat rekene hem alle though I wolde.
    The statue of Mars upon a carte stood
Armed, and looked grym as he were wood;
And over his heed ther shynen two figures
Of sterres, that been cleped in scriptures,
2045 That oon Puella, that oother Rubeus –
This god of armes was arrayed thus.
A wolf ther stood biforn hym at his feet
With eyen rede, and of a man he eet;
With soutil pencel was depeynted this storie
2050 In redoutynge of Mars and of his glorie.
    Now to the temple of Dyane the chaste,
As shortly as I kan, I wol me haste,
To telle yow al the descripsioun.
Depeynted been the walles up and doun
2055 Of huntyng and of shamefast chastitee.
Ther saugh I how woful Calistopee,

agreved angered
bere bear
loode-sterre lode-star, pole star*
2060 *sey* tell   *ferre* further
sone son   *eek* also
Dane Daphne*
mene mean
But the daughter of Peneus that was called Daphne*
2065 There I saw Actaeon turned into a hart*
For vengeaunce that he saugh in revenge for having seen

freeten devour   *for that* because
forther moor further on
2070 *Atthalante* Atalanta*   *boor* boar
Meleagre Meleager   *mo* more
wroghte caused

me list it pleases me   *drawen to* commit
2075 *hert* hart*   *hye* high   *seet* sat

Wexynge waxing   *wanye* wane
gaude yellowish-green
2080 *cas* quiver

Ther where
travaillynge in labour
for because
2085 *pitously* piteously   *Lucyna* Lucina*
mayst best art best able
He that made it knew well how to paint to the life
floryn florin   *hewes* pigments
The lists were now complete . . .
2090
theatre amphitheatre   *every deel* in every respect
hym lyked it pleased him

Whan that Diane agreved was with here,
Was turned from a womman til a bere,
And after was she maad the loode-sterre.
2060 Thus was it peynted; I kan sey yow no ferre.
Hir sone is eek a sterre, as men may see.
Ther saugh I Dane, yturned til a tree –
I mene nat the goddesse Diane,
But Penneus doghter, which that highte Dane.
2065 Ther saugh I Attheon an hert ymaked,
For vengeaunce that he saugh Diane al naked;
I saugh how that his houndes have hym caught
And freeten hym, for that they knewe hym naught.
Yet peynted was a litel forther moor
2070 How Atthalante hunted the wilde boor,
And Meleagre, and many another mo,
For which Dyane wroghte hym care and wo.
Ther saugh I many another wonder storie,
The which me list nat drawen to memorie.
2075   This goddesse on an hert ful hye seet,
With smale houndes al aboute hir feet,
And undernethe hir feet she hadde a moone –
Wexynge it was and sholde wanye soone.
In gaude grene hir statue clothed was,
2080 With bowe in honde and arwes in a cas.
Hir eyen caste she ful lowe adoun
Ther Pluto hath his derke regioun.
A womman travaillynge was hire biforn;
But for hir child so longe was unborn,
2085 Ful pitously Lucyna gan she calle
And seyde, 'Help, for thou mayst best of alle!'
Wel koude he peynten lifly that it wroghte;
With many a floryn he the hewes boghte.
   Now been thise lystes maad, and Theseus,
2090 That at his grete cost arrayed thus
The temples and the theatre every deel,
Whan it was doon, hym lyked wonder weel.

stynte leave off   *lite* little

2095

everich each
darreyne decide
til to   *hold* keep
hem them
2100 *at alle rightes* in all points
And many a man there certainly believed
sithen since
hir hond their hands, prowess

2105 *Nas* there had (not) been   *of* from
wight man
his thankes with a will   *passant* surpassing
preyed prayed
wel was hym happy was he
2110 *fille* befell   *cas* thing

paramours passionately   *myght* strength

hir thankes with a will   *wilnen* wish
2115 *benedicitee* bless you

ferden did   *they* those
many on many a one
Som one   *haubergeoun* coat of mail
2120 *gypoun* tunic
paire plates set of plate armour
Pruce Prussian   *targe* shield
weel well

2125 *gyse* fashion   *nas* has not been

maistow might you have

But stynte I wole of Theseus a lite,
And speke of Palamon and of Arcite.
2095   The day approcheth of hir retournynge,
That everich sholde an hundred knyghtes brynge
The bataille to darreyne, as I yow tolde.
And til Atthenes, hir covenant for to holde,
Hath everich of hem broght an hundred knyghtes,
2100 Wel armed for the werre at alle rightes.
And sikerly ther trowed many a man
That nevere, sithen that the world bigan,
As for to speke of knyghthod of hir hond,
As fer as God hath maked see or lond,
2105 Nas of so fewe so noble a compaignye.
For every wight that lovede chivalrye
And wolde, his thankes, han a passant name,
Hath preyed that he myghte been of that game;
And wel was hym that therto chosen was,
2110 For if ther fille tomorwe swich a cas,
Ye knowen wel that every lusty knyght
That loveth paramours and hath his myght,
Were it in Engelond or elleswhere,
They wolde, hir thankes, wilnen to be there –
2115 To fighte for a lady, benedicitee!
It were a lusty sighte for to see.
    And right so ferden they with Palamon.
With hym ther wenten knyghtes many on;
Som wol ben armed in an haubergeoun,
2120 And in a brestplate and a light gypoun;
And som wol have a paire plates large;
And som wol have a Pruce sheeld or a targe;
Som wol ben armed on his legges weel,
And have an ax, and som a mace of steel –
2125 Ther is no newe gyse that it nas old.
Armed were they, as I have yow told,
Everych after his opinioun.
    Ther maistow seen, comynge with Palamoun,

Lygurge Lycurgus*   *Trace* Thrace

2130

cercles irises

grifphon gryphon*
kempe shaggy

2135   *lymes* limbs   *brawnes* muscles

gyse fashion
chaar chariot
boles bulls   *trays* traces

2140   *cote-armure* a heraldic tunic   *harnays* armour

beres bear's   *for old* with age
kembd combed
for blak because of blackness

2145   *wrethe* wreath   *arm-greet* thick as an arm   *wighte* weight

alauntz wolf-hounds

2150

mosel muzzle
With collars of gold and round filed rings
route following
stierne stern

2155

*Emetreus** *Inde* India
Upon a bay steed with trappings of steel
dyapred with a diamond pattern

2160   *cote-armure* heraldic tunic   *clooth of Tars* Tartary silk
Couched set
brend refined   *ybete* adorned
mantelet short cloak
Bret-ful brim-full, encrusted

Lygurge hymself, the grete kyng of Trace.
2130 Blak was his berd, and manly was his face;
The cercles of his eyen in his heed,
They gloweden bitwixen yelow and reed,
And lik a grifphon looked he aboute,
With kempe heeris on his browes stoute;
2135 His lymes grete, his brawnes harde and stronge,
His shuldres brode, his armes rounde and longe;
And as the gyse was in his contree,
Ful hye upon a chaar of gold stood he,
With foure white boles in the trays.
2140 In stede of cote-armure over his harnays,
With nayles yelewe and brighte as any gold,
He hadde a beres skyn, col-blak for old.
His longe heer was kembd bihynde his bak;
As any ravenes fethere it shoon for blak;
2145 A wrethe of gold, arm-greet, of huge wighte,
Upon his heed, set ful of stones brighte,
Of fyne rubyes and of dyamauntz.
Aboute his chaar ther wenten white alauntz,
Twenty and mo, as grete as any steer,
2150 To hunten at the leoun or the deer,
And folwed hym with mosel faste ybounde,
Colered of gold, and tourettes fyled rounde.
An hundred lordes hadde he in his route,
Armed ful wel, with hertes stierne and stoute.
2155   With Arcita, in stories as men fynde,
The grete Emetreus, the kyng of Inde,
Upon a steede bay trapped in steel,
Covered in clooth of gold, dyapred weel,
Cam ridynge lyk the god of armes, Mars.
2160 His cote-armure was of clooth of Tars
Couched with perles white and rounde and grete;
His sadel was of brend gold newe ybete;
A mantelet upon his shulder hangynge,
Bret-ful of rubyes rede as fyr sparklynge;

2165   *crispe* curly   *was yronne* grew

        citryn lemon-coloured

        frakenes freckles   *yspreynd* sprinkled
2170   *somdel* somewhat   *ymeynd* mingled
        lookyng gaze
        I caste I guess

        trompe trumpet
2175   *laurer* laurel

        deduyt delight

2180

        encrees increase
2185   *part* side

        alle and some one and all

        pryme nine o'clock   *alight* alighted
2190

        inned gave lodging   *degree* rank
        festeth feasts   *dooth* makes   *labour* effort
        esen entertain   *doon* do
2195   *yet men wenen* people still believe
        Of any estate could improve it

        meeste greatest

2200   *deys* dais

2165   His crispe heer lyk rynges was yronne,
        And that was yelow, and glytered as the sonne.
        His nose was heigh, his eyen bright citryn,
        His lippes rounde, his colour was sangwyn;
        A fewe frakenes in his face yspreynd,
2170   Bitwixen yelow and somdel blak ymeynd;
        And as a leon he his lookyng caste.
        Of fyve and twenty yeer his age I caste.
        His berd was wel bigonne for to sprynge;
        His voys was as a trompe thonderynge.
2175   Upon his heed he wered of laurer grene
        A gerland, fressh and lusty for to sene.
        Upon his hand he bar for his deduyt
        An egle tame, as any lilye whyt.
        An hundred lordes hadde he with hym there,
2180   Al armed, save hir heddes, in al hir gere,
        Ful richely in alle maner thynges.
        For trusteth wel that dukes, erles, kynges
        Were gadered in this noble compaignye,
        For love and for encrees of chivalrye.
2185   Aboute this kyng ther ran on every part
        Ful many a tame leon and leopart.
        And in this wise thise lordes, alle and some,
        Been on the Sonday to the citee come
        Aboute pryme, and in the toun alight.
2190   This Theseus, this duc, this worthy knyght,
        Whan he had broght hem into his citee,
        And inned hem, everich at his degree,
        He festeth hem, and dooth so greet labour
        To esen hem and doon hem al honour
2195   That yet men wenen that no mannes wit
        Of noon estaat ne koude amenden it.
            The mynstralcye, the service at the feeste,
        The grete yiftes to the meeste and leeste,
        The riche array of Theseus paleys,
2200   Ne who sat first ne last upon the deys,

felyngly sensitively

2205   *liggen* lie

al th'effect only of the result   *thynketh* seems
leste it please
er before

2210

nere nat was not
tho then

2215   *Citherea* she of Cythera*
digne worthy
hir her*   *a pas* at a slow pace
ther where
cheere mien

2220   *soor* sore

gladere gladdener   *Citheron* Cithaeron
For thilke for the sake of that same   *Adoon* Adonis*

2225   *smerte* painful
at to

biwreye reveal

2230

harmes sorrows
rewe take pity   *soore* pain
wisly surely

2235   *Emforth* to the extent of
holden werre wage war

What ladyes fairest been or best daunsynge,
Or which of hem kan dauncen best and synge,
Ne who moost felyngly speketh of love;
What haukes sitten on the perche above,
2205 What houndes liggen on the floor adoun –
Of al this make I now no mencioun,
But al th'effect; that thynketh me the beste.
Now cometh the point, and herkneth if yow leste.
    The Sonday nyght, er day bigan to sprynge,
2210 Whan Palamon the larke herde synge
(Although it nere nat day by houres two,
Yet song the larke) and Palamon right tho
With hooly herte and with an heigh corage,
He roos to wenden on his pilgrymage
2215 Unto the blisful Citherea benigne –
I mene Venus, honurable and digne.
And in hir houre he walketh forth a pas
Unto the lystes ther hire temple was,
And doun he kneleth, and with humble cheere
2220 And herte soor he seyde as ye shal heere:
    'Faireste of faire, O lady myn, Venus,
Doughter to Jove and spouse of Vulcanus,
Thow gladere of the mount of Citheron,
For thilke love thow haddest to Adoon,
2225 Have pitee of my bittre teeris smerte,
And taak myn humble preyere at thyn herte.
Allas! I ne have no langage to telle
Th'effectes ne the tormentz of myn helle;
Myn herte may myne harmes nat biwreye;
2230 I am so confus that I kan noght seye
But "Mercy, lady bright, that knowest weele
My thought and seest what harmes that I feele!"
Considere al this and rewe upon my soore,
As wisly as I shal for everemoore,
2235 Emforth my myght, thy trewe servant be,
And holden werre alwey with chastitee.

avow vow   *so* providing
kepe care   *to yelpe* to boast
Ne I ne . . . nat nor do I

2240

pris reputation   *blowen* proclaimed

hou how   *wyse* manner
2245   *recche* care   *but* whether
hem them

vertu power
2250   *yow list* it please you
worshipe honour
auter altar   *where* whether   *go* walk
beete kindle

2255

bere pierce
Thanne then   *rekke* care

effect upshot
2260   *Yif* give
When Palamon's prayer was finished
anon directly
pitously piously   *circumstaunces* ceremony
Al although

2265

wherby that from which

wiste knew   *boone* boon, request
2270

thridde third   *inequal* unequal, variable*   *that* after

That make I myn avow, so ye me helpe!
I kepe noght of armes for to yelpe,
Ne I ne axe nat tomorwe to have victorie,
2240 Ne renoun in this cas, ne veyne glorie
Of pris of armes blowen up and doun;
But I wolde have fully possessioun
Of Emelye, and dye in thy servyse.
Fynd thow the manere hou and in what wyse:
2245 I recche nat but it may bettre be
To have victorie of hem, or they of me,
So that I have my lady in myne armes.
For though so be that Mars is god of armes,
Youre vertu is so greet in hevene above
2250 That if yow list, I shal wel have my love.
Thy temple wol I worshipe everemo,
And on thyn auter, where I ride or go,
I wol doon sacrifice and fires beete.
And if ye wol nat so, my lady sweete,
2255 Thanne preye I thee, tomorwe with a spere
That Arcita me thurgh the herte bere.
Thanne rekke I noght, whan I have lost my lyf,
Though that Arcita wynne hire to his wyf.
This is th'effect and ende of my preyere:
2260 Yif me my love, thow blisful lady deere.'
      Whan the orison was doon of Palamon,
His sacrifice he dide, and that anon,
Ful pitously, with alle circumstaunces,
Al telle I noght as now his observaunces;
2265 But atte laste the statue of Venus shook,
And made a signe, wherby that he took
That his preyere accepted was that day.
For thogh the signe shewed a delay,
Yet wiste he wel that graunted was his boone,
2270 And with glad herte he wente hym hoom ful soone.
      The thridde houre inequal that Palamon
Bigan to Venus temple for to gon,

gan hye hastened

2275   *ladde* led

encens incense   *clothes* hangings   *remenant* rest
longen shal should belong
meeth mead   *gyse* custom

2280   Nothing was lacking for the performance of . . .
Smokynge censing   *clothes* hangings

wessh washed   *welle* spring
ryte rite

2285   Unless it were in a general way
a game intriguing
meneth means   *no charge* no burden, no matter
at his large free (to speak or not)
kembd combed   *untressed* loose

2290   *coroune* crown   *ook cerial* evergreen oak
meete suitable
auter altar   *beete* kindle
thynges observances
Stace of Thebes Statius' *Thebaid*

2295   *pitous* pious   *cheere* countenance
Dyane Diana

sene visible
Queen of Pluto's dark realm below

2300   *knowe* known
woost knowest
As keepe may you preserve
aboughte suffered for (see 2065)
wostow knowest thou

2305

love mistress
woost knowest   *yet* still
venerye the chase

Up roos the sonne, and up roos Emelye
And to the temple of Dyane gan hye.
2275 Hir maydens, that she thider with hire ladde,
Ful redily with hem the fyr they hadde,
Th'encens, the clothes, and the remenant al
That to the sacrifice longen shal;
The hornes fulle of meeth, as was the gyse –
2280 Ther lakked noght to doon hir sacrifise.
Smokynge the temple, ful of clothes faire,
This Emelye, with herte debonaire,
Hir body wessh with water of a welle.
But hou she dide hir ryte I dar nat telle,
2285 But it be any thing in general;
And yet it were a game to heeren al.
To hym that meneth wel it were no charge;
But it is good a man been at his large.
Hir brighte heer was kembd, untressed al;
2290 A coroune of a grene ook cerial
Upon hir heed was set ful fair and meete.
Two fyres on the auter gan she beete,
And dide hir thynges, as men may biholde
In Stace of Thebes and thise bookes olde.
2295 Whan kyndled was the fyr, with pitous cheere
Unto Dyane she spak as ye may heere:
    'O chaste goddesse of the wodes grene,
To whom bothe hevene and erthe and see is sene,
Queene of the regne of Pluto derk and lowe,
2300 Goddesse of maydens, that myn herte hast knowe
Ful many a yeer, and woost what I desire,
As keepe me fro thy vengeaunce and thyn ire,
That Attheon aboughte cruelly.
Chaste goddesse, wel wostow that I
2305 Desire to ben a mayden al my lyf,
Ne nevere wol I be no love ne wyf.
I am, thow woost, yet of thy compaignye,
A mayde, and love huntynge and venerye,

2310

Noght wol I not at all do I wish
sith since
By those three forms . . .*

2315   *soore* painfully
moore more (words)
As sende may you send

hire hoote their hot
2320

queynt extinguished   *place* direction
do show
shapen shaped, determined
shal nedes must needs
2325   *As sende* may you send   *desireth* desires*

kepere guardian
maydenhede maidenhood
2330

brenne burn   *auter* altar   *cleere* brightly

queynte curious
right anon straightaway   *queynte* went out
2335   *quyked* revived   *anon* shortly
queynt extinguished   *agon* gone out

As do these wet brands as they burn

2340   *blody dropes**
agast frightened
ny nigh   *crye* cry out
wiste knew
the feere fear

And for to walken in the wodes wilde,
2310 And noght to ben a wyf and be with childe.
Noght wol I knowe compaignye of man.
Now help me, lady, sith ye may and kan,
For tho thre formes that thou hast in thee.
And Palamon, that hath swich love to me,
2315 And eek Arcite, that loveth me so soore,
This grace I preye thee withoute moore,
As sende love and pees bitwixe hem two,
And fro me turne awey hir hertes so
That al hire hoote love and hir desir,
2320 And al hir bisy torment, and hir fir
Be queynt, or turned in another place.
And if so be thou wolt nat do me grace,
Or if my destynee be shapen so
That I shal nedes have oon of hem two,
2325 As sende me hym that moost desireth me.
Bihoold, goddesse of clene chastitee,
The bittre teeris that on my chekes falle.
Syn thou art mayde and kepere of us alle,
My maydenhede thou kepe and wel conserve,
2330 And whil I lyve, a mayde I wol thee serve.'
    The fires brenne upon the auter cleere,
Whil Emelye was thus in hir preyere.
But sodeynly she saugh a sighte queynte,
For right anon oon of the fyres queynte
2335 And quyked agayn, and after that anon
That oother fyr was queynt and al agon;
And as it queynte it made a whistelynge,
As doon thise wete brondes in hir brennynge,
And at the brondes ende out ran anon
2340 As it were blody dropes many oon;
For which so soore agast was Emelye
That she was wel ny mad and gan to crye,
For she ne wiste what it signyfied,
But oonly for the feere thus hath she cried,

2345   *weep* wept

        stynt cease   *hevynesse* sorrowing
        goddes hye high gods
2350
        tho those

        dwelle stay
2355   *brenne* burn
        Shall tell thee, before you go hence
        aventure of fortune in
        caas quiver
        faste loudly
2360
        astoned astonished

        disposicioun disposal
2365   *nexte* nearest
        effect outcome
        nexte first

2370   *payen* pagan   *wyse* custom
        pitous pious

        regnes realms
        Trace Thrace   *yholde* considered
2375
        Of armes al the brydel control of the fortunes of war
        And award them whatever fortune it pleases you to devise
        pitous pious

2380

2345   And weep that it was pitee for to heere.
And therwithal Dyane gan appeere,
With bowe in honde, right as an hunteresse,
And seyde, 'Doghter, stynt thyn hevynesse.
Among the goddes hye it is affermed,
2350   And by eterne word writen and confermed,
Thou shalt ben wedded unto oon of tho
That han for thee so muchel care and wo,
But unto which of hem I may nat telle.
Farwel, for I ne may no lenger dwelle.
2355   The fires which that on myn auter brenne
Shulle thee declaren, er that thou go henne,
Thyn aventure of love, as in this cas.'
And with that word, the arwes in the caas
Of the goddesse clateren faste and rynge,
2360   And forth she wente and made a vanysshynge;
For which this Emelye astoned was,
And seyde, 'What amounteth this, allas?
I putte me in thy proteccioun,
Dyane, and in thy disposicioun.'
2365   And hoom she goth anon the nexte weye.
This is th'effect; ther is namoore to seye.
        The nexte houre of Mars folwynge this,
Arcite unto the temple walked is
Of fierse Mars to doon his sacrifise,
2370   With alle the rytes of his payen wyse.
With pitous herte and heigh devocioun,
Right thus to Mars he seyde his orisoun:
        'O stronge god, that in the regnes colde
Of Trace honoured art and lord yholde,
2375   And hast in every regne and every lond
Of armes al the brydel in thyn hond,
And hem fortunest as thee lyst devyse,
Accepte of me my pitous sacrifise.
If so be that my youthe may deserve,
2380   And that my myght be worthy for to serve

oon of thyne one of thy servants
rewe pity   *pyne* torture
thilke peyne that same pain
whilom brendest once burned
2385   *usedest* didst enjoy
free noble

thee . . . mysfille misfortune befell thee
Vulcanus Vulcan*   *las* net
2390   *liggynge* lying
For by
routhe pity   *smerte* painful
unkonnynge ignorant   *woost* knowest
trowe think   *offended* assailed
2395   *lyves* living
dooth makes
Cares not whether I sink or swim
woot know   *er* before   *heete* promise
moot must   *place* lists
2400   *woot* know

For for the sake of   *brente* burnt

2405   *do* make it
travaille labour

For your pleasure and (exert myself in) your hardy activities
2410   *my baner honge* hang up my banner

fynde provide
avow vow
2415

offensioun injury

Thy godhede, that I may been oon of thyne,
Thanne preye I thee to rewe upon my pyne.
For thilke peyne and thilke hoote fir
In which thow whilom brendest for desir,
2385 Whan that thow usedest the beautee
Of faire, yonge, fresshe Venus free,
And haddest hire in armes at thy wille —
Although thee ones on a tyme mysfille,
Whan Vulcanus hadde caught thee in his las
2390 And foond thee liggynge by his wyf, allas! —
For thilke sorwe that was in thyn herte,
Have routhe as wel upon my peynes smerte.
I am yong and unkonnynge, as thow woost,
And, as I trowe, with love offended moost
2395 That evere was any lyves creature,
For she that dooth me al this wo endure
Ne reccheth nevere wher I synke or fleete.
And wel I woot, er she me mercy heete,
I moot with strengthe wynne hire in the place,
2400 And wel I woot, withouten help or grace
Of thee ne may my strengthe noght availle.
Thanne help me, lord, tomorwe in my bataille,
For thilke fyr that whilom brente thee,
As wel as thilke fyr now brenneth me,
2405 And do that I tomorwe have victorie.
Myn be the travaille, and thyn be the glorie!
Thy sovereyn temple wol I moost honouren
Of any place, and alwey moost labouren
In thy plesaunce and in thy craftes stronge,
2410 And in thy temple I wol my baner honge
And alle the armes of my compaignye,
And everemo, unto that day I dye,
Eterne fir I wol bifore thee fynde.
And eek to this avow I wol me bynde:
2415 My beerd, myn heer, that hongeth long adoun,
That nevere yet ne felte offensioun

shere shears

2420

stynt having ceased

hym agaste took fright
2425

yaf gave
haf raised

2430

his *hauberk rynge* to make its mail-coat ring

seyde it said
yaf gave
2435   *wel to fare* of doing well
in is fare lodging has gone
fayn glad   *fowel* bird
swich such
For thilke grauntyng because of that promise

2440

stierne stern   *armypotente* mighty in arms
stente stop
Saturnus Saturn*
aventures happenings
2445   *art* device
part part
elde old age
usage experience
Men may one can   *atrenne* outrun   *atrede* outwit
2450   *stynten* stop
agayn his kynde against his nature
Of for

Of rasour nor of shere, I wol thee yive,
And ben thy trewe servant whil I lyve.
Now, lord, have routhe upon my sorwes soore;
2420   Yif me [victorie]; I aske thee namoore.'
          The preyere stynt of Arcita the stronge,
The rynges on the temple dore that honge,
And eek the dores, clatereden ful faste,
Of which Arcita somwhat hym agaste.
2425   The fyres brenden upon the auter brighte
That it gan al the temple for to lighte;
A sweete smel the ground anon up yaf,
And Arcita anon his hand up haf,
And moore encens into the fyr he caste,
2430   With othere rytes mo; and atte laste
The statue of Mars bigan his hauberk rynge,
And with that soun he herde a murmurynge
Ful lowe and dym, and seyde thus, 'Victorie!'
For which he yaf to Mars honour and glorie.
2435   And thus with joye and hope wel to fare
Arcite anon unto his in is fare,
As fayn as fowel is of the brighte sonne.
          And right anon swich strif ther is bigonne,
For thilke grauntyng, in the hevene above,
2440   Bitwixe Venus, the goddesse of love,
And Mars, the stierne god armypotente,
That Juppiter was bisy it to stente,
Till that the pale Saturnus the colde,
That knew so manye of aventures olde,
2445   Foond in his olde experience an art
That he ful soone hath plesed every part.
As sooth is seyd, elde hath greet avantage;
In elde is bothe wysdom and usage;
Men may the olde atrenne and noght atrede.
2450   Saturne anon, to stynten strif and drede,
Al be it that it is agayn his kynde,
Of al this strif he gan remedie fynde.

doghter child*   *quod* said
cours course, orbit
2455   *woot* knows
drenchyng drowning*   *wan* dark
prison imprisonment   *cote* cell

murmure murmuring   *cherles* churls', peasants'*
2460   *groynynge* grumbling   *pryvee* secret
do engineer   *pleyn* full   *correccioun* punishment
the leoun Leo*
ruyne ruin

2465   *mynour* miner
slow slew   *Sampsoun* Samson*   *piler* pillar

castes olde long-laid plots
lookyng aspect   *fader* cause
2470   *doon diligence* take care

hight promised
nathelees nonetheless
moot must   *pees* peace
2475   *Al* although   *o* one   *compleccioun* temperament*

aiel grandfather
lust pleasure
stynten stop
2480

effect outcome

Explicit tercia pars Here ends the third part

'My deere doghter Venus,' quod Saturne,
'My cours, that hath so wyde for to turne,
2455 Hath moore power than woot any man.
Myn is the drenchyng in the see so wan;
Myn is the prison in the derke cote;
Myn is the stranglyng and hangyng by the throte,
The murmure and the cherles rebellyng,
2460 The groynynge, and the pryvee empoysonyng;
I do vengeance and pleyn correccioun,
Whil I dwelle in the signe of the leoun.
Myn is the ruyne of the hye halles,
The fallynge of the toures and of the walles
2465 Upon the mynour or the carpenter.
I slow Sampsoun, shakynge the piler;
And myne be the maladyes colde,
The derke tresons, and the castes olde;
My lookyng is the fader of pestilence.
2470 Now weep namoore; I shal doon diligence
That Palamon, that is thyn owene knyght,
Shal have his lady, as thou hast him hight.
Though Mars shal helpe his knyght, yet nathelees
Bitwixe yow ther moot be som tyme pees,
2475 Al be ye noght of o compleccioun,
That causeth al day swich divisioun.
I am thyn aiel, redy at thy wille;
Weep now namoore; I wol thy lust fulfille.'
Now wol I stynten of the goddes above,
2480 Of Mars, and of Venus, goddesse of love,
And telle yow as pleynly as I kan
The grete effect, for which that I bygan.

Explicit tercia pars

Sequitur pars quarta Here follows the fourth part*

Atthenes Athens
lusty joyful
2485   *wight* man   *plesaunce* delight
justen joust

by the cause because   *sholde* had to

2490
the morwe*
harneys armour

route company
2495
maystow canst thou   *devisynge* preparing of   *harneys* equipment
unkouth rare   *wroght* fashioned
browdynge embroidery
testeres head-pieces (for horses)   *trappures* horse-armour
2500   Gold-coloured helmets, mailshirts, heraldic tunics
parementz rich array
of retenue in service
Nailing spearheads to shafts and buckling on helmets
Fitting straps to shields, and lacing thongs
2505   *There as* wherever   *no thyng ydel* by no means idle

faste quickly
fyle file   *prikynge* riding
Yemen yeomen   *communes* common people
2510   *thikke* (crowding) closely   *goon* walk
nakers kettledrums   *clariounes* bugles

holdynge hir questioun debating

Sequitur pars quarta

Greet was the feeste in Atthenes that day,
And eek the lusty seson of that May
2485 Made every wight to been in swich plesaunce
That al that Monday justen they and daunce,
And spenden it in Venus heigh servyse.
But by the cause that they sholde ryse
Eerly, for to seen the grete fight,
2490 Unto hir reste wenten they at nyght.
And on the morwe, whan that day gan sprynge,
Of hors and harneys noyse and claterynge
Ther was in hostelryes al aboute,
And to the paleys rood ther many a route
2495 Of lordes upon steedes and palfreys.
Ther maystow seen devisynge of harneys
So unkouth and so riche, and wroght so weel
Of goldsmythrye, of browdynge, and of steel;
The sheeldes brighte, testeres, and trappures,
2500 Gold-hewen helmes, hauberkes, cote-armures;
Lordes in parementz on hir courseres,
Knyghtes of retenue, and eek squieres
Nailynge the speres, and helmes bokelynge;
Giggynge of sheeldes, with layneres lacynge –
2505 There as nede is they weren no thyng ydel;
The fomy steedes on the golden brydel
Gnawynge, and faste the armurers also
With fyle and hamer prikynge to and fro;
Yemen on foote, and communes many oon
2510 With shorte staves, thikke as they may goon;
Pypes, trompes, nakers, clariounes,
That in the bataille blowen blody sounes;
The paleys ful of peple up and doun,
Heere thre, ther ten, holdynge hir questioun,

2515   *Dyvynynge of* speculating about

    helden sided
    balled bald one   *herd* haired
    he this one   *he wolde* that one would
2520   *sparth* battle-axe   *wighte* weight

    gan to sprynge rose

2525   *Heeld yet* remained in   *chambre* bedchamber
    yliche alike
    fet brought

    trone throne*
2530   *preesseth* crowds
    doon heigh reverence pay profound respect
    herkne listen to   *heste* command   *sentence* order
    heraud herald
    ydo ceased
2535

    tho then
    discrecioun judgement

    gentil noble   *gyse* manner
2540   *emprise* undertaking
    shapen contrive
    firste original
    up on
    shot arrow   *polax* battle-axe
2545

    stoke thrust
    ne drawe neither draw one
    Ne no man shal nor shall any man   *unto* against
    But o cours more than one course*
2550   He may, if it please him, once on foot, thrust to defend himself

2515 Dyvynynge of thise Thebane knyghtes two.
Somme seyden thus, somme seyde 'it shal be so';
Somme helden with hym with the blake berd,
Somme with the balled, somme with the thikke herd;
Somme seyde he looked grymme, and he wolde fighte:
2520 'He hath a sparth of twenty pound of wighte.'
Thus was the halle ful of divynynge,
Longe after that the sonne gan to sprynge.

    The grete Theseus, that of his sleep awaked
With mynstralcie and noyse that was maked,
2525 Heeld yet the chambre of his paleys riche
Til that the Thebane knyghtes, bothe yliche
Honured, were into the paleys fet.
Duc Theseus was at a wyndow set,
Arrayed right as he were a god in trone.
2530 The peple preesseth thiderward ful soone
Hym for to seen, and doon heigh reverence,
And eek to herkne his heste and his sentence.
An heraud on a scaffold made an 'Oo!'
Til al the noyse of peple was ydo,
2535 And whan he saugh the peple of noyse al stille,
Tho shewed he the myghty dukes wille:
    'The lord hath of his heigh discrecioun
Considered that it were destruccioun
To gentil blood to fighten in the gyse
2540 Of mortal bataille now in this emprise.
Wherfore, to shapen that they shal nat dye,
He wol his firste purpos modifye.
No man therfore, up peyne of los of lyf,
No maner shot, ne polax, ne short knyf
2545 Into the lystes sende or thider brynge;
Ne short swerd, for to stoke with poynt bitynge,
No man ne drawe, ne bere it by his syde.
Ne no man shal unto his felawe ryde
But o cours with a sharpe ygrounde spere;
2550 Foyne, if hym list, on foote, hymself to were.

at meschief overpowered   *take* taken

ordeyned set up
shal must go
2555
sleen his make slay his counterpart
turneiynge tournament
spede yow give you success
fighteth fight (imperative)
2560

stevene voice

wilneth desires
2565   *Up* loudly   *trompes* trumpets
rit rides
ordinance order
sarge serge

2570

after hir degree according to their rank

2575   *by tyme* in time
pryme 9 a.m.
set seated

degrees aboute the tiers around them
2580   *seetes* seats   *route* crowd
under Marte under the temple of Mars
parte side
baner banner
selve same
2585   *under Venus* under the temple of Venus
hardy chiere valiant air

And he that is at meschief shal be take
And noght slayn, but be broght unto the stake
That shal ben ordeyned on either syde;
But thider he shal by force, and there abyde.
2555   And if so falle the chieftayn be take
On outher syde, or elles sleen his make,
No lenger shal the turneiynge laste.
God spede you! Gooth forth and ley on faste!
With long swerd and with mace fighteth youre fille.
2560   Gooth now youre wey; this is the lordes wille.'
    The voys of peple touchede the hevene,
So loude cride they with murie stevene,
'God save swich a lord, that is so good
He wilneth no destruccion of blood!'
2565   Up goon the trompes and the melodye,
And to the lystes rit the compaignye,
By ordinance, thurghout the citee large,
Hanged with clooth of gold, and nat with sarge.
    Ful lik a lord this noble duc gan ryde,
2570   Thise two Thebans upon either syde,
And after rood the queene and Emelye,
And after that another compaignye
Of oon and oother, after hir degree.
And thus they passen thurghout the citee,
2575   And to the lystes come they by tyme.
It nas nat of the day yet fully pryme
Whan set was Theseus ful riche and hye,
Ypolita the queene, and Emelye,
And othere ladys in degrees aboute.
2580   Unto the seetes preesseth al the route.
And westward, thurgh the gates under Marte,
Arcite, and eek the hondred of his parte,
With baner reed is entred right anon;
And in that selve moment Palamon
2585   Is under Venus, estward in the place,
With baner whyt and hardy chiere and face.

evene well-matched
nere were not
2590

worthynesse valour   *estaat* rank
for to gesse one would guess
And they draw themselves up in two fine ranks
2595   *rad* read   *everichon* each one
That so that   *gyle* cheating
Tho then   *shet* shut
devoir duty
hir prikyng their riding
2600   *clarioun* bugle

sadly in arrest firmly into the socket
spore spur
juste joust
2605   *shyveren* splinter   *shaftes* spearshafts*
He one   *herte-spoon* base of the breastbone

as the silver brighte bright as silver
tohewen cut to pieces   *toshrede* cut to shreds
2610   *brest* bursts   *stierne* violent
tobreste smash
He one   *threste* thrust

2615   *foyneth* thrusts   *tronchoun* broken spearshaft
And one knocks down another, man and horse
sithen afterwards
Maugree his heed in spite of all he can do
forward the agreement   *abyde* stay
2620   *Another lad is* another is brought in
dooth hem Theseus Theseus makes them
leste should please

In al the world, to seken up and doun,
So evene, withouten variacioun,
Ther nere swiche compaignyes tweye,
2590 For ther was noon so wys that koude seye
That any hadde of oother avauntage
Of worthynesse, ne of estaat, ne age,
So evene were they chosen, for to gesse.
And in two renges faire they hem dresse.
2595 Whan that hir names rad were everichon,
That in hir nombre gyle were ther noon,
Tho were the gates shet, and cried was loude:
'Do now youre devoir, yonge knyghtes proude!'
    The heraudes lefte hir prikyng up and doun;
2600 Now ryngen trompes loude and clarioun.
Ther is namoore to seyn, but west and est
In goon the speres ful sadly in arrest;
In gooth the sharpe spore into the syde.
Ther seen men who kan juste and who kan ryde;
2605 Ther shyveren shaftes upon sheeldes thikke;
He feeleth thurgh the herte-spoon the prikke.
Up spryngen speres twenty foot on highte;
Out goon the swerdes as the silver brighte;
The helmes they tohewen and toshrede;
2610 Out brest the blood with stierne stremes rede;
With myghty maces the bones they tobreste.
He thurgh the thikkeste of the throng gan threste;
Ther stomblen steedes stronge, and doun gooth al,
He rolleth under foot as dooth a bal;
2615 He foyneth on his feet with his tronchoun,
And he hym hurtleth with his hors adoun;
He thurgh the body is hurt and sithen take,
Maugree his heed, and broght unto the stake;
As forward was, right there he moste abyde.
2620 Another lad is on that oother syde.
And some tyme dooth hem Theseus to reste,
Hem to refresshe and drynken, if hem leste.

a day that day   *han* have
wroght his felawe wo done his comrade harm

2625

nas no tygre was no tigress   *Galgopheye* Gargaphia*
hir whelp her cub   *lite* little
on the hunte towards the hunter

2630 Nor in Morocco is there so fierce a lion*
wood mad
praye prey
sleen slay

2635 *renneth* runs
dede deed

gan hente caught

2640

Unyolden without having surrendered   *ydrawen* dragged
rescus (attempted) rescue
born adoun made to fall

2645
born knocked
he Palamon

2650 *abyde* remain
composicioun the agreement
sorweth grieves
moot could

2655 *echon* each one, each and all
Hoo stop   *doon* over
partie partisan

Ful ofte a day han thise Thebanes two
Togydre ymet, and wroght his felawe wo;
2625 Unhorsed hath ech oother of hem tweye.
Ther nas no tygre in the vale of Galgopheye,
Whan that hir whelp is stole whan it is lite,
So crueel on the hunte as is Arcite
For jelous herte upon this Palamon.
2630 Ne in Belmarye ther nys so fel leon,
That hunted is, or for his hunger wood,
Ne of his praye desireth so the blood,
As Palamon to sleen his foo Arcite.
The jelous strokes on hir helmes byte;
2635 Out renneth blood on bothe hir sydes rede.
    Som tyme an ende ther is of every dede.
For er the sonne unto the reste wente,
The stronge kyng Emetreus gan hente
This Palamon, as he faught with Arcite,
2640 And made his swerd depe in his flessh to byte,
And by the force of twenty is he take
Unyolden, and ydrawen to the stake.
And in the rescus of this Palamoun
The stronge kyng Lygurge is born adoun,
2645 And kyng Emetreus, for al his strengthe,
Is born out of his sadel a swerdes lengthe,
So hitte him Palamoun er he were take.
But al for noght; he was broght to the stake.
His hardy herte myghte hym helpe naught:
2650 He moste abyde, whan that he was caught,
By force and eek by composicioun.
    Who sorweth now but woful Palamoun,
That moot namoore goon agayn to fighte?
And whan that Theseus hadde seyn this sighte,
2655 Unto the folk that foghten thus echon
He cryde, 'Hoo! namoore, for it is doon!
I wol be trewe juge, and no partie.
Arcite of Thebes shal have Emelie,

faire fairly

2660

heighe great

2665   *wantynge* lacking
Until her tears fell in the lists
ashamed put to shame
pees peace
boone request

2670   *heed* head   *esed* relieved
trompours trumpeters   *mynstralcie* music

wele happiness   *daun* Don (*dominus*, lord)
But listen to me and hold your noise a little

2675   *Which* what
of his helm ydon taken off his helmet

He rides the length of the spacious arena

2680   *agayn* towards   *freendlich ye* friendly eye*
in comune in general*
folwen alle all follow
chiere happiness*
sterte started*

2685

fere fear
leep leapt   *foundred* stumbled
keep heed
He pitched him on the top of his head

2690

tobrosten shattered
cole coal
yronnen in run into
yborn carried

That by his fortune hath hire faire ywonne.'
2660   Anon ther is a noyse of peple bigonne
For joye of this, so loude and heighe withalle
It semed that the lystes sholde falle.
     What kan now faire Venus doon above?
What seith she now? What dooth this queene of love,
2665   But wepeth so, for wantynge of hir wille,
Til that hir teeres in the lystes fille?
She seyde, 'I am ashamed, doutelees.'
     Saturnus seyde, 'Doghter, hoold thy pees!
Mars hath his wille, his knyght hath al his boone,
2670   And, by myn heed, thow shalt been esed soone.'
     The trompours, with the loude mynstralcie,
The heraudes, that ful loude yelle and crie,
Been in hire wele for joye of daun Arcite.
But herkneth me, and stynteth noyse a lite,
2675   Which a myracle ther bifel anon.
     This fierse Arcite hath of his helm ydon,
And on a courser, for to shewe his face,
He priketh endelong the large place
Lokynge upward upon this Emelye;
2680   And she agayn hym caste a freendlich ye
(For wommen, as to speken in comune,
Thei folwen alle the favour of Fortune)
And was al his chiere, as in his herte.
     Out of the ground a furie infernal sterte,
2685   From Pluto sent at requeste of Saturne,
For which his hors for fere gan to turne,
And leep aside, and foundred as he leep;
And er that Arcite may taken keep,
He pighte hym on the pomel of his heed,
2690   That in the place he lay as he were deed,
His brest tobrosten with his sadel-bowe.
As blak he lay as any cole or crowe,
So was the blood yronnen in his face.
Anon he was yborn out of the place,

2695   *With herte soor* with grief at heart
    Tho then   *korven* carved, cut
    blyve quickly
    in memorie conscious
    criynge calling
2700

    solempnitee ceremony
    aventure misadventure
    disconforten dismay
2705

    fayn glad
    noon none
    Al were they although they were   *namely oon* one especially
2710   Whose breastbone was pierced by a spear
    To for

    Fermacies medicines   *save* sage*
    lymes limbs   *have* keep
2715

    made revel kept up the cheer
    straunge foreign
    Nor was it regarded as any defeat
2720   Except as (in) a joust or a tournament
    soothly truly   *disconfiture* defeat
    aventure misfortune
    lad led
    Unyolden without having surrendered   *with* by
2725   *O* one   *mo* more
    haryed dragged   *too* toe

    knaves servants
    No disgrace was imputed to him
2730   *clepen* call   *cowardye* cowardice

2695 With herte soor, to Theseus paleys.
     Tho was he korven out of his harneys
     And in a bed ybrought ful faire and blyve,
     For he was yet in memorie and alyve,
     And alwey criynge after Emelye.

2700   Duc Theseus, with al his compaignye,
     Is comen hoom to Atthenes his citee,
     With alle blisse and greet solempnitee.
     Al be it that this aventure was falle,
     He nolde noght disconforten hem alle.

2705 Men seyde eek that Arcite shal nat dye;
     He shal been heeled of his maladye.
     And of another thyng they weren as fayn,
     That of hem alle was ther noon yslayn,
     Al were they soore yhurt, and namely oon,

2710 That with a spere was thirled his brest boon.
     To othere woundes and to broken armes
     Somme hadden salves, and somme hadden charmes;
     Fermacies of herbes, and eek save
     They dronken, for they wolde hir lymes have.

2715 For which this noble duc, as he wel kan,
     Conforteth and honoureth every man,
     And made revel al the longe nyght
     Unto the straunge lordes, as was right.
     Ne ther was holden no disconfitynge

2720 But as a justes or a tourneiynge;
     For soothly ther was no disconfiture.
     For fallyng nys nat but an aventure,
     Ne to be lad by force unto the stake
     Unyolden, and with twenty knyghtes take,

2725 O persone allone, withouten mo,
     And haryed forth by arme, foot, and too,
     And eke his steede dryven forth with staves
     With footmen, bothe yemen and eek knaves –
     It nas arretted hym no vileynye;

2730 Ther may no man clepen it cowardye.

leet crye had proclaimed
stynten stop   *envye* ill-will
gree worth

2735   *yiftes* gifts   *hir degree* their rank

a journee largely a good day's journey

2740

endite write

soore pain

2745   In spite of any medical skill, the clotted blood
corrupteth putrefies   *bouk* trunk   *ylaft* left
veyne-blood blood let from a vein   *ventusynge* cupping*

The expulsive or animal power*
2750   Deriving from the power called natural*
venym poison*   *voyden* clear
pipes tubes   *longes* lungs
lacerte muscle   *adoun* deep inside
shent destroyed
2755   There avail him neither, to preserve his life
Vomyt emetic
tobrosten shattered
dominacioun power
ther where   *wirche* work
2760   *phisik* medicine   *ber* carry
This is the long and short, that Arcite must die

2765   *Naught* not at all
o point a fraction   *smerte* painful

For which anon duc Theseus leet crye,
To stynten alle rancour and envye,
The gree as wel of o syde as of oother,
And eyther syde ylik as ootheres brother;
2735 And yaf hem yiftes after hir degree,
And fully heeld a feeste dayes three,
And conveyed the kynges worthily
Out of his toun a journee largely.
And hoom wente every man the righte way.
2740 Ther was namoore but 'Fare wel, have good day!'
Of this bataille I wol namoore endite,
But speke of Palamon and of Arcite.

   Swelleth the brest of Arcite, and the soore
Encreesseth at his herte moore and moore.
2745 The clothered blood, for any lechecraft,
Corrupteth, and is in his bouk ylaft,
That neither veyne-blood, ne ventusynge,
Ne drynke of herbes may ben his helpynge.
The vertu expulsif, or animal,
2750 Fro thilke vertu cleped natural
Ne may the venym voyden ne expelle.
The pipes of his longes gonne to swelle,
And every lacerte in his brest adoun
Is shent with venym and corrupcioun.
2755 Hym gayneth neither, for to gete his lif,
Vomyt upward, ne dounward laxatif.
Al is tobrosten thilke regioun;
Nature hath now no dominacioun.
And certeinly, ther Nature wol nat wirche,
2760 Fare wel phisik! Go ber the man to chirche!
This al and som, that Arcita moot dye;
For which he sendeth after Emelye,
And Palamon, that was his cosyn deere.
Thanne seyde he thus, as ye shal after heere:
2765 'Naught may the woful spirit in myn herte
Declare o point of alle my sorwes smerte

But yet   *biquethe* bequeath   *goost* spirit

2770   *dure* endure, last

2775   *my wyf* *
       endere ender
       What asketh men what is it men want

2780   *foo* foe
       softe gently
       herkneth hear

       agon now passed
2785
       And as surely as (I hope) Jupiter may guide my soul
       servaunt servant in love
       circumstances qualities
       trouthe fidelity, integrity
2790   *estaat* rank   *heigh kynrede* noble lineage
       Fredom generosity   *art* art (of love)
       As Jupiter may take my soul's part

2795
       ben be
       Foryet forget   *gentil* virtuous
       faille gan began to fail

2800
       yet mooreover still further
       ago gone

To yow, my lady, that I love moost,
But I biquethe the servyce of my goost
To yow aboven every creature,
2770 Syn that my lyf may no lenger dure.
Allas, the wo! Allas, the peynes stronge,
That I for yow have suffred, and so longe!
Allas, the deeth! Allas, myn Emelye!
Allas, departynge of oure compaignye!
2775 Allas, myn hertes queene! Allas, my wyf,
Myn hertes lady, endere of my lyf!
What is this world? What asketh men to have?
Now with his love, now in his colde grave
Allone, withouten any compaignye.
2780 Fare wel, my sweete foo, myn Emelye!
And softe taak me in youre armes tweye,
For love of God, and herkneth what I seye.
     'I have heer with my cosyn Palamon
Had strif and rancour many a day agon
2785 For love of yow, and for my jalousye.
And Juppiter so wys my soule gye,
To speken of a servaunt proprely,
With alle circumstances trewely –
That is to seyen, trouthe, honour, knyghthede,
2790 Wysdom, humblesse, estaat, and heigh kynrede,
Fredom, and al that longeth to that art –
So Juppiter have of my soule part,
As in this world right now ne knowe I non
So worthy to ben loved as Palamon,
2795 That serveth yow, and wol doon al his lyf.
And if that evere ye shul ben a wyf,
Foryet nat Palamon, the gentil man.'
And with that word his speche faille gan,
For from his feet up to his brest was come
2800 The coold of deeth, that hadde hym overcome,
And yet mooreover, for in his armes two
The vital strengthe is lost and al ago.

withouten moore with no delay

2805

Dusked grew dark
yet still

hous abode*   *ther* to a place
2810   *As* where   *cam* went
stynte stop   *nam* am not   *divinistre* theologian
Of concerning   *registre* table of contents of a book
me ne list it does not please me   *thilke* the
Of those who may have written of the dwelling-place of souls
2815   *ther Mars his soule gye* may Mars guide his soul

Shrighte shrieked*
suster sister-in-law
baar carried
2820   *tarien forth* waste
weep wept
swich cas such a situation

sorwen so grieve so much
2825

2830

Ector Hector

Cracchynge scratching   *rentynge* tearing
2835   *Why woldestow be deed* why did you want to die
And when you

Oonly the intellect, withouten moore,
That dwelled in his herte syk and soore,
2805 Gan faillen whan the herte felte deeth.
Dusked his eyen two, and failled breeth,
But on his lady yet caste he his ye;
His laste word was, 'Mercy, Emelye!'
His spirit chaunged hous and wente ther,
2810 As I cam nevere, I kan nat tellen wher.
Therfore I stynte; I nam no divinistre;
Of soules fynde I nat in this registre,
Ne me ne list thilke opinions to telle
Of hem, though that they writen wher they dwelle.
2815 Arcite is coold, ther Mars his soule gye!
Now wol I speken forth of Emelye.
    Shrighte Emelye, and howleth Palamon,
And Theseus his suster took anon
Swownynge, and baar hire fro the corps away.
2820 What helpeth it to tarien forth the day
To tellen how she weep bothe eve and morwe?
For in swich cas wommen have swich sorwe,
Whan that hir housbondes ben from hem ago,
That for the moore part they sorwen so,
2825 Or ellis fallen in swich maladye
That at the laste certeinly they dye.
    Infinite been the sorwes and the teeres
Of olde folk and folk of tendre yeeres
In al the toun for deeth of this Theban.
2830 For hym ther wepeth bothe child and man;
So greet wepyng was ther noon, certayn,
Whan Ector was ybroght, al fressh yslayn,
To Troye. Allas, the pitee that was ther,
Cracchynge of chekes, rentynge eek of heer.
2835 'Why woldestow be deed,' thise wommen crye,
'And haddest gold ynough, and Emelye?'
    No man myghte gladen Theseus,
Savynge his olde fader Egeus,

2840

ensamples examples   *liknesse* analogies
Right just   *quod* said
ne lyvede had not lived   *degree* rank of life
2845   *Right* just

nys but is only   *thurghfare* thoroughfare*

2850   *over* in addition to
enhorte exhort
hem reconforte take comfort
cure care
Caste considered   *sepulture* tomb
2855

in his degree according to his rank

ther as where

2860   *selve* same   *swoote* sweet

compleynte lament
office rite
accomplice accomplish
2865   *leet comande* had orders given
on a rewe in a row
colpons bundles   *arrayed* arranged

2870

After for   *beere* bier

suyte material

That knew this worldes transmutacioun,
2840 As he hadde seyn it chaunge bothe up and doun,
Joye after wo, and wo after gladnesse,
And shewed hem ensamples and liknesse.
    'Right as ther dyed nevere man,' quod he,
'That he ne lyvede in erthe in some degree,
2845 Right so ther lyvede never man,' he seyde,
'In al this world, that som tyme he ne deyde.
This world nys but a thurghfare ful of wo,
And we been pilgrymes, passynge to and fro.
Deeth is an ende of every worldly soore.'
2850 And over al this yet seyde he muchel moore
To this effect, ful wisely to enhorte
The peple that they sholde hem reconforte.
    Duc Theseus, with al his bisy cure,
Caste now wher that the sepulture
2855 Of goode Arcite may best ymaked be,
And eek moost honurable in his degree.
And at the laste he took conclusioun
That ther as first Arcite and Palamoun
Hadden for love the bataille hem bitwene,
2860 That in that selve grove, swoote and grene,
Ther as he hadde his amorouse desires,
His compleynte, and for love his hoote fires,
He wolde make a fyr in which the office
Funeral he myghte al accomplice.
2865 And leet comande anon to hakke and hewe
The okes olde, and leye hem on a rewe
In colpons wel arrayed for to brenne.
His officers with swifte feet they renne
And ryde anon at his comandement.
2870 And after this, Theseus hath ysent
After a beere, and it al overspradde
With clooth of gold, the richeste that he hadde.
And of the same suyte he cladde Arcite;
Upon his hondes hadde he gloves white,

2875   *laurer* laurel

He Theseus   *bare the visage* with face uncovered
weep wept
And so that all the people might see him
2880

Tho then
With fluttering beard and shaggy, ash-strewn hair

2885   *passynge othere of* surpassing others in
rewefulleste saddest

leet forth . . . brynge had brought forth
2890   *trapped* fitted out
armes heraldic arms   *daun* Don

seten sat
up on his hondes heeld held up in his hands
2895   *Turkeys* Turkish
brend refined   *caas* quiver   *harneys* fittings
a paas at a walk   *cheere* countenance

2900   *beere* bier
With slakke paas at a slow pace
Thurghout right through   *maister strete* main street
sprad spread   *wonder hye* to a wonderful height
The street (front) is covered in that same colour
2905

2910

2875 Eek on his heed a coroune of laurer grene,
      And in his hond a swerd ful bright and kene.
      He leyde hym, bare the visage, on the beere;
      Therwith he weep that pitee was to heere.
      And for the peple sholde seen hym alle,
2880 Whan it was day, he broghte hym to the halle,
      That roreth of the criyng and the soun.
          Tho cam this woful Theban Palamoun,
      With flotery berd and ruggy, asshy heeres,
      In clothes blake, ydropped al with teeres;
2885 And, passynge othere of wepynge, Emelye,
      The rewefulleste of al the compaignye.
      In as muche as the servyce sholde be
      The moore noble and riche in his degree,
      Duc Theseus leet forth thre steedes brynge,
2890 That trapped were in steel al gliterynge,
      And covered with the armes of daun Arcite.
      Upon thise steedes, that weren grete and white,
      Ther seten folk, of whiche oon baar his sheeld,
      Another his spere up on his hondes heeld,
2895 The thridde baar with hym his bowe Turkeys
      (Of brend gold was the caas and eek the harneys);
      And riden forth a paas with sorweful cheere
      Toward the grove, as ye shul after heere.
      The nobleste of the Grekes that ther were
2900 Upon hir shuldres caryeden the beere,
      With slakke paas and eyen rede and wete,
      Thurghout the citee by the maister strete,
      That sprad was al with blak, and wonder hye
      Right of the same is the strete ywrye.
2905 Upon the right hond wente olde Egeus,
      And on that oother syde duc Theseus,
      With vessels in hir hand of gold ful fyn,
      Al ful of hony, milk, and blood, and wyn;
      Eek Palamon, with ful greet compaignye;
2910 And after that cam woful Emelye,

gyse custom
office rite
Heigh great   *apparaillynge* preparation

2915   *raughte* reached
And the sides stretched twenty fathoms in breadth
That is to say, the boughs were so broad
stree straw   *leyd* laid   *lode* load
But how the fire was built up so high*
2920   *Ne eek* nor also   *highte* were called
aspe aspen   *holm* holm-oak*
Wylugh willow   *chasteyn* chestnut   *lynde* lime
bech beech   *ew* yew   *whippeltree* cornel
feld felled   *for me* for my part
2925   *ronnen* ran*

woneden used to dwell
fawnes fauns   *amadrides* hamadryads

2930   *Fledden* fled   *falle* felled
agast was of was frightened of
That which
couched laid   *stree* straw
stikkes sticks   *cloven* split   *a* in
2935   *spicerye* spices
perrye precious stones

mirre myrrh   *encens* incense   *odour* fragrance

2940

Putte in applied

2945
brente burnt

With fyr in honde, as was that tyme the gyse,
To do the office of funeral servyse.

 Heigh labour and ful greet apparaillynge
Was at the service and the fyr-makynge,
2915 That with his grene top the hevene raughte;
And twenty fadme of brede the armes straughte –
This is to seyn, the bowes weren so brode.
Of stree first ther was leyd ful many a lode.
But how the fyr was maked upon highte,
2920 Ne eek the names that the trees highte,
As ook, firre, birch, aspe, alder, holm, popler,
Wylugh, elm, plane, assh, box, chasteyn, lynde, laurer,
Mapul, thorn, bech, hasel, ew, whippeltree –
How they weren feld shal nat be toold for me;
2925 Ne hou the goddes ronnen up and doun,
Disherited of hire habitacioun,
In which they woneden in reste and pees,
Nymphes, fawnes and amadrides;
Ne hou the beestes and the briddes alle
2930 Fledden for fere, whan the wode was falle;
Ne how the ground agast was of the light,
That was nat wont to seen the sonne bright;
Ne how the fyr was couched first with stree,
And thanne with drye stikkes cloven a thre,
2935 And thanne with grene wode and spicerye,
And thanne with clooth of gold and with perrye,
And gerlandes, hangynge with ful many a flour;
The mirre, th'encens, with al so greet odour;
Ne how Arcite lay among al this,
2940 Ne what richesse aboute his body is;
Ne how that Emelye, as was the gyse,
Putte in the fyr of funeral servyse;
Ne how she swowned whan men made the fyr,
Ne what she spak, ne what was hir desir;
2945 Ne what jeweles men in the fyre caste,
Whan that the fyr was greet and brente faste;

And part of the garments they were wearing
coppes cups
2950   *wood* mad
route company
Thries thrice

And thrice clattering their spears
2955
lad led

lyche-wake wake   *yholde* held

2960   *wake-pleyes* funeral games   *kepe* care
wrastleth wrestles
baar acquitted   *no disjoynt* no trouble

pley game
2965   *wende* journey

processe course   *certeyn* a number of
stynted ceased

2970   *semed me* it seemed to me   *parlement* parliament
caas situations, matters

obeisaunce obedience
2975
Leet senden after ordered to be sent for
Unwist of unknown to

hye haste
2980   *Tho* then
set seated   *hust* hushed
abiden hadde had waited   *space* moment

Ne how somme caste hir sheeld, and somme hir spere,
And of hire vestimentz, whiche that they were,
And coppes fulle of wyn, and milk, and blood,
2950 Into the fyr, that brente as it were wood;
Ne how the Grekes, with an huge route,
Thries riden al the fyr aboute
Upon the left hand, with a loud shoutynge,
And thries with hir speres claterynge;
2955 And thries how the ladyes gonne crye;
And how that lad was homward Emelye;
Ne how Arcite is brent to asshen colde;
Ne how that lyche-wake was yholde
Al thilke nyght; ne how the Grekes pleye
2960 The wake-pleyes; ne kepe I nat to seye
Who wrastleth best naked with oille enoynt,
Ne who that baar hym best, in no disjoynt.
I wol nat tellen eek how that they goon
Hoom til Atthenes, whan the pley is doon;
2965 But shortly to the point thanne wol I wende
And maken of my longe tale an ende.

By processe and by lengthe of certeyn yeres,
Al stynted is the moornynge and the teres
Of Grekes, by oon general assent.
2970 Thanne semed me ther was a parlement
At Atthenes, upon certein pointz and caas;
Among the whiche pointz yspoken was,
To have with certein contrees alliaunce,
And have fully of Thebans obeisaunce.
2975 For which this noble Theseus anon
Leet senden after gentil Palamon,
Unwist of hym what was the cause and why,
But in his blake clothes sorwefully
He cam at his comandement in hye.
2980 Tho sente Theseus for Emelye.
Whan they were set, and hust was al the place,
And Theseus abiden hadde a space

Er before
lest pleasure
2985   *sad* serious   *siked stille* sighed quietly

Moevere Mover   *the cause* causing, causality*
faire cheyne beautiful chain
heigh exalted   *entente* purpose
2990   He well knew why he did it and what he meant by it
bond bound
eyr air
boundes boundaries   *flee* wander
quod said
2995   *adoun* below
Certeyne a certain number of
engendred brought to life
Over the whiche beyond which   *pace* pass
Although they may easily cut these days short
3000   There is no need to cite authority
preeved proved
Yet I wish to make my meaning clear
by from
thilke that same
3005   Everybody who is not a fool knows well
dirryveth from his hool derives from its whole

partie part   *cantel* portion

3010   Which thus descends until it becomes corruptible
of by   purveiaunce providence
biset established   *ordinaunce* decree
speces species   *progressiouns* processes
enduren live   *successiouns* turns
3015   *nat eterne* not be eternal   *lye* lie
at ye at a glance
Loo the ook behold the oak*   *norisshynge* growing up

Er any word cam fram his wise brest,
His eyen sette he ther as was his lest.
2985 And with a sad visage he siked stille,
And after that right thus he seyde his wille:
   'The Firste Moevere of the cause above,
Whan he first made the faire cheyne of love,
Greet was th'effect, and heigh was his entente.
2990 Wel wiste he why, and what thereof he mente,
For with that faire cheyne of love he bond
The fyr, the eyr, the water, and the lond
In certeyn boundes, that they may nat flee.
That same Prince and that Moevere,' quod he,
2995 'Hath stablissed in this wrecched world adoun
Certeyne dayes and duracioun
To al that is engendred in this place,
Over the whiche day they may nat pace,
Al mowe they yet tho dayes wel abregge.
3000 Ther nedeth noght noon auctoritee t'allegge,
For it is preeved by experience,
But that me list declaren my sentence.
Thanne may men by this ordre wel discerne
That thilke Moevere stable is and eterne.
3005 Wel may men knowe, but it be a fool,
That every part dirryveth from his hool,
For nature hath nat taken his bigynnyng
Of no partie or cantel of a thyng,
But of a thyng that parfit is and stable,
3010 Descendynge so til it be corrumpable.
And therfore, of his wise purveiaunce,
He hath so wel biset his ordinaunce
That speces of thynges and progressiouns
Shullen enduren by successiouns,
3015 And nat eterne, withouten any lye.
This maystow understonde and seen at ye.
   'Loo the ook, that hath so long a norisshynge
From tyme that it first bigynneth to sprynge,

3020   *wasted* perished
        Considereth eek consider too
        goon walk
        lyth lies
        wexeth dreye becomes dry
3025   *wende* pass
        Thanne then

        nedes necessarily   *termes* periods

3030   *moot be deed* must die
        Som one
        large feeld open field (of battle)
        Ther helpeth noght nothing avails   *ilke* same
        Thanne then
3035   *maketh* makes happen

        Turning everything back into its own source
        sooth truth
        And against this, no creature alive
3040   Of no degree, does it avail to strive
        thynketh me seems to me

        And take in good part what we may not avoid
        namely that especially what
3045   And anyone who complains at all is acting foolishly
        hym that al may gye him who can govern everything

        flour flower
        siker sure
3050   *hym* himself

        yolden yielded
        apalled faded
        vassellage noble service

And hath so long a lif, as we may see,
3020 Yet at the laste wasted is the tree.
    'Considereth eek how that the harde stoon
Under oure feet, on which we trede and goon,
Yet wasteth it as it lyth by the weye.
The brode ryver somtyme wexeth dreye;
3025 The grete tounes se we wane and wende.
Thanne may ye se that al this thyng hath ende.
    'Of man and womman seen we wel also
That nedes, in oon of thise termes two –
This is to seyn, in youthe or elles age –
3030 He moot be deed, the kyng as shal a page;
Som in his bed, som in the depe see,
Som in the large feeld, as men may see;
Ther helpeth noght; al goth that ilke weye.
Thanne may I seyn that al this thyng moot deye.
3035 'What maketh this but Juppiter, the kyng,
That is prince and cause of alle thyng,
Convertynge al unto his propre welle
From which it is dirryved, sooth to telle?
And heer-agayns no creature on lyve,
3040 Of no degree, availleth for to stryve.
    'Thanne is it wysdom, as it thynketh me,
To maken vertu of necessitee,
And take it weel that we may nat eschue,
And namely that to us alle is due.
3045 And whoso gruccheth ought, he dooth folye,
And rebel is to hym that al may gye.
And certeinly a man hath moost honour
To dyen in his excellence and flour,
Whan he is siker of his goode name;
3050 Thanne hath he doon his freend, ne hym, no shame:
And gladder oghte his freend been of his deeth,
Whan with honour up yolden is his breeth,
Than whan his name apalled is for age,
For al forgeten is his vassellage.

3055

That a man die when his reputation is at its height

grucchen complain   *hevynesse* grief

3060   *duetee* due respect

grucchen complain
Of about, for
woot knows   *never a deel* not a bit
3065   Who respect neither his soul nor themselves
mowe can   *hir lustes* their happiness   *amende* advance
serye sequence of argument
rede advise

3070

O one
herinne in this matter
amenden amend
3075   *assent* desire
avys advice

syn since
3080   *rewe* take pity

Lene lend   *oure accord* our resolve
Now let your womanly compassion be seen
brother brother's   *pardee* by God
3085   Even if he were a poor young knight

leeveth believe
For noble mercy ought to prevail over right*

3090

3055 Thanne is it best, as for a worthy fame,
     To dyen whan that he is best of name.
          'The contrarie of al this is wilfulnesse.
     Why grucchen we, why have we hevynesse,
     That goode Arcite, of chivalrie flour,
3060 Departed is with duetee and honour
     Out of this foule prisoun of this lyf?
     Why grucchen heere his cosyn and his wyf
     Of his welfare, that loved hem so weel?
     Kan he hem thank? Nay, God woot, never a deel,
3065 That both his soule and eek hemself offende,
     And yet they mowe hir lustes nat amende.
          'What may I conclude of this longe serye,
     But after wo I rede us to be merye
     And thanken Juppiter of al his grace?
3070 And er that we departen from this place
     I rede that we make of sorwes two
     O parfit joye, lastynge everemo.
     And looketh now, wher moost sorwe is herinne,
     Ther wol we first amenden and bigynne.
3075   'Suster,' quod he, 'this is my fulle assent,
     With al th'avys heere of my parlement,
     That gentil Palamon, youre owene knyght,
     That serveth yow with wille, herte, and myght,
     And ever hath doon syn ye first hym knewe,
3080 That ye shul of youre grace upon hym rewe,
     And taken hym for housbonde and for lord.
     Lene me youre hond, for this is oure accord.
     Lat se now of youre wommanly pitee.
     He is a kynges brother sone, pardee;
3085 And though he were a povre bacheler,
     Syn he hath served yow so many a yeer,
     And had for yow so greet adversitee,
     It moste been considered, leeveth me,
     For gentil mercy oghte to passen right.'
3090   Thanne seyde he thus to Palamon the knight:

trowe believe   *sermonyng* talk

3095 *highte* is called
conseil council

3100 *it deere aboght* dearly paid for it
alle wele all happiness
heele well-being

3105

teene vexation
endeth ends

'I trowe ther nedeth litel sermonyng
To make yow assente to this thyng.
Com neer, and taak youre lady by the hond.'
    Bitwixen hem was maad anon the bond
3095 That highte matrimoigne or mariage,
By al the conseil and the baronage.
And thus with alle blisse and melodye
Hath Palamon ywedded Emelye.
And God, that al this wyde world hath wroght,
3100 Sende hym his love that hath it deere aboght;
For now is Palamon in alle wele,
Lyvynge in blisse, in richesse, and in heele,
And Emelye hym loveth so tendrely,
And he hire serveth so gentilly,
3105 That nevere was ther no word hem bitwene
Of jalousie or any oother teene.
Thus endeth Palamon and Emelye;
And God save al this faire compaignye! Amen.

Heere is ended the Knyghtes Tale.

3110   *route* company   *nas* was not

     drawen to memorie remember
     namely especially   *the gentils* the well-born   *everichon* every one
     lough laughed   *So moot I gon* I must say
3115   It's going well; the bag is opened*
     Lat se let's see

     sir Monk   *konne* know
     to quite with with which to match
3120   *for dronken* because he was drunk*
     unnethe not easily
     nolde avalen would not take off
     Nor had he the grace to give way to another man
     Pilates Pontius Pilate's*   *crie* shout
3125   *By armes* by (Christ's) arms*
     kan know   *nones* occasion
     quite match, repay
     saugh saw   *dronke of* drunk with
     Abyd wait   *leeve* dear
3130

     werken thriftily go about things properly
     quod said   *that wol nat I* I shall not

THE MILLER'S PROLOGUE

Heere folwen the wordes bitwene the Hoost and the Millere.

    Whan that the Knyght had thus his tale ytoold,
3110 In al the route nas ther yong ne oold
That he ne seyde it was a noble storie
And worthy for to drawen to memorie,
And namely the gentils everichon.
Oure Hooste lough and swoor, 'So moot I gon,
3115 This gooth aright; unbokeled is the male.
Lat se now who shal telle another tale;
For trewely the game is wel bigonne.
Now telleth ye, sir Monk, if that ye konne,
Somwhat to quite with the Knyghtes tale.'
3120 The Millere, that for dronken was al pale,
So that unnethe upon his hors he sat,
He nolde avalen neither hood ne hat,
Ne abyde no man for his curteisie,
But in Pilates voys he gan to crie,
3125 And swoor, 'By armes, and by blood and bones,
I kan a noble tale for the nones,
With which I wol now quite the Knyghtes tale.'
Oure Hooste saugh that he was dronke of ale,
And seyde, 'Abyd, Robyn, my leeve brother;
3130 Som bettre man shal telle us first another.
Abyd, and lat us werken thriftily.'
    'By Goddes soule,' quod he, 'that wol nat I;

a devel wey in the devil's name*

3135

herkneth listen   *alle and some* one and all

my soun the sound of my voice
mysspeke or seye stumble in speech or word

3140 *Wyte it* blame it on   *preye* beseech
legende saint's life*
*carpenter**
How a student made a fool of the carpenter*
Stynt thy clappe stop your claptrap

3145 *Lat be* leave   *lewed* coarse   *harlotrye* ribaldry

apeyren injure
swich fame such (ill) repute
You can say enough about other things

3150 *ageyn* back
Leve dear
cokewold cuckold*
oon one

3155

but if unless   *madde* go mad
artow art thou
pardee by God
for in exchange for

3160 *moore* more (cares)   *ynogh* enough
demen believe   *oon* one
wol am willing to   *noon* not one

pryvetee secrets*

3165 *So as   foyson* plenty*
There is no need to enquire about the rest
sholde I moore more should I*
nolde . . . forbere would not forbear

For I wol speke or elles go my wey.'
Oure Hoost answerde, 'Tel on, a devel wey!
3135 Thou art a fool; thy wit is overcome.'
        'Now herkneth,' quod the Millere, 'alle and some!
But first I make a protestacioun
That I am dronke; I knowe it by my soun.
And therfore if that I mysspeke or seye,
3140 Wyte it the ale of Southwerk, I you preye.
For I wol telle a legende and a lyf
Bothe of a carpenter and of his wyf,
How that a clerk hath set the wrightes cappe.'
        The Reve answerde and seyde, 'Stynt thy clappe!
3145 Lat be thy lewed dronken harlotrye.
It is a synne and eek a greet folye
To apeyren any man, or hym defame,
And eek to bryngen wyves in swich fame.
Thou mayst ynogh of othere thynges seyn.'
3150   This dronke Millere spak ful soone ageyn
And seyde, 'Leve brother Osewold,
Who hath no wyf, he is no cokewold.
But I sey nat therfore that thou art oon;
Ther been ful goode wyves many oon,
3155 And evere a thousand goode ayeyns oon badde.
That knowestow wel thyself, but if thou madde.
Why artow angry with my tale now?
I have a wyf, pardee, as wel as thow;
Yet nolde I, for the oxen in my plogh,
3160 Take upon me moore than ynogh,
As demen of myself that I were oon;
I wol bileve wel that I am noon.
An housbonde shal nat been inquisityf
Of Goddes pryvetee, nor of his wyf.
3165 So he may fynde Goddes foyson there,
Of the remenant nedeth nat enquere.'
        What sholde I moore seyn, but this Millere
He nolde his wordes for no man forbere,

3170   I regret that I have to repeat it here
        wight creature
        demeth nat do not believe
        Out of evil intention but because I must repeat

3175   *falsen* misrepresent
        list prefer
        leef leaf, page*   *chese* choose
        ynowe enough
        storial historical   *toucheth* concerns
3180
        Blameth nat me do not blame me   *amys* wrongly
        cherl churl
        othere mo others beside
        harlotrie ribaldry, dirty stories
3185   *Avyseth yow* be advised, consider
        maken ernest of game take a joke seriously

        Whilom once   *Oxenford* Oxford*
        gnof churl*   *gestes* lodgers   *to bord* as boarders

3190   *poure scoler* poor scholar*
        lerned art studied Arts*   *fantasye* fancy
        *astrologye**
        And knew a certain number of propositions
        To work out by calculations

But tolde his cherles tale in his manere.
3170　M'athynketh that I shal reherce it heere.
And therfore every gentil wight I preye,
For Goddes love, demeth nat that I seye
Of yvel entente, but for I moot reherce
Hir tales alle, be they bettre or werse,
3175　Or elles falsen som of my mateere.
And therfore, whoso list it nat yheere,
Turne over the leef and chese another tale;
For he shal fynde ynowe, grete and smale,
Of storial thyng that toucheth gentillesse,
3180　And eek moralitee and hoolynesse.
Blameth nat me if that ye chese amys.
The Millere is a cherl; ye knowe wel this.
So was the Reve eek and othere mo,
And harlotrie they tolden bothe two.
3185　Avyseth yow, and put me out of blame;
And eek men shal nat maken ernest of game.

THE MILLER'S TALE

Heere bigynneth the Millere his tale.

Whilom ther was dwellynge at Oxenford
A riche gnof, that gestes heeld to bord,
And of his craft he was a carpenter.
3190　With hym ther was dwellynge a poure scoler,
Hadde lerned art, but al his fantasye
Was turned for to lerne astrologye,
And koude a certeyn of conclusiouns,
To demen by interrogaciouns,

3195   *in certein houres* at certain hours
         droghte dry weather   *elles shoures* else showers

         clerk clerk, student   *cleped* called   *hende* gentle*
3200   He knew about secret love and about its reward*
         therto in addition   *sleigh* sly   *privee* discreet
         meke for to see meek to look at
         hostelrye lodging
         *compaignye**
3205   Very neatly set about with sweet herbs

         lycorys licorice   *cetewale* zedoary, a ginger spice
         Almageste Ptolemy's *Great Treatise* of astronomy*
         astrelabie astrolabe*   *longynge for* belonging to
3210   His arithmetical counters lay neatly to one side*
         couched arranged
         presse cupboard   *faldyng* woollen cloth
         sautrie psaltery*

3215
         Angelus ad virginem 'The Angel to the Virgin'*
         Kynges Noote King's Tune
         throte throat

3220   According to his friends' provision and his income

         narwe closely
3225
         demed thought   *cokewold* cuckold
         Catoun the Maxims of Cato*   *rude* untutored
         bad advised
         after hire according to their
3230   *elde* old age

3195   If that men asked hym, in certein houres
       Whan that men sholde have droghte or elles shoures,
       Or if men asked hym what sholde bifalle
       Of every thyng; I may nat rekene hem alle.
           This clerk was cleped hende Nicholas.
3200   Of deerne love he koude and of solas;
       And therto he was sleigh and ful privee,
       And lyk a mayden meke for to see.
       A chambre hadde he in that hostelrye
       Allone, withouten any compaignye,
3205   Ful fetisly ydight with herbes swoote;
       And he hymself as sweete as is the roote
       Of lycorys or any cetewale.
       His Almageste, and bookes grete and smale,
       His astrelabie, longynge for his art,
3210   His augrym stones layen faire apart,
       On shelves couched at his beddes heed;
       His presse ycovered with a faldyng reed;
       And al above ther lay a gay sautrie,
       On which he made a-nyghtes melodie
3215   So swetely that all the chambre rong;
       And *Angelus ad virginem* he song;
       And after that he song the Kynges Noote.
       Ful often blessed was his myrie throte.
       And thus this sweete clerk his tyme spente
3220   After his freendes fyndyng and his rente.
           This carpenter hadde wedded newe a wyf,
       Which that he lovede moore than his lyf;
       Of eighteteene yeer she was of age.
       Jalous he was, and heeld hire narwe in cage,
3225   For she was wylde and yong, and he was old
       And demed hymself been lik a cokewold.
       He knew nat Catoun, for his wit was rude,
       That bad man sholde wedde his simylitude.
       Men sholde wedden after hire estaat,
3230   For youthe and elde is often at debaat.

sith since   *snare* trap
care trouble

wezele weasel   *gent* graceful   *smal* slender
3235   *ceynt* belt   *werede* wore   *barred al* all striped
barmclooth apron   *morne* morning
lendes loins   *goore* slash
smok dress   *broyden* embroidered   *bifoore* in front
coler collar   *aboute* around
3240   *Of* in
tapes ribbons   *voluper* cap
Matched her collar
filet headband
sikerly certainly   *likerous* wanton
3245   *smale ypulled* narrow plucked
sloo sloe
on to see to look at
Than the early-ripe pear tree newly in blossom
wolle wool   *wether* ram
3250   *heeng* hung
perled studded   *latoun* metal
seken seek
thenche imagine
popelote poppet, doll   *wenche* lower-class girl
3255   *hewe* complexion
Tour Tower Mint   *noble* coin   *newe* newly
of as for   *yerne* lively
swalwe swallow   *berne* barn
koude knew how   *skippe* frolic   *make game* play
3260   *kyde* kid   *his dame* its mother
bragot country ale   *meeth* mead
leyd laid   *hey* hay   *heeth* heather
Wynsynge skittish   *joly* fresh
upright straight   *bolt* bolt of a crossbow
3265   *baar* wore
boos boss   *bokeler* shield

But sith that he was fallen in the snare,
He moste endure, as oother folk, his care.
   Fair was this yonge wyf, and therwithal
As any wezele hir body gent and smal.
3235 A ceynt she werede, barred al of silk,
A barmclooth as whit as morne milk
Upon hir lendes, ful of many a goore.
Whit was hir smok, and broyden al bifoore
And eek bihynde, on hir coler aboute,
3240 Of col-blak silk, withinne and eek withoute.
The tapes of hir white voluper
Were of the same suyte of hir coler;
Hir filet brood of silk, and set ful hye.
And sikerly she hadde a likerous ye;
3245 Ful smale ypulled were hire browes two,
And tho were bent and blake as any sloo.
She was ful moore blisful on to see
Than is the newe pere-jonette tree,
And softer than the wolle is of a wether.
3250 And by hir girdel heeng a purs of lether,
Tasseled with silk and perled with latoun.
In al this world, to seken up and doun,
There nys no man so wys that koude thenche
So gay a popelote or swich a wenche.
3255 Ful brighter was the shynyng of hir hewe
Than in the Tour the noble yforged newe.
But of hir song, it was as loude and yerne
As any swalwe sittynge on a berne.
Therto she koude skippe and make game,
3260 As any kyde or calf folwynge his dame.
Hir mouth was sweete as bragot or the meeth,
Or hoord of apples leyd in hey or heeth.
Wynsynge she was, as is a joly colt,
Long as a mast, and upright as a bolt.
3265 A brooch she baar upon hir lowe coler,
As brood as is the boos of a bokeler.

on hir legges hye high on her legs
prymerole primrose   piggesnye pig's eye*
leggen lay
3270   yeman yeoman
eft again   so bifel the cas it so happened

rage sport
Oseneye Osney*
3275   subtile artful   queynte sly
prively stealthily   queynte the pleasing thing
Ywis, but if ich truly, unless I
deerne secret   spille die

3280   Lemman sweetheart   atones at once
also as
sproong sprang   trave shoeing-frame
wryed twisted
fey faith
3285   lat be leave off   quod said
out, harrow help!
Do wey take away

And spoke so nicely and offered his service so eagerly
3290

Thomas Thomas of Canterbury

leyser chance   espie perceive

3295   wayte watch   privee discreet
woot know   nam but I'm as good as
deerne secretive
therof care thee noght don't worry about that
litherly biset his whyle poorly used his time
3300   koude knew how to   bigyle beguile, deceive
accorded agreed
wayte wait

Hir shoes were laced on hir legges hye.
She was a prymerole, a piggesnye,
For any lord to leggen in his bedde,
3270   Or yet for any good yeman to wedde.
    Now, sire, and eft, sire, so bifel the cas
That on a day this hende Nicholas
Fil with this yonge wyf to rage and pleye,
Whil that hir housbonde was at Oseneye,
3275   As clerkes ben ful subtile and ful queynte;
And prively he caughte hire by the queynte,
And seyde, 'Ywis, but if ich have my wille,
For deerne love of thee, lemman, I spille.'
And heeld hire harde by the haunchebones,
3280   And seyde, 'Lemman, love me al atones,
Or I wol dyen, also God me save!'
And she sproong as a colt dooth in the trave,
And with hir heed she wryed faste awey,
And seyde, 'I wol nat kisse thee, by my fey!
3285   Why, lat be!' quod she. 'Lat be, Nicholas,
Or I wol crie "out, harrow" and "allas"!
Do wey youre handes, for youre curteisye!'
    This Nicholas gan mercy for to crye,
And spak so faire, and profred him so faste,
3290   That she hir love hym graunted atte laste,
And swoor hir ooth, by Seint Thomas of Kent,
That she wol been at his comandement,
Whan that she may hir leyser wel espie.
'Myn housbonde is so ful of jalousie
3295   That but ye wayte wel and been privee,
I woot right wel I nam but deed,' quod she.
'Ye moste been ful deerne, as in this cas.'
    'Nay, therof care thee noght,' quod Nicholas.
'A clerk hadde litherly biset his whyle,
3300   But if he koude a carpenter bigyle.'
And thus they been accorded and ysworn
To wayte a tyme, as I have told biforn.

everideel completely
thakked patted   *lendes* loins
3305   *sweete* sweetly   *sawtrie* psaltery*
faste eagerly

werkes works   *wirche* do
haliday holy day
3310   *forheed shoon* forehead shone
leet left

ycleped called   *Absolon**
Crul curly
3315   *strouted* stuck out   *fanne* fan
joly shode lovely parting
rode complexion   *eyen* eyes   *goos* goose-feather*
Poules St Paul's (Cathedral)   *corven* cut out*
hoses stockings   *fetisly* elegantly
3320   *smal* fine   *proprely* neatly
kirtel tunic   *waget* blue
poyntes laces
surplys surplice (clerical gown)
rys twig
3325   *child* young fellow
laten let   *clippe* cut hair*
chartre charter   *acquitaunce* release of property*

After the scole in the fashion
3330   *casten* shoot
rubible rebeck, fiddle
quynyble high treble
giterne cithern, guitar
nas there was not
3335   *solas* entertainment
Wherever there was a merry barmaid
But truth to tell he was rather squeamish
of speche daungerous fastidious in speech

    Whan Nicholas had doon thus everideel
    And thakked hire aboute the lendes weel,
3305 He kiste hire sweete and taketh his sawtrie,
    And pleyeth faste, and maketh melodie.
      Thanne fil it thus, that to the paryssh chirche,
    Cristes owene werkes for to wirche,
    This goode wyf went on an haliday.
3310 Hir forheed shoon as bright as any day,
    So was it wasshen whan she leet hir werk.
    Now was ther of that chirche a parissh clerk,
    The which that was ycleped Absolon.
    Crul was his heer, and as the gold it shoon,
3315 And strouted as a fanne large and brode;
    Ful streight and evene lay his joly shode.
    His rode was reed, his eyen greye as goos.
    With Poules wyndow corven on his shoos,
    In hoses rede he wente fetisly.
3320 Yclad he was ful smal and proprely
    Al in a kirtel of a lyght waget;
    Ful faire and thikke been the poyntes set.
    And therupon he hadde a gay surplys
    As whit as is the blosme upon the rys.
3325 A myrie child he was, so God me save.
    Wel koude he laten blood, and clippe and shave,
    And maken a chartre of lond or acquitaunce.
    In twenty manere koude he trippe and daunce
    After the scole of Oxenforde tho,
3330 And with his legges casten to and fro,
    And pleyen songes on a smal rubible;
    Therto he song som tyme a loud quynyble;
    And as wel koude he pleye on a giterne.
    In al the toun nas brewhous ne taverne
3335 That he ne visited with his solas,
    Ther any gaylard tappestere was.
    But sooth to seyn, he was somdeel squaymous
    Of fartyng, and of speche daungerous.

jolif pretty
3340 *sencer* censer, thurible
Sensynge censing*
lovely loving   *hem* them
namely especially

3345 *propre* smart   *likerous* flirtatious
seyn say
he would have seized her immediately

3350 *of* from   *wyf* woman   *offrynge* church offering*

gyterne guitar
paramours for love's sake   *wake* stay awake
3355

cokkes cocks   *ycrowe* crowed
dressed hym placed himself   *shot-wyndowe* casement

3360 *smal* high
thy wille be it be thy will
rewe take pity
In harmony with his playing on the guitar

3365

Herestow do you hear
chaunteth sings   *boures* bedroom's

Yes indeed, God knows, John, I hear it every bit
3370 *what wol ye bet than weel* what more would you have?

woweth woos
waketh remains awake
kembeth combs   *brode* out

This Absolon, that jolif was and gay,
3340 Gooth with a sencer on the haliday,
Sensynge the wyves of the parisshe faste;
And many a lovely look on hem he caste,
And namely on this carpenteris wyf.
To looke on hire hym thoughte a myrie lyf,
3345 She was so propre and sweete and likerous.
I dar wel seyn, if she hadde been a mous,
And he a cat, he wolde hire hente anon.
This parissh clerk, this joly Absolon,
Hath in his herte swich a love-longynge
3350 That of no wyf took he noon offrynge;
For curteisie, he seyde, he wolde noon:
    The moone, whan it was nyght, ful brighte shoon,
And Absolon his gyterne hath ytake;
For paramours he thoghte for to wake.
3355 And forth he gooth, jolif and amorous,
Til he cam to the carpenteres hous
A litel after cokkes hadde ycrowe,
And dressed hym up by a shot-wyndowe
That was upon the carpenteris wal.
3360 He syngeth in his voys gentil and smal,
'Now, deere lady, if thy wille be,
I praye yow that ye wole rewe on me,'
Ful wel acordaunt to his gyternynge.
This carpenter awook, and herde him synge,
3365 And spak unto his wyf, and seyde anon,
'What! Alison! Herestow nat Absolon,
That chaunteth thus under oure boures wal?'
And she answerde hir housbonde therwithal,
'Yis, God woot, John, I heere it every deel.'
3370   This passeth forth; what wol ye bet than weel?
Fro day to day this joly Absolon
So woweth hire that hym is wo bigon.
He waketh al the nyght and al the day;
He kembeth his lokkes brode, and made hym gay;

3375   *meenes* go-betweens   *brocage* use of an agent

      brokkynge trilling
      pyment sweetened wine   *meeth* mead
      wafres wafers, waffles   *gleede* embers
3380   *of town* a town girl   *meede* money
      wonnen won
      strokes blows
      lightnesse agility   *maistrye* skill
      He acts the part of Herod high on a stage*
3385   *availleth* does it help

      blowe the bukkes horn go whistle

      ape monkey
3390   *jape* joke
      lye lie
      nye slye sly one near at hand
      ferre leeve far-off dear one   *looth* hated
      wood mad   *wrooth* angry
3395

      ber thee wel do your best

3400   *Osenay* Osney

      shapen hym a wyle work out a plan for himself
      sely hapless*   *bigyle* beguile
3405

      hire hers

      wolde tarie wished to delay
3410   *softe* quietly

3375   He woweth hire by meenes and brocage,
    And swoor he wolde been hir owene page;
    He syngeth, brokkynge as a nyghtyngale;
    He sente hire pyment, meeth, and spiced ale,
    And wafres, pipyng hoot out of the gleede;
3380   And, for she was of town, he profred meede;
    For som folk wol ben wonnen for richesse,
    And somme for strokes, and somme for gentillesse.
       Somtyme, to shewe his lightnesse and maistrye,
    He pleyeth Herodes upon a scaffold hye.
3385   But what availleth hym as in this cas?
    She loveth so this hende Nicholas
    That Absolon may blowe the bukkes horn;
    He ne hadde for his labour but a scorn.
    And thus she maketh Absolon hire ape,
3390   And al his ernest turneth til a jape.
    Ful sooth is this proverbe, it is no lye,
    Men seyn right thus: 'Alwey the nye slye
    Maketh the ferre leeve to be looth.'
    For though that Absolon be wood or wrooth,
3395   By cause that he fer was from hire sight,
    This nye Nicholas stood in his light.
       Now ber thee wel, thou hende Nicholas,
    For Absolon may waille and synge 'allas.'
    And so bifel it on a Saterday,
3400   This carpenter was goon til Osenay;
    And hende Nicholas and Alisoun
    Acorded been to this conclusioun,
    That Nicholas shal shapen hym a wyle
    This sely jalous housbonde to bigyle;
3405   And if so be the game wente aright,
    She sholde slepen in his arm al nyght,
    For this was his desir and hire also.
    And right anon, withouten wordes mo,
    This Nicholas no lenger wolde tarie,
3410   But dooth ful softe unto his chambre carie

mete food
bad told

nyste did not know
3415   Hadn't set eyes on him all day
trowed believed   *in maladye* ill
cry shout
In any event, he would not answer
thilke that
3420   *stille* quiet
hym leste pleased him

hath greet merveyle wondered greatly
Of about   *eyle* ail
3425   *adrad* scared

shilde forbid   *deyde* should die
tikel unstable, ticklish   *sikerly* surely
cors corpse   *yborn* carried
3430   *saugh* saw   *wirche* work
knave servant
Clepe call
boldely plainly
sturdily boldly
3435

cride shouted   *wood* mad

may can
he the servant
3440   *foond* found

capyng gaping
3445   *kiked* gazed

Bothe mete and drynke for a day or tweye,
And to hire housbonde bad hire for to seye,
If that he axed after Nicholas,
She sholde seye she nyste where he was;

3415 Of al that day she saugh hym nat with ye;
She trowed that he was in maladye,
For, for no cry hir mayde koude hym calle,
He nolde answere for thyng that myghte falle.

This passeth forth al thilke Saterday,

3420 That Nicholas stille in his chambre lay,
And eet and sleep, or dide what hym leste,
Til Sonday, that the sonne gooth to reste.
This sely carpenter hath greet merveyle
Of Nicholas, or what thyng myghte hym eyle,

3425 And seyde, 'I am adrad, by Seint Thomas,
It stondeth nat aright with Nicholas.
God shilde that he deyde sodeynly!
This world is now ful tikel, sikerly.
I saugh today a cors yborn to chirche

3430 That now, on Monday last, I saugh hym wirche.
'Go up,' quod he unto his knave anoon,
'Clepe at his dore, or knokke with a stoon.
Looke how it is, and tel me boldely.'

This knave gooth hym up ful sturdily,

3435 And at the chambre dore whil that he stood,
He cride and knokked as that he were wood,
'What, how! What do ye, maister Nicholay?
How may ye slepen al the longe day?'

But al for noght; he herde nat a word.

3440 An hole he foond, ful lowe upon a bord,
Ther as the cat was wont in for to crepe,
And at that hole he looked in ful depe,
And at the laste he hadde of hym a sight.
This Nicholas sat evere capyng upright,

3445 As he had kiked on the newe moone.
Adoun he gooth, and tolde his maister soone

array state
blessen make the sign of the cross
Frydeswyde Frideswide*
3450   *woot* knows   *bityde* befall
astromye astro(no)my*
woodnesse madness
I always thought it might turn out like this
pryvetee secrets*
3455   *lewed* simple, unlearned
Who knows nothing except his Creed
ferde fared
prye spy
sterres stars   *ther sholde* was going to
3460   *marle-pit* clay-pit

Me reweth soore I feel very sorry
rated told off
hevene heaven's
3465   *underspore* push under
hevest heave   *dore* door*

gan hym dresse position himself
carl fellow   *nones* job
3470   *haaf* heaved   *of* off   *atones* at once
fil fell
ay ever
caped gaped
wende supposed
3475   *hente* seized
spitously violently
adoun down
passioun passion*
crouche make sign of the cross over*   *elves* evil spirits   *wightes* creatures
3480   *nyght-spel* night-spell*   *anon-rightes* straightaway
halves sides
thresshfold threshold   *withoute* outside

In what array he saugh this ilke man.
      This carpenter to blessen hym bigan,
      And seyde, 'Help us, Seinte Frydeswyde!
3450 A man woot litel what hym shal bityde.
      This man is falle, with his astromye,
      In some woodnesse or in som agonye.
      I thoghte ay wel how that it sholde be!
      Men sholde nat knowe of Goddes pryvetee.
3455 Ye, blessed be alwey a lewed man
      That noght but oonly his bileve kan!
      So ferde another clerk with astromye;
      He walked in the feeldes for to prye
      Upon the sterres, what ther sholde bifalle,
3460 Til he was in a marle-pit yfalle;
      He saugh nat that. But yet, by Seint Thomas,
      Me reweth soore of hende Nicholas.
      He shal be rated of his studiyng,
      If that I may, by Jhesus, hevene kyng!
3465 Get me a staf, that I may underspore,
      Whil that thou, Robyn, hevest up the dore.
      He shal out of his studiyng, as I gesse.'
      And to the chambre dore he gan hym dresse.
      His knave was a strong carl for the nones,
3470 And by the haspe he haaf it of atones;
      Into the floor the dore fil anon.
      This Nicholas sat ay as stille as stoon,
      And evere caped upward into the eir.
      This carpenter wende he were in despeir,
3475 And hente hym by the sholdres myghtily,
      And shook hym harde, and cride spitously,
      'What! Nicholay! What, how! What, looke adoun!
      Awak, and thenk on Cristes passioun!
      I crouche thee from elves and fro wightes.'
3480 Therwith the nyght-spel seyde he anon-rightes
      On foure halves of the hous aboute,
      And on the thresshfold of the dore withoute:

Benedight Benedict
wight creature
3485   Against the night's demon, the white pater-noster!
Saint Peter's sister, where did you go?

sik sigh   *soore* sorrowfully
eftsoones so soon again
3490   *seystow* are you saying
swynke labour

in pryvetee in secrecy
toucheth concerns
3495   *certeyn* certainly
ageyn back
myghty powerful   *large* full

shette shut
3500
lief beloved
trouthe honour   *swere* swear
wight creature   *conseil* secret   *wreye* reveal

3505   *man* to man   *forlore* lost
vengeaunce punishment
wreye me give me away   *wood* mad
forbede forbid
sely innocent   *nam* am not   *labbe* blab
3510   Nor, though I say it myself, am I fond of gossip

hym that harwed helle Him that harrowed hell*

3515
quarter quarter-way through
reyn rain   *wood* furious
Noes Noe's, Noah's

'Jhesu Crist and Seinte Benedight,
Blesse this hous from every wikked wight,
3485 For nyghtes verye, the white *pater-noster*!
Where wentestow, Seinte Petres soster?'
     And atte laste this hende Nicholas
Gan for to sik soore, and seyde, 'Allas!
Shal al the world be lost eftsoones now?'
3490   This carpenter answerde, 'What seystow?
What! Thynk on God, as we doon, men that swynke.'
     This Nicholas answerde, 'Fecche me drynke,
And after wol I speke in pryvetee
Of certeyn thyng that toucheth me and thee.
3495 I wol telle it noon oother man, certeyn.'
     This carpenter goth doun, and comth ageyn,
And broghte of myghty ale a large quart;
And whan that ech of hem had dronke his part,
This Nicholas his dore faste shette,
3500 And doun the carpenter by hym he sette.
     He seyde 'John, myn hooste, lief and deere,
Thou shalt upon thy trouthe swere me heere
That to no wight thou shalt this conseil wreye,
For it is Cristes conseil that I seye,
3505 And if thou telle it man, thou art forlore;
For this vengeaunce thou shalt han therfore,
That if thou wreye me, thou shalt be wood.'
'Nay, Crist forbede it, for his hooly blood!'
Quod tho this sely man, 'I nam no labbe,
3510 Ne, though I seye, I nam nat lief to gabbe.
Sey what thou wolt, I shal it nevere telle
To child ne wyf, by hym that harwed helle!'
     'Now John,' quod Nicholas, 'I wol nat lye;
I have yfounde in myn astrologye,
3515 As I have looked in the moone bright,
That now a Monday next, at quarter nyght,
Shal falle a reyn, and that so wilde and wood
That half so greet was nevere Noes flood.

3520 *dreynt* drowned   *shour* shower
　　　drenche drown   *lese hir lyf* lose their lives

　　　fil fell
3525 *cas* situation
　　　yis yes indeed   *for* by
　　　If you are willing to act on instruction and advice
　　　heed head, thinking
　　　Salomon Solomon*   *trewe* truthful
3530 Do everything by counsel, and you shall not be sorry

　　　seyl sail
　　　Yet still   *saven* save   *hire* her
　　　*Noe**
3535
　　　lorn lost
　　　Yis yes indeed   *yoore ago* long ago

　　　sorwe troubles*   *felaweshipe* company
3540 *Er that* before
　　　He would have been happier, I dare affirm
　　　thilke that   *wetheres* *blake* black rams
　　　hirself to herself
　　　woostou do you know   *doone* do
3545 *asketh* calls for   *hastif* urgent

　　　Anon immediately   *in* house
　　　knedyng trogh kneading trough   *kymelyn* brewing vat

3550 *swymme* float   *barge* sailing vessel
　　　vitaille *suffisant* enough food
　　　But just   *fy on* ignore
　　　aslake slacken off
　　　pryme the first hour, 9 a.m.

This world,' he seyde, 'in lasse than an hour
3520 Shal al be dreynt, so hidous is the shour.
Thus shal mankynde drenche, and lese hir lyf.'
      This carpenter answerde, 'Allas, my wyf!
And shal she drenche? Allas, myn Alisoun!'
For sorwe of this he fil almoost adoun,
3525 And seyde, 'Is ther no remedie in this cas?'
      'Why, yis, for Gode,' quod hende Nicholas,
'If thou wolt werken after loore and reed.
Thou mayst nat werken after thyn owene heed;
For thus seith Salomon, that was ful trewe:
3530 "Werk al by conseil, and thou shalt nat rewe."
And if thou werken wolt by good conseil,
I undertake, withouten mast and seyl,
Yet shal I saven hire and thee and me.
Hastow nat herd hou saved was Noe,
3535 Whan that oure Lord hadde warned hym biforn
That al the world with water sholde be lorn?'
      'Yis,' quod this Carpenter, 'ful yoore ago.'
      'Hastou nat herd,' quod Nicholas, 'also
The sorwe of Noe with his felaweshipe,
3540 Er that he myghte gete his wyf to shipe?
Hym hadde be levere, I dar wel undertake,
At thilke tyme, than alle his wetheres blake
That she hadde had a ship hirself allone.
And therfore, woostou what is best to doone?
3545 This asketh haste, and of an hastif thyng
Men may nat preche or maken tariyng.
      'Anon go gete us faste into this in
A knedyng trogh, or ellis a kymelyn,
For ech of us, but looke that they be large,
3550 In which we mowe swymme as in a barge,
And han therinne vitaille suffisant
But for a day — fy on the remenant!
The water shal aslake and goon away
Aboute pryme upon the nexte day.

3555 *wite* know *knave* manservant
Ne eek nor yet

pryvetee secret purpose
Let it suffice thee, unless your wits go mad
3560
out of without

Ygeten got
3565 *shaltow* must thou *hye* high up
purveiaunce providing *espy* catch sight of

yleyd laid
atwo in two
3570
an heigh high up
Unto the gardyn-ward toward the garden
frely unhindered

3575 *swymme* float
doke duck
clepe call
anon at once

3580 *morwe* morning

o one
avysed warned
3585 *into shippes bord* aboard ship

but be except it be
heeste command
moote must *fer atwynne* far apart
3590 *no synne**

3555 But Robyn may nat wite of this, thy knave,
Ne eek thy mayde Gille I may nat save;
Axe nat why, for though thou aske me,
I wol nat tellen Goddes pryvetee.
Suffiseth thee, but if thy wittes madde,
3560 To han as greet a grace as Noe hadde.
Thy wyf shal I wel saven, out of doute.
Go now thy wey, and speed thee heer-aboute.
    'But whan thou hast, for hire and thee and me,
Ygeten us thise knedyng tubbes thre,
3565 Thanne shaltow hange hem in the roof ful hye,
That no man of oure purveiaunce espye.
And whan thou thus hast doon as I have seyd,
And hast oure vitaille faire in hem yleyd,
And eek an ax to smyte the corde atwo,
3570 Whan that the water comth, that we may go
And breke an hole an heigh, upon the gable,
Unto the gardyn-ward, over the stable,
That we may frely passen forth oure way,
Whan that the grete shour is goon away.
3575 Thanne shaltou swymme as myrie, I undertake,
As dooth the white doke after hire drake.
Thanne wol I clepe, "How, Alison! How, John!
Be myrie, for the flood wol passe anon."
And thou wolt seyn, "Hayl, maister Nicholay!
3580 Good morwe, I se thee wel, for it is day."
And thanne shul we be lordes al oure lyf
Of al the world, as Noe and his wyf.
    'But of o thyng I warne thee ful right:
Be wel avysed on that ilke nyght
3585 That we ben entred into shippes bord,
That noon of us ne speke nat a word,
Ne clepe, ne crie, but be in his preyere;
For it is Goddes owene heeste deere.
    'Thy wyf and thou moote hange fer atwynne;
3590 For that bitwixe yow shal be no synne,

ordinance rule   *speede* give success

3595   *abidyng* awaiting
        space time
        sermonyng discourse

        it needeth thee nat teche no need to teach you
3600   *the biseche* beseech you
        sely innocent
        weylawey alack
        pryvetee secret
        war aware   *bet* better
3605   What all this elaborate contrivance meant
        ferde acted   *wolde* was going to

        echon each one of us

3610
        which what   *affeccioun* emotion*

        take taken
        sely simple   *quake* tremble
3615   *thynketh* seems   *verraily* truly
        walwynge rolling   *see* sea
        drenchen drown
        maketh sory cheere looks wretched
        siketh sighs   *swogh* groan
3620

        pryvely discreetly   *in* house
        heng hung   *in pryvetee* secretly
        His owene hand with his own hand
3625   *ronges* rungs   *stalkes* shafts
        balkes beams

Namoore in lookyng than ther shal in deede.
This ordinance is seyd. Go, God thee speede!
Tomorwe at nyght, whan men ben alle aslepe,
Into oure knedyng-tubbes wol we crepe,
3595   And sitten there, abidyng Goddes grace.
Go now thy wey; I have no lenger space
To make of this no lenger sermonyng.
Men seyn thus, "sende the wise, and sey no thyng."
Thou art so wys, it needeth thee nat teche.
3600   Go, save oure lyf, and that I the biseche.'
         This sely carpenter goth forth his wey.
Ful ofte he seide 'Allas and weylawey,'
And to his wyf he tolde his pryvetee,
And she was war, and knew it bet than he,
3605   What al this queynte cast was for to seye.
But nathelees she ferde as she wolde deye.
And seyde, 'Allas! go forth thy wey anon,
Help us to scape, or we been dede echon!
I am thy trewe, verray wedded wyf;
3610   Go, deere spouse, and help to save oure lyf.'
         Lo, which a greet thyng is affeccioun!
Men may dyen of ymaginacioun,
So depe may impressioun be take.
This sely carpenter bigynneth quake;
3615   Hym thynketh verraily that he may see
Noees flood come walwynge as the see
To drenchen Alisoun, his hony deere.
He wepeth, weyleth, maketh sory cheere;
He siketh with ful many a sory swogh;
3620   He gooth and geteth hym a knedyng trogh,
And after that a tubbe and a kymelyn,
And pryvely he sente hem to his in,
And heng hem in the roof in pryvetee.
His owene hand he made laddres thre,
3625   To clymben by the ronges and the stalkes
Unto the tubbes hangynge in the balkes,

vitailled provisioned
jubbe jug

3630   *er that* before   *array* preparation
knave man   *wenche* maid

drow drew
shette shut
3635   *dressed* arranged
clomben climbed
seten sat   *wel a furlong way* for a good few minutes*
Pater-noster, clom (Say an) Our Father (then) be quiet

3640

sit sits   *biddeth* prays

dede dead   *for* because of   *bisynesse* labour

3645   *corfew-tyme* curfew-time, dusk*
travaille trouble   *goost* spirit   *groneth* groans   *soore* painfully
eft then   *routeth* snores   *myslay* lay wrong
of from   *stalketh* creeps
softe quietly
3650

Ther as where   *wont* accustomed

lith lie
bisynesse   *solas* pleasure
3655   *laudes* Lauds, dawn service*
freres friars   *chauncel* chancel   *gonne* began

3660   *hym to disporte* to amuse himself
upon cas by chance   *cloisterer* monk
prively privately

And hem vitailled, bothe trogh and tubbe,
With breed, and chese, and good ale in a jubbe,
Suffisynge right ynogh as for a day.
3630　But er that he hadde maad al this array,
He sente his knave, and eek his wenche also,
Upon his nede to London for to go.
And on the Monday, whan it drow to nyght,
He shette his dore withoute candel-lyght,
3635　And dressed alle thyng as it sholde be.
And shortly, up they clomben alle thre;
They seten stille wel a furlong way.
　'Now, *Pater-noster*, clom!' seyde Nicholay,
And 'Clom!' quod John, and 'Clom!' seyde Alisoun.
3640　This carpenter seyde his devocioun,
And stille he sit, and biddeth his preyere,
Awaitynge on the reyn, if he it heere.
　The dede sleep, for wery bisynesse,
Fil on this carpenter right, as I gesse,
3645　Aboute corfew-tyme, or litel moore;
For travaille of his goost he groneth soore,
And eft he routeth, for his heed myslay.
Doun of the laddre stalketh Nicholay,
And Alisoun ful softe adoun she spedde;
3650　Withouten wordes mo they goon to bedde,
Ther as the carpenter is wont to lye.
Ther was the revel and the melodye;
And thus lith Alison and Nicholas,
In bisynesse of myrthe and of solas,
3655　Til that the belle of laudes gan to rynge,
And freres in the chauncel gonne synge.
　This parissh clerk, this amorous Absolon,
That is for love alwey so wo bigon,
Upon the Monday was at Oseneye
3660　With compaignye, hym to disporte and pleye,
And axed upon cas a cloisterer
Ful prively after John the carpenter;

he the monk   *drough* drew
I don't know; I've not seen him working here
3665   *Syn* since   *trowe* believe   *be went* has gone
ther where
wont accustomed
grange monastery farm

3670   *soothly* rightly
light delighted
wake be awake
For I certainly have not seen him stirring
syn since
3675   *moot* may
pryvely quietly
stant is set   *boures* bedroom's

3680   *leeste* least
maner kind   *parfay* in faith
icched itched*

me mette I dreamed   *feeste* feast
3685

anon at once
rist rises
arraieth dresses   *at poynt-devys* in every detail
3690   *greyn* Grain of Paradise (cardamom seed)
er before   *kembd* combed
trewe-love true-love (a herb)*   *beer* carried
wende thought
rometh roams
3695   *stant* stands   *shot* hinged
raughte reached
softe quietly   *semy soun* little sound

And he drough hym apart out of the chirche,
And seyde, 'I noot; I saugh hym heere nat wirche
3665 Syn Saterday; I trowe that he be went
For tymber, ther oure abbot hath hym sent;
For he is wont for tymber for to go
And dwellen at the grange a day or two;
Or elles he is at his hous, certeyn.
3670 Where that he be, I kan nat soothly seyn.'
    This Absolon ful joly was and light,
And thoghte, 'Now is tyme to wake al nyght,
For sikirly I saugh hym nat stirynge
Aboute his dore, syn day bigan to sprynge.
3675   'So moot I thryve, I shal, at cokkes crowe,
Ful pryvely knokken at his wyndowe
That stant ful lowe upon his boures wal.
To Alison now wol I tellen al
My love-longynge, for yet I shal nat mysse
3680 That at the leeste wey I shal hire kisse.
Som maner confort shal I have, parfay.
My mouth hath icched al this longe day;
That is a signe of kissyng atte leeste.
Al nyght me mette eek I was at a feeste.
3685 Therfore I wol go slepe an houre or tweye,
And al the nyght thanne wol I wake and pleye.'
    Whan that the firste cok hath crowe, anon
Up rist this joly lovere Absolon,
And hym arraieth gay, at poynt-devys.
3690 But first he cheweth greyn and lycorys,
To smellen sweete, er he hadde kembd his heer.
Under his tonge a trewe-love he beer,
For therby wende he to ben gracious.
He rometh to the carpenteres hous,
3695 And stille he stant under the shot-wyndowe –
Unto his brest it raughte, it was so lowe –
And softe he cougheth with a semy soun:
'What do ye, hony-comb, sweete Alisoun,

bryd bird   cynamome cinnamon*
3700 lemman sweetheart

swete sweat   ther wherever
swelte swoon
moorne yearn   tete teat
3705 Ywis indeed   swich such
turtel turtle-dove
may can   ete eat
Jakke fool you idiot boy
As so   com pa me come and kiss me*

3710

Wel bet much more

a twenty devel way in the name of twenty devils

3715 yvel biset ill bestowed

certes truly   lemman darling
3720 I come anon I'm coming at once
stille softly
hust hush
doun sette hym got down
at alle degrees all right

3725

Lemman sweetheart   bryd bird   oore mercy
undoth undoes
Have do get it over with   of on   speed the faste be quick

3730

pich pitch   cole coal

And Absalom, it befell him no better nor worse
But than that   ers arse

3700 My faire bryd, my sweete cynamome?
Awaketh, lemman myn, and speketh to me!
Wel litel thynken ye upon my wo,
That for youre love I swete ther I go.
No wonder is thogh that I swelte and swete;
I moorne as dooth a lamb after the tete.
3705 Ywis, lemman, I have swich love-longynge
That lik a turtel trewe is my moornynge.
I may nat ete na moore than a mayde.'
    'Go fro the wyndow, Jakke fool,' she sayde;
'As help me God, it wol nat be "com pa me."
3710 I love another – and elles I were to blame –
Wel bet than thee, by Jhesu, Absolon.
Go forth thy wey, or I wol caste a ston,
And lat me slepe, a twenty devel wey!'
    'Allas,' quod Absolon, 'and weylawey,
3715 That trewe love was evere so yvel biset!
Thanne kysse me, syn it may be no bet,
For Jhesus love, and for the love of me.'
    'Wiltow thanne go thy wey therwith?' quod she.
    'Ye, certes, lemman,' quod this Absolon.
3720 'Thanne make thee redy,' quod she, 'I come anon.'
And unto Nicholas she seyde stille,
'Now hust, and thou shalt laughen al thy fille.'
    This Absolon doun sette hym on his knees
And seyde, 'I am a lord at alle degrees;
3725 For after this I hope ther cometh moore.
Lemman, thy grace, and sweete bryd, thyn oore!'
    The wyndow she undoth, and that in haste.
'Have do,' quod she, 'com of, and speed the faste,
Lest that oure neighebores thee espie.'
3730 This Absolon gan wype his mouth ful drie.
Derk was the nyght as pich, or as the cole,
And at the wyndow out she putte hir hole,
And Absolon, hym fil no bet ne wers,
But with his mouth he kiste hir naked ers

3735   *Ful savourly* with relish   *er he were war* before he realized
        stirte started   *it was amys* something was wrong
        wiste knew   *berd* beard
        yherd haired
        do done

3740
        a sory pas with sorry step
        berd beard
        corpus body
        sely hapless   *deel* bit

3745
        quyte pay back
        Who rubbeth*   *froteth* scrapes
        sond sand   *chippes* wood-shavings

3750   *bitake* give   *Sathanas* Satan
        'Sweeter to me than the whole of this town,' he said
        'It would be to be avenged for this insult'
        ne hadde ybleynt did not blench, turn aside
        yqueynt quenched

3755
        For love-making he would not give a water-cress
        heeled cured   *maladie**
        deffie denounce
        weep wept   *ybete* beaten

3760   *A softe paas* with soft step   *over* along
        To a smith men called Mr Gervays
        forge*   *harneys* parts
        Eagerly he sharpens ploughshare and coulter
        esily gently

3765   *Undo* open up   *that anon* at once
        artow are you
        sweete tree dear cross
        rathe early   *benedicitee* bless you

3735 Ful savourly, er he were war of this.
Abak he stirte, and thoughte it was amys,
For wel he wiste a womman hath no berd.
He felte a thyng al rough and long yherd,
And seyde, 'Fy! allas! what have I do?'

3740 'Tehee!' quod she, and clapte the wyndow to,
And Absolon gooth forth a sory pas.
     'A berd! A berd!' quod hende Nicholas,
'By Goddes corpus, this goth faire and weel.'
     This sely Absolon herde every deel,

3745 And on his lippe he gan for anger byte,
And to hymself he seyde, 'I shal thee quyte.'
     Who rubbeth now, who froteth now his lippes
With dust, with sond, with straw, with clooth, with
                                        [chippes,
But Absolon, that seith ful ofte, 'Allas!'

3750 'My soule bitake I unto Sathanas,
But me were levere than al this toun,' quod he,
'Of this despit awroken for to be.
Allas,' quod he, 'allas, I ne hadde ybleynt!'
His hoote love was coold and al yqueynt;

3755 For fro that tyme that he hadde kist hir ers,
Of paramours he sette nat a kers,
For he was heeled of his maladie.
Ful ofte paramours he gan deffie,
And weep as dooth a child that is ybete.

3760 A softe paas he wente over the strete
Until a smyth men cleped daun Gerveys,
That in his forge smythed plough harneys;
He sharpeth shaar and kultour bisily.
This Absolon knokketh al esily,

3765 And seyde, 'Undo, Gerveys, and that anon.'
          'What, who artow?' 'It am I, Absolon.'
'What, Absolon! for Cristes sweete tree,
Why rise ye so rathe? Ey, benedicitee!

eyleth ails   *woot* knows
3770 *viritoot* early rising?*
Note Neot   *woot* know
roghte nat a bene cared not a bean
For all his playfulness; he gave no word in response
tow on his distaf flax on his distaff (work on hand)*
3775

kultour coulter, blade of the plough
As lene lend   *to doone* something to do
agayn back

3780 *poke* bag   *nobles* gold coins   *untold* uncounted
have have (it)
Cristes foo by the Devil

I shall tell you about it all right tomorrow
3785 *stele* handle
softe quietly   *stele* steal

cogheth coughs   *therwithal* then
right just   *er* before
3790

warante believe
woot knows   *leef* beloved
deerelyng darling

3795 *yaf* gave   *so* as
ygrave engraved
yeve give

amenden improve   *jape* joke
3800 *He* Absalom   *ers* arse   *scape* escape
dide put
pryvely secretly

What eyleth yow? Som gay gerl, God it woot,
3770 Hath broght yow thus upon the viritoot.
By Seinte Note, ye woot wel what I mene.'
    This Absolon ne roghte nat a bene
Of al his pley; no word agayn he yaf;
He hadde moore tow on his distaf
3775 Than Gerveys knew, and seyde, 'Freend so deere,
That hoote kultour in the chymenee heere,
As lene it me; I have therwith to doone,
And I wol brynge it thee agayn ful soone.'
    Gerveys answerde, 'Certes, were it gold,
3780 Or in a poke nobles alle untold,
Thou sholdest have, as I am trewe smyth.
Ey, Cristes foo! What wol ye do therwith?'
    'Therof,' quod Absolon, 'be as be may.
I shal wel telle it thee to-morwe day' –
3785 And caughte the kultour by the colde stele.
Ful softe out at the dore he gan to stele,
And wente unto the carpenteris wal.
He cogheth first, and knokketh therwithal
Upon the wyndowe, right as he dide er.
3790   This Alison answerde, 'Who is ther
That knokketh so? I warante it a theef.'
    'Why, nay,' quod he, 'God woot, my sweete leef,
I am thyn Absolon, my deerelyng.
Of gold,' quod he, 'I have thee broght a ryng.
3795 My mooder yaf it me, so God me save;
Ful fyn it is, and therto wel ygrave.
This wol I yeve thee, if thou me kisse.'
    This Nicholas was risen for to pisse,
And thoughte he wolde amenden al the jape;
3800 He sholde kisse his ers er that he scape.
And up the wyndowe dide he hastily,
And out his ers he putteth pryvely
Over the buttok, to the haunche-bon;
And therwith spak this clerk, this Absolon,

3805 Speak, sweet bird, I don't know where you are
      fle fly
      thonder-dent thunderclap*
      strook blast   *he* Absalom   *yblent* blinded

3810

      Off goes the skin a hand's width all around
      brende burnt   *toute* rump
      smert pain   *wende for to dye* thought he would die
      wood mad
3815 *herte* heart
      sterte started
      herde oon heard someone   *wood* mad
      Nowelis Nowel's*
      sit hym sat   *mo* further
3820 *atwo* in two
      al everything   *foond* found   *to selle* for sale
      Neither bread nor ale until he reached the ground
      aswowne in a swoon
      hire themselves
3825 *Harrow* help

      ronnen ran   *gauren on* stare at

      brosten broken
3830 But he had to put up with his injury
      anon at once   *bore doun* shouted down
      With by
      wood mad
      agast frightened   *Nowelis* Nowel's
3835 Through some delusion, so that in his folly
      yboght hym bought himself

      preyed begged
      par compaignye for the sake of company
3840

3805 'Spek, sweete bryd, I noot nat where thou art.'
      This Nicholas anon leet fle a fart
    As greet as it had been a thonder-dent,
    That with the strook he was almoost yblent;
    And he was redy with his iren hoot,
3810 And Nicholas amydde the ers he smoot.
      Of gooth the skyn an hande-brede aboute,
    The hoote kultour brende so his toute,
    And for the smert he wende for to dye.
    As he were wood, for wo he gan to crye,
3815 'Help! Water! Water! Help, for Goddes herte!'
      This carpenter out of his slomber sterte,
    And herde oon crien 'water!' as he were wood,
    And thoughte, 'Allas, now comth Nowelis flood!'
    He sit hym up withouten wordes mo,
3820 And with his ax he smoot the corde atwo,
    And doun gooth al; he foond neither to selle,
    Ne breed ne ale, til he cam to the celle
    Upon the floor, and ther aswowne he lay.
      Up stirte hire Alison and Nicholay,
3825 And criden 'Out' and 'Harrow' in the strete.
    The neighebores, bothe smale and grete,
    In ronnen for to gauren on this man,
    That yet aswowne lay, bothe pale and wan,
    For with the fal he brosten hadde his arm.
3830 But stonde he moste unto his owene harm;
    For whan he spak, he was anon bore doun
    With hende Nicholas and Alisoun.
      They tolden every man that he was wood;
    He was agast so of Nowelis flood
3835 Thurgh fantasie that of his vanytee
    He hadde yboght hym knedyng tubbes thre,
    And hadde hem hanged in the roof above;
    And that he preyed hem, for Goddes love,
    To sitten in the roof, *par compaignye*.
3840   The folk gan laughen at his fantasye;

kiken stare   *cape* gape
jape joke*
what so whatever
It was for nothing; no man listened to what he said

3845   *sworn adoun* overcome by oaths
holde wood believed to be mad
For every scholar immediately agreed with the other
wood mad*   *leeve* dear
wight creature   *stryf* row

3850   *swyved* fucked*
kepyng watching
nether ye nether eye
towte rump
done finished   *rowte* company

Into the roof they kiken and they cape,
And turned al his harm unto a jape.
For what so that this carpenter answerde,
It was for noght; no man his reson herde.
3845   With othes grete he was so sworn adoun
That he was holde wood in al the toun;
For every clerk anonright heeld with oother.
They seyde, 'The man is wood, my leeve brother';
And every wight gan laughen at this stryf.
3850   Thus swyved was this carpenteris wyf,
For al his kepyng and his jalousye,
And Absolon hath kist hir nether ye,
And Nicholas is scalded in the towte.
This tale is doon, and God save al the rowte!

Heere endeth the Millere his tale.

3855   *nyce cas* foolish affair

     Diverse different
     moore greater   *loughe* laughed   *pleyde* jested
     hym greve take offence
3860   Except only for Oswald the Reeve*
     carpenteris craft the carpenter's guild
     ylaft left
     grucche complain   *blamed* criticized   *lite* little
     So theek As I may prosper*
3865   With the hoodwinking of a proud miller*
     me liste it pleased me   *ribaudye* ribaldry
     *ik I**   *pley* fool about   *for* because of
     Grazing time is gone; my feed now is hay
     writeth announces   *yeris* years
3870   *also mowled* as mouldy   *heris* hairs
     open-ers the fruit of the medlar*
     That is the fruit which the older it is the worse it gets
     mullok muck-heap   *stree* straw
     drede fear
3875   We cannot be ripe until we are rotten
     We dance on always, as long as the world will pipe
     For there is always a nail to hinder our desire*
     hoor hoary, grey   *grene tayl* green tail
     myght strength
3880   *wyl* will   *evere in oon* always the same

THE REEVE'S PROLOGUE

3855   Whan folk hadde laughen at this nyce cas
Of Absolon and hende Nicholas,
Diverse folk diversely they seyde,
But for the moore part they loughe and pleyde.
Ne at this tale I saugh no man hym greve,
3860 But it were oonly Osewold the Reve.
By cause he was of carpenteris craft,
A litel ire is in his herte ylaft;
He gan to grucche, and blamed it a lite.
     'So theek,' quod he, 'ful wel koude I thee quite
3865 With bleryng of a proud milleres ye,
If that me liste speke of ribaudye.
But ik am oold; me list not pley for age;
Gras tyme is doon; my fodder is now forage;
This white top writeth myne olde yeris;
3870 Myn herte is also mowled as myne heris,
But if I fare as dooth an open-ers –
That ilke fruyt is ever lenger the wers,
Til it be roten in mullok or in stree.
We olde men, I drede, so fare we:
3875 Til we be roten, kan we nat be rype;
We hoppen alwey whil that the world wol pype.
For in oure wyl ther stiketh evere a nayl,
To have an hoor heed and a grene tayl,
As hath a leek; for thogh oure myght be goon,
3880 Oure wyl desireth folie evere in oon.

doon do

Yet still　*asshen* ashes　*yreke* raked over, hidden
gleedes embers　*devyse* list
Avauntyng boasting　*liyng* lying　*coveitise* greed

3885　*sparkles* sparks　*longen* belong　*eelde* old age
lemes limbs　*mowe* may　*unweelde* weak
wyl will, desire　*sooth* the truth
yet still　*ik* I　*coltes tooth* a colt's appetite
Although it is many a year that has passed away

3890　*tappe* tap, spigot　*renne* run*
sikerly surely　*bore* born; *also* bored　*anon* at once
Deeth Death　*drough* drew, turned on
sithe since
tonne tun, cask

3895　*chymbe* rim of the cask
sely foolish　*tonge* tongue　*chymbe* chime
wrecchednesse ignoble matter　*ful yoore* long ago
save except　*is namoore* there is nothing else

3900

What does all this wisdom add up to?
What shul why must　*writ* Scripture*
for to　to
Or (made) a sailor or a doctor/out of a shoemaker*

3905

Depeford Deptford　*half-wey pryme* 7.30 a.m.*
Grenewych Greenwich　*shrewe* rascal
al high

3910　*nat yow greve* not vex yourselves
somdeel sette his howve somewhat rumple his hood*
It is lawful to repel force with force*

bigyled tricked *carpenteer*

3915　*Peraventure* perhaps　*for* because　*oon* one*
leve leave　*quite* repay*

For whan we may nat doon, than wol we speke;
Yet in oure asshen olde is fyr yreke.
     'Foure gleedes han we, which I shal devyse –
Avauntyng, liyng, anger, coveitise;
3885 Thise foure sparkles longen unto eelde.
Oure olde lemes mowe wel been unweelde,
But wyl ne shal nat faillen, that is sooth.
And yet ik have alwey a coltes tooth,
As many a yeer as it is passed henne
3890 Syn that my tappe of lif bigan to renne.
For sikerly, whan I was bore, anon
Deeth drough the tappe of lyf and leet it gon,
And ever sithe hath so the tappe yronne
Til that almoost al empty is the tonne.
3895 The streem of lyf now droppeth on the chymbe.
The sely tonge may wel rynge and chymbe
Of wrecchednesse that passed is ful yoore;
With olde folk, save dotage, is namoore!'
     Whan that oure Hoost hadde herd this sermonyng,
3900 He gan to speke as lordly as a kyng.
He seide, 'What amounteth al this wit?
What shul we speke alday of hooly writ?
The devel made a reve for to preche,
Or of a soutere a shipman or a leche.
3905 Sey forth thy tale, and tarie nat the tyme.
Lo Depeford, and it is half-wey pryme!
Lo Grenewych, ther many a shrewe is inne!
It were al tyme thy tale to bigynne.'
     'Now, sires,' quod this Osewold the Reve,
3910 'I pray yow alle that ye nat yow greve,
Thogh I answere, and somdeel sette his howve;
For leveful is with force force of-showve.
     'This dronke Millere hath ytoold us heer
How that bigyled was a carpenteer,
3915 Peraventure in scorn, for I am oon.
And, by youre leve, I shal hym quite anoon;

      *cherles termes**
      mote may
      stalke straw*
3920 *balke* beam

      Trumpyngtoun Trumpington*   *Cantebrigge* Cambridge
      brigge bridge
      stant stands   *melle* mill
      verray sooth genuine truth*
3925 *was* had been
      pecok peacock
      Pipen play the bagpipes* *beete* mend
      And turn cups, and wrestle and shoot well*
      Ay ever *panade* cutlass
3930 *trenchant* sharp
      poppere dagger *pouche* pocket

      In his stocking he kept a Sheffield knife
      camus flat*
3935 *piled* bald
      market-betere a swaggering bully at market *atte fulle* out and out
      legge lay
      abegge pay for it
      mele ground meal
3940 And that a sly one, accustomed to steal
      hoote called *deynous Symkyn* scornful Symkyn*
      ycomen descended

Right in his cherles termes wol I speke.
I pray to God his nekke mote to-breke;
He kan wel in myn eye seen a stalke,
3920   But in his owene he kan nat seen a balke.'

THE REEVE'S TALE

Heere bigynneth the Reves Tale.

At Trumpyngtoun, nat fer fro Cantebrigge,
Ther gooth a brook, and over that a brigge,
Upon the whiche brook ther stant a melle;
And this is verray sooth that I yow telle:
3925   A millere was ther dwellynge many a day.
As any pecok he was proud and gay.
Pipen he koude and fisshe, and nettes beete,
And turne coppes, and wel wrastle and sheete;
Ay by his belt he baar a long panade,
3930   And of a swerd ful trenchant was the blade.
A joly poppere baar he in his pouche;
Ther was no man, for peril, dorste hym touche
A Sheffeld thwitel baar he in his hose.
Round was his face, and camus was his nose;
3935   As piled as an ape was his skulle.
He was a market-betere atte fulle.
Ther dorste no wight hand upon hym legge,
That he ne swoor he sholde anon abegge.
A theef he was for sothe of corn and mele,
3940   And that a sly, and usaunt for to stele.
His name was hoote deynous Symkyn.
A wyf he hadde, ycomen of noble kyn;

person parson   *toun* village   *fader**
He gave along with her (as dowry) many a brass pan*
3945 In order that Symkyn should ally himself by marriage with his family*
yfostred fostered out

Unless she were well brought up,*and a virgin
To protect his rank as a freeman
3950 *peert* pert, impudent   *pye* magpie
upon hem two (to look) upon the two of them
halydayes holy days   *biforn* in front of
typet the point of the hood
gyte gown   *reed* red*
3955 *hosen* stockings
dame Lady
by the weye along the road
rage flirt   *ones* once
Unless he wished to be killed by Symkyn
3960 *panade* cutlass   *boidekyn* dagger
perilous dangerous*
At any rate they would like their wives to think so
somdel smoterlich somewhat besmirched in reputation
She was as grand as ditch-water*
3965 *hoker* scorn   *bisemare* disdain
Hir thoughte it seemed to her   *hire spare* hold back
What for by reason of   *kynrede* family   *nortelrie* upbringing

3970 *mo* more (children)
Savynge except for
propre page fine boy
ygrowen grown*
kamus pug*
3975

for because   *feir* fair
In purpos intending

The person of the toun hir fader was.
With hire he yaf ful many a panne of bras,
3945 For that Symkyn sholde in his blood allye.
She was yfostred in a nonnerye;
For Symkyn wolde no wyf, as he sayde,
But she were wel ynorissed and a mayde,
To saven his estaat of yomanrye.
3950 And she was proud, and peert as is a pye.
A ful fair sighte was it upon hem two;
On halydayes biforn hire wolde he go
With his typet wounde aboute his heed,
And she cam after in a gyte of reed;
3955 And Symkyn hadde hosen of the same.
Ther dorste no wight clepen hire but 'dame';
Was noon so hardy that wente by the weye
That with hire dorste rage or ones pleye,
But if he wolde be slayn of Symkyn
3960 With panade, or with knyf, or boidekyn.
For jalous folk ben perilous everemo –
Algate they wolde hire wyves wenden so.
And eek, for she was somdel smoterlich,
She was as digne as water in a dich,
3965 And ful of hoker and of bisemare.
Hir thoughte that a lady sholde hire spare,
What for hire kynrede and hir nortelrie
That she hadde lerned in the nonneric.
    A doghter hadde they bitwixe hem two
3970 Of twenty yeer, withouten any mo,
Savynge a child that was of half yeer age;
In cradel it lay and was a propre page.
This wenche thikke and wel ygrowen was,
With kamus nose and eyen greye as glas,
3975 With buttokes brode and brestes rounde and hye.
But right fair was hire heer; I wol nat lye.
    This person of the toun, for she was feir,
In purpos was to maken hire his heir,

catel property   *mesuage* house and contents
3980 And he made difficulties about her marriage
hye nobly
auncetrye ancestry
*hooly** *good* property   *moot* must   *despended* bestowed
On descendants of the blood of Holy Church
3985

Greet sokene a profitable monopoly
malt barley
nameliche especially
3990 *clepen* call   *Soler Halle* Solar Hall*
Ther at the mill   *hir* their*
in a stounde at one time
maunciple manciple, steward*
wenden wisly thought for certain
3995 *stal* stole

therbiforn beforehand   *curteisly* politely

For which the Master chided (him) and made a fuss*
4000 *sette* valued   *tare* weed*
craketh boost spoke boastfully
povre scolers poor scholars

Testif headstrong   *lusty for to pleye* keen on a lark
4005 *oonly* purely   *hire* their
bisily eagerly
To give them leave, for a short time only
hir their
And they would certainly wager their necks
4010 *pekke* peck, quarter of a bushel of corn
sleighte cunning   *reve* rob

highte was called
o one   *Strother* a village as yet unidentified*

Bothe of his catel and his mesuage,
3980 And straunge he made it of hir mariage.
His purpos was for to bistowe hire hye
Into som worthy blood of auncetrye;
For hooly chirches good moot been despended
On hooly chirches blood, that is descended.
3985 Therfore he wolde his hooly blood honoure,
Though that he hooly chirche sholde devoure.
    Greet sokene hath this millere, out of doute,
With whete and malt of al the land aboute;
And nameliche ther was a greet collegge
3990 Men clepen the Soler Halle at Cantebregge;
Ther was hir whete and eek hir malt ygrounde.
And on a day it happed, in a stounde,
Sik lay the maunciple on a maladye;
Men wenden wisly that he sholde dye.
3995 For which this millere stal bothe mele and corn
An hundred tyme moore than biforn;
For therbiforn he stal but curteisly,
But now he was a theef outrageously,
For which the wardeyn chidde and made fare.
4000 But therof sette the millere nat a tare;
He craketh boost, and swoor it was nat so.
    Thanne were ther yonge povre scolers two,
That dwelten in this halle, of which I seye.
Testif they were, and lusty for to pleye,
4005 And, oonly for hire myrthe and revelrye,
Upon the wardeyn bisily they crye
To yeve hem leve, but a litel stounde,
To goon to mille and seen hir corn ygrounde;
And hardily they dorste leye hir nekke
4010 The millere sholde not stele hem half a pekke
Of corn by sleighte, ne by force hem reve;
And at the laste the wardeyn yaf hem leve.
John highte that oon, and Aleyn highte that oother;
Of o toun were they born, that highte Strother,

4015   *Fer* far
       gere gear

4020   *hem nedede* they needed
       layth lays
       Al hayl All hail! (N = a Northern form)*   *y-fayth* in faith

4025   *do ye* are you doing
       nede has na peer need has no equal, *i.e.* must rule
       Hym boes It behoves him, he must (N)   *swayn* servant

       hope believe (N)
4030   *werkes* ache (N)   *ay* ever   *wanges* back teeth
       forthy therefore
       ham home (N)
       heythen hence (N)

4035

       hopur hopper*
       howgates in what way (N)   *gas* goes (N)
       Never have I seen, by my father's family (honour)*
       wagges til and fra wags to and fro (N)
4040   *wiltow swa* wilt thou (do) so (N)
       bynethe underneath   *croun* head

       sal shall (N)   *disport* entertainment
       sort kind
4045   *ille* poor
       of hir nycetee at their foolishness
       nys doon but for a wyle is done only for a trick
       wene think   *bigyle* deceive
       thrift welfare, life   *blere hir ye* delude their eyes
4050   *sleighte* cunning   *philosophye* study*

4015 Fer in the north; I kan nat telle where.
    This Aleyn maketh redy al his gere,
And on an hors the sak he caste anon.
Forth goth Aleyn the clerk, and also John,
With good swerd and with bokeler by hir syde.
4020 John knew the wey – hem nedede no gyde –
And at the mille the sak adoun he layth.
Aleyn spak first: 'Al hayl, Symond, y-fayth!
Hou fares thy faire doghter and thy wyf?'
    'Aleyn, welcome,' quod Symkyn, 'by my lyf!
4025 And John also, how now, what do ye heer?'
    'Symond,' quod John, 'by God, nede has na peer.
Hym boes serve hymself that has na swayn,
Or elles he is a fool, as clerkes sayn.
Oure manciple, I hope he wil be deed,
4030 Swa werkes ay the wanges in his heed;
And forthy is I come, and eek Alayn,
To grynde oure corn and carie it ham agayn;
I pray yow spede us heythen that ye may.'
    'It shal be doon,' quod Symkyn, 'by my fay!
4035 What wol ye doon whil that it is in hande?'
    'By God, right by the hopur wil I stande,'
Quod John, 'and se howgates the corn gas in.
Yet saugh I nevere, by my fader kyn,
How that the hopur wagges til and fra.'
4040   Aleyn answerde, 'John, and wiltow swa?
Thanne wil I be bynethe, by my croun,
And se how that the mele falles doun
Into the trough; that sal be my disport.
For John, y-faith, I may been of youre sort;
4045 I is as ille a millere as ar ye.'
    This millere smyled of hir nycetee,
And thoghte, 'Al this nys doon but for a wyle.
They wene that no man may hem bigyle,
But by my thrift, yet shal I blere hir ye,
4050 For al the sleighte in hir philosophye.

queynte cunning   *crekes* tricks

stide stead   *bren* bran
*The gretteste clerkes . . .**
4055   *whilom* once
Of for   *art* learning   *tare* weed
pryvely secretly
softely quietly

4060   *ybounde* tied up
levesel arbour

strepeth of strips off
laus loose   *he gynneth gon* he made off
4065   *ther* where   *wilde mares** *renne* run
wehee a whinnying cry*
gooth agayn returns
note work, job   *pleyde* joked

4070
fynt finds
Harrow help   *Weylaway* alas
lorn lost   *banes* bones (N)
Com of hurry up   *al atanes* at once (N)
4075
al everything
housbondrie careful management
whilk which (N)   *geen* gone (N)
lepynge leaping   *ren* run*
4080

Unthank bad luck   *boond* tethered
knyt wove, tied
peyne pain, passion
4085   *alswa* also (N)
is am (N)   *wight* strong   *waat* knows (N)   *raa* roe (N)

The moore queynte crekes that they make,
The moore wol I stele whan I take.
In stide of flour yet wol I yeve hem bren.
"The gretteste clerkes been noght wisest men,"
4055 As whilom to the wolf thus spak the mare.
Of al hir art counte I noght a tare.'
   Out at the dore he gooth ful pryvely,
Whan that he saugh his tyme, softely.
He looketh up and doun til he hath founde
4060 The clerkes hors, ther as it stood ybounde
Bihynde the mille, under a levesel;
And to the hors he goth hym faire and wel;
He strepeth of the brydel right anon.
And whan the hors was laus, he gynneth gon
4065 Toward the fen, ther wilde mares renne,
And forth with 'wehee', thurgh thikke and thurgh thenne.
   This millere gooth agayn, no word he seyde,
But dooth his note, and with the clerkes pleyde
Til that hir corn was faire and weel ygrounde.
4070 And whan the mele is sakked and ybounde,
This John goth out and fynt his hors away,
And gan to crie 'Harrow!' and 'Weylaway!
Oure hors is lorn, Alayn, for Goddes banes,
Step on thy feet! Com of, man, al atanes!
4075 Allas, our wardeyn has his palfrey lorn.'
This Aleyn al forgat, bothe mele and corn;
Al was out of his mynde his housbondrie.
'What, whilk way is he geen?' he gan to crie.
   The wyf cam lepynge inward with a ren.
4080 She seyde, 'Allas! youre hors goth to the fen
With wilde mares, as faste as he may go.
Unthank come on his hand that boond hym so,
And he that bettre sholde han knyt the reyne!'
   'Allas,' quod John, 'Aleyn, for Cristes peyne
4085 Lay doun thy swerd, and I wil myn alswa.
I is ful wight, God waat, as is a raa;

sal shall (N)   *bathe* both (N)
pit put   *capul* horse   *lathe* barn (N)
Ilhayl bad luck   *fonne* fool
4090 *sely* poor

busshel bushel, measúre of wheat*
bad told   *knede* knead
4095 *trowe* think   *aferd* suspicious
make a . . . berd outwit
art skill
he the horse
gete get   *croun* head
4100 *sely* hapless   *rennen* run
Keep watch, stop   *Jossa* down   *warderere* watch out behind
Ga go (N)   *kepe* watch
til until   *verray* true

4105 *Hir capul* their horse
dych ditch
Weary and wet, as an animal out in the rain
Comth comes

4110 *dryve til hethyng* brought into contempt

Bathe both (N)   *felawes* fellow-students
namely particularly
pleyneth complains   *gooth* walks
4115 *Bayard* horse's name*

forther further   *myghte* could (go)

For shelter and hospitality in return for their penny
4120 *agayn* in reply   *eny* any

streit small   *lerned art* studied the arts*

By Goddes herte, he sal nat scape us bathe!
Why ne had thow pit the capul in the lathe?
Ilhayl! By God, Alayn, thou is a fonne!'
4090   Thise sely clerkes han ful faste yronne
Toward the fen, bothe Aleyn and eek John.
And whan the millere saugh that they were gon,
He half a busshel of hir flour hath take,
And bad his wyf go knede it in a cake.
4095   He seyde, 'I trowe the clerkes were aferd.
Yet kan a millere make a clerkes berd,
For al his art; now lat hem goon hir weye!
Lo, wher he gooth! Ye, lat the children pleye.
They gete hym nat so lightly, by my croun.'
4100   Thise sely clerkes rennen up and doun
With 'Keep! Keep! Stand! Stand! Jossa, warderere,
Ga whistle thou, and I shal kepe hym heere!'
But shortly, til that it was verray nyght,
They koude nat, though they dide al hir myght,
4105   Hir capul cacche, he ran alwey so faste,
Til in a dych they caughte hym atte laste.
Wery and weet, as beest is in the reyn,
Comth sely John, and with him comth Aleyn.
'Allas,' quod John, 'the day that I was born!
4110   Now are we dryve til hethyng and til scorn.
Oure corn is stoln; men wil us fooles calle,
Bathe the wardeyn and oure felawes alle,
And namely the millere, weylaway!'
Thus pleyneth John as he gooth by the way
4115   Toward the mille, and Bayard in his hond.
The millere sittynge by the fyr he fond,
For it was nyght, and forther myghte they noght;
But for the love of God they hym bisoght
Of herberwe and of ese, as for hir peny.
4120   The millere seyde agayn, 'If ther be eny,
Swich as it is, yet shal ye have youre part.
Myn hous is streit, but ye han lerned art;

konne know how to   argumentes logic
brood across   of out of

4125

rowm roomy   with speche by talking   gise custom
Cutberd Cuthbert (N)*
Ay is thou myrie you're always very amusing
sal must (N)   taa take (N)   of from

4130   Slyk such*

mete food   make us cheere entertain us

na haukes tulle lure no hawks*

4135

toun the village

boond tethered   hire their

4140   chalons blankets   yspred spread
Noght not

by and by side by side
It could be no better arranged, and for what reason?

4145   roumer roomier   herberwe lodging
soupen sup   hem to solace to cheer themselves up
atte of the

vernysshed his heed made his head shine*

4150   for dronken with drink   reed red
yexeth hiccups
on the quakke hoarse   pose head-cold

light lively

4155   ywet wetted*
hir their
rokken rock   sowke suck
crowke crock

Ye konne by argumentes make a place
A myle brood of twenty foot of space.
4125 Lat se now if this place may suffise,
Or make it rowm with speche, as is youre gise.'
'Now, Symond,' seyde John, 'by Seint Cutberd,
Ay is thou myrie, and this is faire answerd.
I have herd seyd, "Man sal taa of twa thynges:
4130 Slyk as he fyndes, or taa slyk as he brynges."
But specially I pray thee, hooste deere,
Get us som mete and drynke, and make us cheere,
And we wil payen trewely atte fulle.
With empty hand men may na haukes tulle;
4135 Loo, heere oure silver, redy for to spende.'
    This millere into toun his doghter sende
For ale and breed, and rosted hem a goos,
And boond hire hors, it sholde namoore go loos,
And in his owene chambre hem made a bed,
4140 With sheetes and with chalons faire yspred
Noght from his owene bed ten foot or twelve.
His doghter hadde a bed, al by hirselve,
Right in the same chambre by and by.
It myghte be no bet, and cause why?
4145 Ther was no roumer herberwe in the place.
They soupen and they speke, hem to solace,
And drynken evere strong ale atte beste.
Aboute mydnyght wente they to reste.
    Wel hath this millere vernysshed his heed;
4150 Ful pale he was for dronken, and nat reed.
He yexeth, and he speketh thurgh the nose
As he were on the quakke, or on the pose.
To bedde he goth, and with hym goth his wyf.
As any jay she light was and jolyf,
4155 So was hir joly whistle wel ywet.
The cradel at hir beddes feet is set,
To rokken, and to yeve the child to sowke.
And whan that dronken al was in the crowke,

4160

dwale sleeping draught
wisely surely   *bibbed* imbibed
fnorteth snorts
Nor did he pay attention to his tail behind

4165   *bar* kept   *burdon* bass accompaniment
Their snoring could be heard two furlongs off*
eek too   *par compaignye* for company's sake*

Slepestow are you asleep

4170   *slyk a sang* such a song (N)
swilk such   *complyn* compline, evensong   *ymel* amongst (N)
wilde fyr a skin disease   *thair* their
Wha who (N)   *ferly* amazing
flour of il endyng best of a bad end*

4175   *tydes* is destined
na fors no matter   *sal* shall (N)
moot I thryve may I thrive
swyve fuck
esement redress   *lawe* equity   *yshapen* destined

4180   *lawe**
gif if   *a* one   *agreved* injured
releved compensated
it is na nay there is no denying it
il fit hard time

4185   *neen* no (N)   *amendement* recompense
esement redress
sale soul (N)
avyse thee be advised, beware
perilous dangerous

4190   *abreyde* start
bathe both (N)   *vileynye* harm
nat a flye not worth a fly
rist rises
uprighte on her back

To bedde wente the doghter right anon;
4160 To bedde goth Aleyn and also John;
Ther nas na moore – hem nedede no dwale.
This millere hath so wisely bibbed ale
That as an hors he fnorteth in his sleep,
Ne of his tayl bihynde he took no keep.
4165 His wyf bar hym a burdon, a ful strong;
Men myghte hir rowtyng heere two furlong;
The wenche rowteth eek, *par compaignye.*

Aleyn the clerk, that herde this melodye,
He poked John, and seyde, 'Slepestow?
4170 Herdestow evere slyk a sang er now?
Lo, swilk a complyn is ymel hem alle;
A wilde fyr upon thair bodyes falle!
Wha herkned evere slyk a ferly thyng?
Ye, they sal have the flour of il endyng.
4175 This lange nyght ther tydes me na reste;
But yet, na fors, al sal be for the beste.
For, John,' seyde he, 'als evere moot I thryve,
If that I may, yon wenche wil I swyve.
Som esement has lawe yshapen us,
4180 For, John, ther is a lawe that says thus:
That gif a man in a point be agreved,
That in another he sal be releved.
Oure corn is stoln, sothly, it is na nay,
And we han had an il fit al this day;
4185 And syn I sal have neen amendement
Agayn my los, I will have esement.
By Goddes sale, it sal neen other bee!'

This John answerde, 'Alayn, avyse thee!
The millere is a perilous man,' he seyde,
4190 'And gif that he out of his sleep abreyde,
He myghte doon us bathe a vileynye.'

Aleyn answerde, 'I counte hym nat a flye.'
And up he rist, and by the wenche he crepte.
This wenche lay uprighte and faste slepte,

4195   *ny close   er* before
        had been would have been   *to* too
        aton at one

        stille quiet   *a furlong wey* for a few moments
4200   *to hymself he maketh routhe* he laments to himself
        wikked jape bad joke
        ape imitator, fool

4205   *auntred hym* took a chance   *nedes sped* needs satisfied
        draf-sak sack of dirty straw

        halde held   *daf* fool   *cokenay* weakling
        auntre risk
4210   *Unhardy is unseely* Unplucky is unlucky
        roos rose
        it hente picked it up
        baar carried
        hir rowtyng leet left off her snoring
4215

        noon not one (cradle)
        mysgoon gone astray

4220   *benedicite* bless us   *foule ysped* fared badly

        forther further
        noght nothing

4225   *nyste (ne wiste)* knew not
        creep crept
        lith lies
        leep leapt
        leith on soore set to vigorously
4230   She had not had so merry a bout for ages

4195 Til he so ny was, er she myghte espie,
That it had been to late for to crie,
And shortly for to seyn, they were aton.
Now pley, Aleyn, for I wol speke of John.
     This John lith stille a furlong wey or two,
4200 And to hymself he maketh routhe and wo.
'Allas!' quod he, 'this is a wikked jape;
Now may I seyn that I is but an ape.
Yet has my felawe somwhat for his harm;
He has the milleris doghter in his arm.
4205 He auntred hym, and has his nedes sped,
And I lye as a draf-sak in my bed;
And when this jape is tald another day,
I sal been halde a daf, a cokenay!
I wil arise and auntre it, by my fayth!
4210 "Unhardy is unseely," thus men sayth.'
And up he roos, and softely he wente
Unto the cradel, and in his hand it hente,
And baar it softe unto his beddes feet.
     Soone after this the wyf hir rowtyng leet,
4215 And gan awake, and wente hire out to pisse,
And cam agayn, and gan hir cradel mysse,
And groped heer and ther, but she foond noon.
'Allas!' quod she, 'I hadde almoost mysgoon;
I hadde almoost goon to the clerkes bed.
4220 Ey, benedicte! Thanne hadde I foule yspedl'
And forth she gooth til she the cradel fond.
She gropeth alwey forther with hir hond,
And foond the bed, and thoghte noght but good,
By cause that the cradel by it stood,
4225 And nyste wher she was, for it was derk;
But faire and wel she creep in to the clerk,
And lith ful stille, and wolde han caught a sleep.
Withinne a while this John the clerk up leep,
And on this goode wyf he leith on soore.
4230 So myrie a fit ne hadde she nat ful yoore;

priketh pierces
lad led
thridde cok third crow of the cock, heralding dawn*
wax grew   *wery* weary
4235   *swonken* laboured
*Malyne** *wight* creature
byde stay
wher so wheresoever
awen own (N)   *swa have I seel* as I may have luck (N)
4240   *lemman* sweetheart   *far* fare
o one
wendest make your way

cake loaf
4245   *mele* meal
heelp helped   *sire* father

dawe dawns
4250

wrang wrong (N)   *mysgon* strayed
toty fuddled*   *swynk* labour
ga walk (N)   *aright* straight
4255   I can tell from the cradle that I have gone astray

a twenty devel way in the name of twenty devils
ther as where
wende have cropen thought to have crept in
4260   *creep* crept

swynes-heed swine's head, sluggard
saule soul   *heer* hear
Jame James*
4265   *thries* thrice
Swyved fucked   *bolt upright* flat on her back

He priketh harde and depe as he were mad.
This joly lyf han thise two clerkes lad
Til that the thridde cok bigan to synge.
 Aleyn wax wery in the dawenynge,
4235 For he had swonken al the longe nyght,
And seyde, 'Fare weel, Malyne, sweete wight!
The day is come; I may no lenger byde;
But everemo, wher so I go or ryde,
I is thyn awen clerk, swa have I seel!'
4240 'Now, deere lemman,' quod she, 'go, far weel!
But er thow go, o thyng I wol thee telle:
Whan that thou wendest homward by the melle,
Right at the entree of the dore bihynde
Thou shalt a cake of half a busshel fynde
4245 That was ymaked of thyn owene mele,
Which that I heelp my sire for to stele.
And, goode lemman, God thee save and kepe!'
And with that word almoost she gan to wepe.
 Aleyn up rist, and thoughte, 'Er that it dawe,
4250 I wol go crepen in by my felawe,'
And fond the cradel with his hand anon.
'By God,' thoughte he, 'al wrang I have mysgon.
Myn heed is toty of my swynk to-nyght,
That makes me that I ga nat aright.
4255 I woot wel by the cradel I have mysgo;
Heere lith the millere and his wyf also.'
And forth he goth, a twenty devel way,
Unto the bed ther as the millere lay.
He wende have cropen by his felawe John,
4260 And by the millere in he creep anon,
And caughte hym by the nekke, and softe he spak.
He seyde, 'Thou John, thou swynes-heed, awak,
For Cristes saule, and heer a noble game.
For by that lord that called is Seint Jame,
4265 As I have thries in this shorte nyght
Swyved the milleres doghter bolt upright,

agast frightened
Ye yes   *harlot* rascal   *hast* have you

4270

disparage dishonour*
swich lynage such a lineage
throte-bolle Adam's apple
hente hym despitously agayn grabbed him fiercely in return

4275   *smoot* struck   *fest* fist

walwe wallow   *poke* bag (N)
goon get   *anon* then

4280   *sporned at* tripped over

That wiste who knew   *nyce* silly
lite wight little time

4285   *hir* her   *breyde* started*
croys cross   *Bromeholm* a Norfolk shrine*
In manus tuas Into thy hands (I commend my spirit)*
feend devil   *falle* fallen
I nam but I am almost

4290   *oon* one   *wombe* stomach

stirte leaped
graspeth by gropes along

4295   *estres* interior   *bet* better

4300   *sikerly* certainly   *nyste* did not know
But as but   *whit* white   *ye* eye
gan did   *espye* catch sight of

Whil thow hast, as a coward, been agast.'
    'Ye, false harlot,' quod the millere, 'hast?
A, false traitour! False clerk!' quod he,
4270 'Thow shalt be deed, by Goddes dignitee!
Who dorste be so boold to disparage
My doghter, that is come of swich lynage?'
And by the throte-bolle he caughte Alayn,
And he hente hym despitously agayn,
4275 And on the nose he smoot hym with his fest.
Doun ran the blody streem upon his brest;
And in the floor, with nose and mouth tobroke,
They walwe as doon two pigges in a poke;
And up they goon, and doun agayn anon,
4280 Til that the millere sporned at a stoon,
And doun he fil bakward upon his wyf,
That wiste no thyng of this nyce stryf;
For she was falle aslepe a lite wight
With John the clerk, that waked hadde al nyght,
4285 And with the fal out of hir sleep she breyde.
'Help! hooly croys of Bromeholm,' she seyde,
'In manus tuas! Lord, to thee I calle!
Awak, Symond! The feend is on me falle.
Myn herte is broken; help! I nam but deed!
4290 Ther lyth oon upon my wombe and on myn heed.
Help, Symkyn, for the false clerkes fighte!'
    This John stirte up as faste as ever he myghte,
And graspeth by the walles to and fro,
To fynde a staf; and she stirte up also,
4295 And knew the estres bet than dide this John,
And by the wal a staf she foond anon,
And saugh a litel shymeryng of a light,
For at an hole in shoon the moone bright,
And by that light she saugh hem bothe two,
4300 But sikerly she nyste who was who,
But as she saugh a whit thyng in hir ye.
And whan she gan this white thyng espye,

wende thought   *wered* worn   *volupeer* nightcap
drow drew   *ay neer and neer* ever nearer
4305   *wende han* thought to have   *at the fulle* with full force
smoot struck   *pyled* bald
So that down he goes, and shouted 'Help! I die!'
beete beat   *lete* let
greythen hem dress   *anon* then
4310   *mele* meal
yet moreover   *cake* loaf
ybake baked
ybete beaten*
ylost lost (the fee for)
4315   *everideel* every bit of
bette had beaten
swyved fucked   *als* too
swich it is a millere thus it is for a miller
sooth truly
4320   He need not expect good who does evil
gylour deceiver   *bigyled* deceived

quyt repaid

She wende the clerk hadde wered a volupeer,
And with the staf she drow ay neer and neer,
4305 And wende han hit this Aleyn at the fulle,
And smoot the millere on the pyled skulle,
That doun he gooth, and cride, 'Harrow! I dye!'
Thise clerkes beete hym weel and lete hym lye,
And greythen hem, and tooke hir hors anon,
4310 And eek hire mele, and on hir wey they gon.
And at the mille yet they tooke hir cake
Of half a busshel flour, ful wel ybake.

Thus is the proude millere wel ybete,
And hath ylost the gryndynge of the whete,
4315 And payed for the soper everideel
Of Aleyn and of John, that bette hym weel.
His wyf is swyved, and his doghter als.
Lo, swich it is a millere to be fals!
And therfore this proverbe is seyd ful sooth,
4320 'Hym thar nat wene wel that yvele dooth.'
A gylour shal hymself bigyled be.
And God, that sitteth heighe in magestee,
Save al this compaignye, grete and smale!
Thus have I quyt the Millere in my tale.

Heere is ended the Reves Tale.

In his joy, it seemed to him that the Reeve was scratching his back

For by

To his dispute concerning lodging

4330 *Salomon**

herberwynge harbouring, giving lodging
avysed for to be be wary
pryvetee privacy

4335 *so yeve* may give
If ever, since I was called Hodge (Roger) of Ware*
I heard of a miller put to better employment
hadde a jape of malice was played a nasty trick
stynte stop

4340 *vouche-sauf* vouchsafe, agree

fil happened

4345 *looke* make sure
pastee pasty, meat pie   *laten blood* let blood (juice)*
Jakke of Dovere a kind of pie*
twies twice
hastow hast thou had

4350 For they are still the worse off from your parsley*

THE COOK'S PROLOGUE

The prologe of the Cokes Tale.

4325   The Cook of Londoun, whil the Reve spak,
For joye him thoughte he clawed him on the bak.
'Ha! ha!' quod he, 'For Cristes passion,
This millere hadde a sharp conclusion
Upon his argument of herbergage!
4330 Wel seyde Salomon in his langage,
"Ne bryng nat every man into thyn hous,"
For herberwynge by nyghte is perilous.
Wel oghte a man avysed for to be
Whom that he broghte into his pryvetee.
4335 I pray to God, so yeve me sorwe and care
If evere, sitthe I highte Hogge of Ware,
Herde I a millere bettre yset a-werk.
He hadde a jape of malice in the derk.
But God forbede that we stynte heere;
4340 And therfore, if ye vouche-sauf to heere
A tale of me, that am a povre man,
I wol yow telle, as wel as evere I kan,
A litel jape that fil in oure citee.'
    Oure Hoost answerde and seide, 'I graunte it thee.
4345 Now telle on, Roger; looke that it be good,
For many a pastee hastow laten blood,
And many a Jakke of Dovere hastow soold
That hath been twies hoot and twies coold.
Of many a pilgrym hastow Cristes curs,
4350 For of thy percely yet they fare the wors,

stubbel goos goose raised on stubble
loos loose
by thy name in accordance with your name
wroth for game angry at a joke*

4355   *seye ful sooth* tell the truth
fey faith
sooth pley, quaad pley true jest, bad jest
*Herry Bailly**

4360   *Though that* if   *hostileer* innkeeper
yit yet
parte separate   *ywis* certainly   *quit* answered
lough laughed

4365   *prentys* apprentice*   *whilom* once   *oure citee* London
craft guild   *vitailliers* victuallers, caterers
Gaillard merry   *goldfynch**   *shawe* grove
Broun dark-skinned   *berye* berry   *propre* good-looking
ykembd combed   *fetisly* neatly

4370   *koude* knew how to
cleped called   *Perkyn Revelour* Perkyn the Reveller*
paramour love-making
hyve hive
Wel lucky

4375   *bridale* wedding party   *hoppe* dance
bet better

That they han eten with thy stubbel goos,
For in thy shoppe is many a flye loos.
Now telle on, gentil Roger by thy name.
But yet I pray thee, be nat wroth for game;

4355   A man may seye ful sooth in game and pley.'
    'Thou seist ful sooth,' quod Roger, 'by my fey!
But "sooth pley, quaad pley," as the Flemyng seith.
And therfore, Herry Bailly, by thy feith,
Be thou nat wrooth, er we departen heer,

4360   Though that my tale be of an hostileer.
But nathelees I wol nat telle it yit;
But er we parte, ywis, thou shalt be quit.'
And therwithal he lough and made cheere,
And seyde his tale, as ye shul after heere.

THE COOK'S TALE

Heere bigynneth the Cookes Tale.

4365   A prentys whilom dwelled in oure citee,
And of a craft of vitailliers was hee.
Gaillard he was as goldfynch in the shawe,
Broun as a berye, a propre short felawe,
With lokkes blake, ykembd ful fetisly.

4370   Dauncen he koude so wel and jolily
That he was cleped Perkyn Revelour.
He was as ful of love and paramour
As is the hyve ful of hony sweete;
Wel was the wenche with hym myghte meete.

4375   At every bridale wolde he synge and hoppe;
He loved bet the taverne than the shoppe.

ridyng procession   Chepe Cheapside*
lepe leap
Til that until
4380   ayeyn back
gadered hym a meynee gathered round him a following
maken swich disport have that kind of fun
setten steven made a time
the dys dice   swich such and such
4385

fairer koude knew better how to

Of his expenditure, on the quiet
chaffare business
4390   box strongbox
sikerly certainly   revelour partying
Who makes a habit of dice, debauchery or wenching*
abye pay for
Al have he though he (the master) have
4395   riot debauchery   convertible interchangeable
Even though he (the apprentice) know how to play a cithern or a fiddle*
Revelling and honesty, in a man of low degree
been ful wrothe al day can never agree ('are angry')
bood remained
4400   Until he was near the end of his apprenticeship
Al although   snybbed reprimanded
And sometimes conducted with minstrelsy to prison*
hym bithoghte called to mind
when Perkyn asked for his certificate of service
4405

Wel bet far better*
rotie should rot
fareth goes   by with   riotous dissolute
ful lasse much less   pace go
4410   shende ruin
yaf gave   acquitance release
bad ordered   with meschance bad luck to him

For whan ther any ridyng was in Chepe,
Out of the shoppe thider wolde he lepe –
Til that he hadde al the sighte yseyn,
4380 And daunced wel, he wolde nat come ayeyn –
And gadered hym a meynee of his sort
To hoppe and synge and maken swich disport;
And ther they setten stevene for to meete,
To pleyen at the dys in swich a streete.
4385 For in the toune nas ther no prentys
That fairer koude caste a paire of dys
Than Perkyn koude, and therto he was free
Of his dispense, in place of pryvetee.
That fond his maister wel in his chaffare,
4390 For often tyme he foond his box ful bare.
For sikerly a prentys revelour
That haunteth dys, riot, or paramour,
His maister shal it in his shoppe abye,
Al have he no part of the mynstralcye.
4395 For thefte and riot, they been convertible,
Al konne he pleye on gyterne or ribible.
Revel and trouthe, as in a lowe degree,
They been ful wrothe al day, as men may see.
    This joly prentys with his maister bood,
4400 Til he were ny out of his prentishood,
Al were he snybbed bothe erly and late,
And somtyme lad with revel to Newegate.
But atte laste his maister hym bithoghte,
Upon a day, whan he his papir soghte,
4405 Of a proverbe that seith this same word:
'Wel bet is roten appul out of hoord
Than that it rotie al the remenaunt.'
So fareth it by a riotous servaunt;
It is ful lasse harm to lete hym pace,
4410 Than he shende alle the servantz in the place.
Therfore his maister yaf hym acquitance,
And bad hym go, with sorwe and with meschance!

leve leave

riote revel   *leve* leave off, stop

4415   *for* since   *lowke* accomplice

wasten waste   *sowke* suck up

Of from   *brybe* steal

array clothing

compeer companion

4420   *disport* fun

heeld kept   *contenance* the sake of appearances

swyved fucked   *sustenance* living*

And thus this joly prentys hadde his leve.
Now lat hym riote al the nyght or leve.
4415 And for ther is no theef withoute a lowke,
That helpeth hym to wasten and to sowke
Of that he brybe kan or borwe may,
Anon he sente his bed and his array
Unto a compeer of his owene sort,
4420 That lovede dys, and revel, and disport,
And hadde a wyf that heeld for contenance
A shoppe, and swyved for hir sustenance.

Notes

Notes are keyed to the line numbers of the First Fragment, from 1 to 4422. (These line numbers may not agree with the line numbers other editors have given to Tales in the Fragment, which may start with the first line of the Tale or of the Tale's own Prologue.) When a cross-reference is made within the same Tale, simple line numbers are given, but cross-references to other parts of the Fragment preface the line numbers with the following abbreviations: GP General Prologue; KT Knight's Tale; MP Miller's Prologue; MT Miller's Tale; RP Reeve's Prologue; RT Reeve's Tale; CP Cook's Prologue; CT Cook's Tale. R: The Riverside Chaucer. Bible quotations are from the Douay-Rheims Bible (1582–1609), which, being translated from the Latin Vulgate, is closest to the Bible Chaucer knew.

GENERAL PROLOGUE

1–18 A Spring opening was a tradition of medieval romance writing. Here Chaucer combines it with a *chronographia*, an indication of time by means of an astronomical periphrasis, favoured by Dante. This 18-line sentence is built on an elaborate *chronographia*: *Whan . . . whan thanne . . . and specially*.

1 *soote* 'gentle' as well as 'sweet'.

2 *droghte* A dry March is good for sowing.

7 *yonge* The sun's year begins on the Spring equinox, 12 March in the Julian Calendar.

8 *the Ram* The sun had completed its transit of Aries, the first sign of the zodiac, on 11 April. The opening of Fragment II of the *Tales* gives the date as 18 April.

10 *open ye* A way of saying that the birds are light sleepers.

11 *nature* Chaucer had presented Nature as a goddess who presides over the mating of birds in his early work *The Parliament of Fowls* (c.1381).

13 *palmeres* The palm carried by pilgrims to the Holy Land gave a name to pilgrims in general. From the fourth century onwards, pilgrimages

to sacred sites became more and more popular, not only for penitential or pious purposes but also as excursions.

17   *The . . . martir* St Thomas of Canterbury, Archbishop and defender of the rights of the Church. Killed at the altar of his Cathedral by knights of Henry II in 1170. Canterbury, two days' ride from London into Kent, became one of the chief places of pilgrimage in Europe. Henry VIII suppressed the pilgrimage in 1537.

18   *holpen* A saint can intercede with God for sick people who pray to him. *seke/seeke* is an identical rhyme, known as *rime riche*.

20   *Southwerk* Southwark, a borough across the Thames from the City of London proper, to which it was linked by London Bridge. *The Tabard* was a large inn in Chaucer's day. A tabard is a short sleeveless heraldic jacket.

43   *The KNYGḢT* is a professional soldier, leader of the military Estate among the pilgrims. His virtues, campaign record, modesty and piety recall the original ideals of Christian chivalry of the twelfth century.

49   The knight has fought for *oure feith* on the eastern, southern and northern borders of the Christian West from Egypt round to Russia. It is notable that he fights against Muslims, heathens and schismatics, rather than, as many Englishmen had, against fellow Catholics in France and Spain.

51   English knights were at the taking of the great city of *Alisaundre* from the Muslims in 1365 by Peter of Lusignan, celebrated in Machaut's *La Prise d'Alexandrie*. Peter, King of Cyprus and sixth Latin king of Jerusalem, is a great chivalric hero in the *Chronicles* of Chaucer's French contemporary, Jean Froissart.

53   The Teutonic Knights launched their campaigns from *Pruce* eastwards into the pagan lands along the south coast of the Baltic and into orthodox Russia from 1228 onwards.

54   *Lettow* Lithuania followed its Prince Jagiello into the Catholic Church after 1386.

57   With the conquest in 1344 of *Algezir*, Algeciras, their chief port in Granada, the Belmarin dynasty returned to their kingdom in Morocco (*Belmarye*), where Christian knights also campaigned.

58   *Lyeys* Ayash, the Armenian port near Antioch, was taken by Peter of Cyprus in 1367. He had taken the rich port of *Satalye* (Adalia, Antalya) in 1361.

63   *lystes* Instead of doing battle, Christian and Muslim forces sometimes agreed to a formal combat of champions.

65   *Palatye* Balat (ancient Miletus), an emirate on the south-west coast of Turkey. The emir for whom the knight fought (against *another hethen*) may be one who is recorded as having paid homage to Peter of Cyprus in 1365.

72   *verray, parfit gentil* Each of the three qualifiers in this oft-quoted line
has changed its sense. All are adjectives.

74   The knight cares more for his *hors*, horses than for his *array*, exemplify-
ing his wisdom (68).

76   His simple tunic is spotted with (honourable) rust from his *habergeon*,
coat of mail.

79   A *SQUIER* is a junior knight in the service of a senior knight. A
knight *bacheler* (80), in the first degree of knighthood, cannot, like a
knight banneret, display his banner and lead others. The father fights
Christian battles far away in his lord's war; the son fights across the
Channel in hope of his lady's grace. Full of youth and gaiety, the
image of fashion and accomplishment, he follows courtly pursuits,
including love and war. He treats his father with honour.

86   *Artoys, and Pycardie*, the parts of France nearest to Kent, often saw
English armies in the Hundred Years War. Chaucer had fought in
France in 1359. The reference to *Flaundres* recalls the Bishop of
Norwich's 'crusade' against the French lords of Flanders in 1361.

98   *nyghtyngale* In lyric poetry the bird of love, which sings all night long
in the season.

100 One duty of a squire was to carve the meat for the knight he
followed; it was an honour for a son to carve for his father.

101 The *YEMAN* is a free servant (the word came to mean a small
landowner in the next century), who completes the military trio; the
six-foot longbow had a range of 290 yards. He is a gamekeeper, a
huntsman rather than a woodsman.

115 St *Cristopher* was popular, as a protector against disaster and sudden
death, with travellers as much as with huntsmen.

118 As head of a convent, the *PRIORESSE* takes precedence over the
Monk. She is a lady – many nuns were dowerless daughters of gentry
families – and her portrait praises the refinement of her manners and
sensibility. This praise is ironical rather than broadly satirical. The
Prioress's shapely nose, grey eyes, small mouth and large unwrinkled
forehead are what *Vogue* prescribed in 1387.

The Benedictine Rule did not prescribe little dogs, or a brooch,
or even going on pilgrimage. The reader should not allow the
ambiguity to be distorted by changes in the sense of words: a 'coy'
smile was not archly inviting, 'counterfeit' (139) did not mean
'fake'.

119 *coy* Derived from Latin *quietus*, quiet.

120 St Eligius (French *Eloi*), bishop, patron saint of goldsmiths, founder
of convents.

121 *Eglentyne* (French *Eglintin*: briar rose), a fashionable name in romance.

122 *service dyvyne* A dignified performance of the Divine Office is

Benedictine practice. The Office has seven canonical hours; a nasal intonation is easier on the throat.

125–6   The Benedictine convent at *Stratford*, Bromley by Bow, Middlesex, was visited by Chaucer in 1354, when the community included Elizabeth of Hainault, sister of Edward III's Queen Philippa. Her will bequeathed gold, jewellery and clothing to her fellow-nuns. The joke about the Prioress's Stratford *Frenssh* may be that it is not court French but Norman French or Hainault French. Chaucer's wife was another Philippa from Hainault. He had a sister, or daughter, who was a nun at the neighbouring aristocratic convent of Barking.

127–36   The table manners are those of a well-bred lady, as prescribed in courtesy books and in *Le Roman de la Rose*.

140   *estatlich* The Rule of St Benedict prescribed dignity to a head of house.

142   That the prioress's *conscience* is touched by the sufferings of mice rather than men shows her as sentimental rather than compassionate. Gauging the irony here is complicated by the consideration that this is also an instance of the narrator's hyperbole, which he uses for heightening as often as for caricature.

151   *wympul* The headdress of Benedictine nuns.

159   The *gauds* are larger beads for the Pater Noster, dividing off decades of Ave Maria beads in a set of rosary beads, used for saying a cycle of prayers meditating on the Fifteen Mysteries. The rosary is a devotional practice which began in the thirteenth century.

161   The *crowned A* was an emblem for Anne of Bohemia, queen to Richard II.

162   *Amor vincit omnia* The motto is of secular origin in Virgil. Usually taken as 'Love conquers all', it can also mean 'Love binds all', with a religious sense. Like much about the the Prioress, it is ambiguous.

164   A Prioress with one attendant and *three* priests? This half-line is usually rejected as a scribe's effort to fill a gap in the text. One Nun's Priest tells a tale; three would bring the number of pilgrims up to thirty-one rather than the twenty-nine of line 24.

165   The *MONK* is the senior cleric after the Prioress, and like her a Benedictine. A fat lord and a hunter, he fulfils the satirists' image of a man who professes to have withdrawn from the world but rejoices in the world and is proud to serve it. Chaucer improves the joke by recording that he, Chaucer, 'seyde his opinion was good' (183).

166   *venerie* hunting; the pursuit of Venus is a later sense.

170   Bells on the *brydel* were a fashion, especially with Canterbury pilgrims. Though Chaucer does not say so, we gather that the Monk prefers their sound to that of the chapel bell.

171–4   Incomplete syntax has led editors to disagree as to how to punctuate.

172   *lord* 'Dominus' is a monk's title (also *Daun* Dom).
the celle A lesser monastic house where this monk is Prior.

173   *St Beneit* Benedict of Nursia (*c.*480–*c.*550), founder of western monasticism. The credit for introducing his Rule into France was attributed to his disciple St Maur.

177–8   *that text* A traditional comment on such Biblical figures as Esau.

179–82   A Benedictine takes a vow of stability: the monastery is a place of liturgical prayer, sacred reading and manual labour.

187   *Austyn* St Augustine of Hippo (354–430) wrote that monks should support themselves by manual work. Augustinian Canons followed a Rule derived from his precepts.

191   *huntyng for the hare* The abbot of Leicester held an annual hare-hunt for Edward III.

194   *grys* The finest squirrel-fur, forbidden to monks.

196   *gold . . . pyn* Pins were forbidden to monks (compare 160).

199   If (as is likely) the monk is a priest he will have been *enoynt* with holy oils at his ordination.

200   *in good poynt* is a phrase used of a horse's condition.

203   Luxury *bootes* were forbidden to monks.

205   *forpyned goost* The monk's idea of asceticism.

206   The Rule forbade monks to eat quadrupeds, *roost* or otherwise; a *swan* was the most expensive of fowls.

207   *as is a berye* Even the Monk's horse is compared with something edible.

208   *FRERE* Latin *frater*, French *frère*, brother. The original mission of the Friars was apostolic: to practise and preach the Gospel in the world, possessing nothing and living off charity. But the followers of SS Francis and Dominic were seen to have abused their privileges and had become the butt of a virulent satirical literature, reflected in the length of the portrait.

209   *lymytour* Convents and individual friars were licensed to beg in a specified district.

210   *ordres foure* The Franciscans, Friars Minor or Grey Friars (founded by St Francis, 1209); the Dominicans, Friars Preachers or Black Friars (founded by St Dominic, 1216); the Carmelites or White Friars; and the Austin Friars.

213–14   *cost/post* The provision of a dowry is an act of generosity; and *post* recalls 'a pillar of the church'. But satirical writers give an indecent innuendo to *post* (= erection), and the rhyme suggests that the Friar pays for the marriages of girls he has seduced.

216   *frankeleyns* On franklins and their hospitality, see 331–60.

220   The Friar's claim to have been licensed with *moore* powers as a confessor than the parish priest sounds suspicious, but is not impossible.

221   The sacrament of *confessioun* or Penance: since the thirteenth century every Christian had been required once a year to confess his sins to a priest. A contrite penitent is absolved of guilt, and, after performing the penance imposed, of punishment.

223   *esy . . . penaunce* The Friar's penances are softer (to the right man) than would be those of a good *Person of a Toun* or parish priest. One penance that could be imposed was a pilgrimage.

224   *pitaunce* charitable alms.

226   Penitential manuals say that tears are a *signe* of true contrition; Friar Hubert says that in hard cases money is just as good a sign.

234   For the popularity of *pynnes*, see 160 and 196.

239   *champioun* Champions were used in the judicial ordeal by battle.

242   *lazar* (called after Lazarus) *or a beggestere* Company kept by those whose example friars professed to follow.

254   *In principio* The opening words of St John's Gospel, and of the Latin mass, used as a devout greeting.

258   *love-dayes*, appointed for the amicable settlement of disputes between those who could not afford lawyers, offered opportunities to force and fraud.

270   The *MARCHANT* is the first non-military lay pilgrim. Feudal social theory had no room for non-military laymen who were not manual workers or skilled tradesmen, but in fact merchants were increasingly important in London as a source of finance for kings' French wars. The merchant heads a large burgher group, nominally part of the third (workers') Estate. Chaucer's family were merchants in wine. Merchants of the Staple held the monopoly on the export of wool, fells and hides, a trade for which Chaucer was Controller of Customs in the 1370s. Merchants were satirized for their secrecy, self-importance and dubious financial dealings.

271   *mottelee* Probably the livery of his guild.

277   *Middelburgh* on the island of Walcheren in the Netherlands was the port for the Staple, 1384–88, and thereafter for the Merchant Adventurers; Orwell is a port near Ipswich, where Chaucer's family came from.

278   *sheeldes* were French *écus*, coins with a shield on one side. Currency trading was regarded as a form of usury, hence condemned by the Church.

280   *dette* Interest-bearing debt, the basis of mercantile enterprise and of international finance, was suspect. The line can be read in two or three senses.

282   *chevyssaunce* A technical term for dealing, including borrowing (as here) and lending. All lending at interest was suspect.

284   *I noot* The Merchant did not give his name away.

285   A university *CLERK* followed the Trivium (grammar, logic, rhetoric) for the BA, then the Quadrivium (arithmetic, geometry, astronomy, music) for the MA.

286   Oxford was strong in logic, the main arts subject.

291   The studious clerk has perhaps deferred taking Holy Orders until he has a benefice or ecclesiastical living.

295   The works of *Aristotle*, the Greek philosopher of the fourth century BC, were translated from Arabic and became the basis of university study from the twelfth century.

293–6   This Oxford clerk buys books; Nicholas in the *Miller's Tale* prefers astrology and has a psaltery.

298   *cofre* The rhyme confirms a worldly joke about the 'philosopher's stone' of the alchemists, which turned base metal into gold. Although 'philosophy' included natural science, there was no money in logic.

309   A *SERGEANT OF THE LAWE* held the highest legal rank, as one of the king's *servientes ad legem*. If not judges, they could act as circuit judges, and, in other cases, as barristers. Some acquired land, including the learned Thomas Pynchbec, who in 1388 as chief baron of the Exchequer signed a writ for Chaucer's arrest for debt. See 326n.

310   The *Parvys* was where clients met Sergeants.

314   Only Sergeants could be judges at the *Assise*, county courts which heard all civil cases.

315   *patente* An open letter of appointment from the king.

317   *fees and robes* A legal formula denoting recurrent annual payments; a Sergeant might get £20 p.a. and a robe at Christmas.

318   *purchasour* It is left unclear whether the Sergeant buys land for clients or for himself.

319   *fee symple* Legal ownership direct from the Crown, without other feudal obligation.

323   *termes* Either in exact legal terms, or in Term Books (law reports).

326   *pynche* Possibly a dig at Pynchbec (see 309n).

328   *medlee* cloth of dyed wool. The Sergeant does not wear his ceremonious travelling dress.

331   *FRANKELEYN* A free-born provincial landholder. Franklins were often knights; two neighbours of Pynchbec in Lincolnshire have been offered as models. The picture of the country squire is more amused than satirical.

333   *complexioun* Not facial colour but temperament or balance of 'humours'. The four humours (hot, cold, moist and dry), themselves combinations of the four elements of earth, air, fire and water,

produced four complexions: melancholy, choleric, phlegmatic and sanguine. Blood predominated in the *sangwyn* man: ruddy of face, pleasure-loving, of good digestion and 'humour'.

334   *a sop in wyn* A common light breakfast.

336   The Greek philosopher *Epicurus* held that pleasure was the chief good. Epicureans were later identified with gourmets.

345   *snewed* Proverbial hyperbole.

353   A permanent table of hospitality, *dormant*, whereas most tables were trestle tables.

355–6   The Franklin served as Justice of the Peace and Member of Parliament, as had Chaucer in the 1380s.

357   *anlaas* and *gipser* denoted a gentleman.

359   The *shirreve* was the king's chief officer in a shire. A *contour* could be responsible for a shire's taxes.

361–2   The five guildsmen wear one livery, presumably of a parish guild, since a single craft guild would not include carpentry with four cloth crafts.

364   *solempne and a greet* The supposed importance of the guild is presented via the consciousness of its members and their wives.

367   *silver* mounts were permitted under sumptuary law to tradesmen with property of over £500.

370   *a yeldehalle* The seat of civic government.

372   Though each is *shaply for to been an alderman*, it was to be a century before a member of these trades became an alderman of London.

376   *madame* The title given an alderman's wife.

378   The *mantel*, carried by a servant walking in front in the procession, was for warmth at the vigil-service of a feast-day, but more for show. See 450.

379   The *COOK*'s portrait is just a list of skills, until we glimpse his *mormal*. Towards the end of the Tales he falls off his horse, drunk. The Cook calls himself *Hogge* (a version of Roger) of Ware. A Roger of Ware, Cook, is recorded as in trouble with the law.

381   *galyngale* is the powdered root of sweet cyperus, said to resemble ginger.

382   *Londoun ale* was extra strong and expensive; the quality of each brewing was tested before release.

386   *mormal* A dry scabbed gangrenous ulcer.

388   The *SHIPMAN* A ship's master. Shipmen do not feature much in estates satire written by urban clerks. Chaucer's family of wine merchants would doubtless have had views on shipmen. Chaucer was himself a customs officer.

389   *Dertemouthe* England's major south-western port. A ship the *Maudelayne* (410) is recorded there, its master in 1391 a Peter Risshenden.

390   The *rouncy*, and the Shipman's unfamiliarity with horses, are comic.

397   *Burdeux* Imports from English Gascony were the heart of the wine-trade in which Chaucer's family engaged. The final words of the line awaken the second sense of *ydrawe* in 396.

400   *By water he sente hem hoom* He drowned his prisoners – not an unknown practice.

403   *lodemenage* From 'lodestar', the North Star which 'leads' navigators.

404   *Hulle* Hull is in Yorkshire.
       Cartage Probably Spanish Cartagena rather than ancient Carthage.

408   *Fynystere* The Spanish rather than the Breton cape.

410   A *barge* of Edward III's time was 80 feet long and 20 feet wide, with a single mast and oars. For *Maudelayne* see 389n.

411   *DOCTOUR OF PHISIK* A Doctorate required studies lasting 15 years or more. The best physician and surgeon in the world, and the most learned, this Doctor (like many in literature) cares for the body rather than the spirit and is too fond of gold.

413   *To speke of* The Doctor excels in the practice of his two professions, rather than in talking about them.

414   *astronomye* The science of planetary influences was part of medical practice, and was taken seriously, e.g. in Chaucer's *Treatise upon the Astrolabe*.

415–16   The Doctor *kepte*, observed, his patient's response to the astrological hours of planetary influence. Magic *natureel* is distinguished from black magic.

417   *fortunen the ascendent* Calculate the planetary position in which the 'lord of the ascendant' was favourable to the stones making up the talismanic figures used in medicine.

420   *hoot, or coold* . . . The four qualities, linked to the four elements (see 333n). Medicine sought to keep the four humours in balance, and these could be affected by planets.

427   *ech of hem made oother for to wynne* An old gibe.

429–34   A list of the most eminent medical authorities, beginning with Aesculapius, the father of Greek medicine; Dioscorides (first century AD) wrote a pharmaceutical encyclopaedia; Rufus of Ephesus, his contemporary; Hippocrates of Cos (fifth century BC), the founder of modern medicine; the works of Galen (second century AD) were medieval textbooks. Greek medicine was transmitted by Middle Eastern writers: Haly is probably Ali ibn Abbas (d. 994), a Persian; there are three medical writers called Serapion; Rhazes wrote a medical manual; Avicenna and Averroes, the most influential Islamic philosophers in the West, both wrote on medicine; Damascenus was a name given to two or three Arabic works; Constantinus (eleventh century) was a North African monk who translated Arabic works. The final trio are modern British authorities: Bernard of Gordon, a thirteenth-century Scot, of Montpellier; John of Gaddesden (d. 1349), fellow of Merton College; Gilbertus Anglicus (*fl.* 1250).

438   *litel on the Bible* Scepticism has long been diagnosed as the occupational disease of doctors.

442   *pestilence* The bubonic plague. The Black Death of 1349, which killed one in three English people, was the worst of four outbreaks in Chaucer's lifetime.

443–4   *gold* was used in medicine, but the last line is a traditional gibe at doctors.

445   *WIF* means woman rather than married woman, although in her Prologue the Wife says that she is looking for a sixth husband. The Wife is the merry widow of clerical satire. Weaving was women's work, and Bath a weaving area. But weaving, like widowhood, is the Wife's means to wealth and display and to her other pursuit, marriage.

446   Her deafness is emblematic as well as physical. Her Prologue tells us she is deaf from a blow on the ear from her fifth husband.

448   *hem of Ypres* English and Flemish weavers were rivals.

450   Offertory: part of the Mass at which the people brought their gifts to the altar.

453   *coverchiefs* could be worn over a wire framework; such headdresses were a target of clerical satire.

454   *ten pound* Comic hyperbole. On Sunday the Wife was a walking advertisement for her wares and for herself.

460   At the civil marriage *at chirche dore* the husband promised to endow his wife if he should die. The Wife's first three rich old husbands made her rich. *Fyve* is the number of husbands had by the woman at the well in John 4:18. D.W. Robertson sees a play on *well* and *Bath*.

461   *compaignye* A hint at promiscuity.

463   *Jerusalem* (pronounced Jersalem) was not an uncommon pilgrimage, but *thries* seems suitably excessive.

465   SS Peter and Paul were martyred at *Rome*; *Boulogne* boasted a miraculous image of the Virgin.

466   The pilgrimage to *Seint-Jame* of Compostela, in Galicia, Spain, was third only to Rome and Jerusalem; *Cologne* had the shrines of the Three Kings and of St Ursula.

468   In her Prologue the Wife associates her *gat-tothed*ness with Venus.

471, 473   *targe*, *spores sharpe* Martial hints developed in the Wife's Prologue.

475   *remedyes of love* 'means of remedying (curing or satisfying) love-sickness, with a possible reference to Ovid's *Remedia amoris*' (R).

476   *the olde daunce* 'la vieille daunce', *Le Roman de la Rose* 3938.

478   The village *PERSOUN* exemplifies Gospel ideals of pastoral virtue, free from the faults satirized earlier in the regular clergy and later in church officials.

486   *tithes* One tenth of each income went to the priest, who was supposed publicly to excommunicate those who refused.

495   *feet . . . staf* According to the example of early Christian pastors.

497   *wroghte . . . taughte* 'But he that shall do and teach, he shall be called great in the kingdom of heaven' (Matthew 5:19).

500   *iren,* unlike gold, is liable to rust. The application is, 'If the priest is corrupt, what hope is there for lay people?'

510   *chaunterie* A chantry chapel priest chanted masses for the soul of its patron.

513   *the wolf* In the parable of the good shepherd and the hireling (*mercenarie*) in John 10:12 the wolf represents the devil.

529   The *PLOWMAN* is a freeman, not a bonded labourer. The willing servant is the ideal of Christianity and of medieval social theory. His brotherhood to the Parson is expressed in the tag *laborare est orare*, to work is to pray. He is very like the Piers Plowman of Langland.

533-5   *God loved he . . . with al his hoole herte* After Matthew 22:37-9: 'Thou shalt love the Lord thy God with thy whole heart . . . Thou shalt love thy neighbour as thyself.'

536   *dyke and delve* also means to work hard.

539-40   The Plowman paid tithes on the produce of his *swynk* and the profit of his *catel.*

542-4   The final group of pilgrims are dishonest rascals, with whom Chaucer includes himself.

545   The *MILLERE* is a bully, a brute and a thief. He is likened to the lower animals, but also has the shattering qualities of his windmill. Millers were disliked for dishonestly abusing their monopoly of the sale of corn and supply of flour on the manorial estate.

552   *sowe* and *fox* Emblems of grossness and stealth.

559   *forneys* Hell-mouth was shown as a furnace with jaws.

560   *janglere* Chatterers were said to 'clap as a mill'.
      goliardeys Originally a clerical jester, here a teller of dirty stories.

562   *tollen* The toll was a fraction of the corn ground, taken in addition to money paid as a fee.

563   *thombe of gold* The miller's gold came from his skill in testing corn by feeling it between thumb and forefinger. There was a proverb that an honest miller has a golden thumb, meaning that honesty would be miraculous in a miller.

565   *baggepipe* A Rabelaisian instrument.

567   The *MAUNCIPLE* is a minor officer who buys provisions for the Inner or the Middle Temple, one of the Inns of Court. There is a

tradition that Chaucer was at the Inner Temple, and he may have known such a *gentil* cheat. Manciples do not feature in other estates satire.

570   The score was notched on a *taille*, tally or tallystick, which was then split between debtor and creditor.

586   To *sette a cappe* is to make its wearer look silly.

587   *REVE* General manager on an estate, responsible for the land, the stock, the work and the accounts. Crafty and sly, dominated by the humour of choler (bile), he is the opposite of the Miller.

611–12   The Reeve earns from his lord the thanks due to an equal – for lending him his own property. Like the Manciple, the Reeve is a dishonest servant.

614   The Reeve is made a *carpenter* because the Miller is to tell a tale against a carpenter.

620   *Baldeswelle* A village in north Norfolk.

622   *hyndreste* At the furthest remove from the Miller.

623   The *SOMONOUR* is a minor non-clerical officer of the arch-deacon's court, who served summonses to appear there (*apparitor* is an alternative title). He could act as beadle, and also as moral police-man, with opportunities for extortion. Physiognomy and medicine bulk large in the later portraits, which are morally and physically unattractive.

624   The faces of the cherubim are shown as *fyr-reed* with God's love, unlike the face of this unangelic messenger.

625   *saucefleem* with an excess of salty phlegm.

627   *piled berd* Hair-loss and swollen eyelids (625) are symptoms of the disease of alopecia.

634–5   *garleek . . . wyn* A diet and a lifestyle bad for the *saucefleem*.

652   Quiet finch-plucking: predatory seduction.

655   *curs* Excommunication was the penalty for moral offences and for non-payment of tithes. Reparation was often by a fine. The *curs* might be avoided by bribing the Summoner.

659–62   Chaucer has said or implied that the opinions of the pilgrims were good (e.g. 183), even when irony is evident. Here he says the Summoner *lyed*, since damnation and salvation are in the Church's power (see Matthew 16:19). But since hell is worse than prison, 662 leads some to find irony in 661.

662   *Significavit* The first word of a writ authorizing civil imprisonment of the excommunicated who have not made reparation.

667   The *ale-stake* stuck out over the inn door, with a *gerland* wreathed to a hoop at the end.
    stake/cake: a hint that the Summoner can't stop eating and drinking.

669   *PARDONER* Seller of pardons. A pardon or indulgence was an

official dispensation of the punishment due to sins on earth or in purgatory (*if* the guilt of sin had first been absolved by contrition and confession). Confessors could impose penance in the form of prayer or pilgrimage, or alms-giving for good works, such as hospitals. After 1300 Rome licensed the giving of pardons in exchange for alms, a system which got out of hand. The credentials of some pardoners were as false as this Pardoner's relics.

670   *Rouncivale* The hospital of St Mary Rouncesval, near Charing Cross, ran a series of fund-raising drives in the 1380s by selling pardons, some of which were found to be unauthorized.

671   *court of Rome* The Roman Curia was the source of authorized pardons.

672   *to me* Note the rhyme with *Rome*. Compare 523.

673   *burdoun* Bass part, accompanying the Pardoner's high voice (688) in a come-hither song. The clerical duet are companions in fraud; also, possibly, in sex.

675–91   A display of *heer* was a sign of effeminacy.

684   The *hare* was believed to sleep with eyes open, and to have the characteristics of both sexes.

685   *vernycle* An image of the veil of St Veronica, a name given to one of the weeping women of Jerusalem at Christ's Passion (Luke 23:28). She wiped his face with her veil, which was then imprinted with its image. The veil was much venerated in Rome in the fourteenth century. Pilgrims wore copies of it.

687   *hoot* Like cakes.

688   The *goat* is proverbially lecherous.

691   If a *geldyng* is a castrated man or eunuch, a *mare* suggests a passive .homosexual.

692   Berwick-on-Tweed and Ware, Hertfordshire, are at the ends of the Great North Road.

694–701   *pilwe-beer* The cult of relics produced many false relics.

699   *latoun* An alloy which looked like gold.

702   The Parson on the pilgrimage is such a resident *person* (478).

708   *ecclesiaste* The Pardoner preaches well (as his Tale shows), but may not be an ordained cleric.

709   A *lessoun* is a reading from Scripture and part of the Mass, but a *storie* may be a Gospel or a saint's life.

710–13   The *offertorie* was sung while the people brought up their gifts, after the Gospel and (in England) before the homily.

725–42   An apology for *vileynye*, coarseness of language, in the tales to follow; compare MP 3167–86.

741   *Plato* A doctrine in the *Timaeus*, which Chaucer would have met in Boethius and in *Le Roman de la Rose*.

743–5   A characteristic apology, for Chaucer does not neglect *degree*.

746   *My wit is short* Chaucer often claims to be an inadequate writer.

751   *OURE HOOSTE* The Host is called Harry Bailly in the Cook's Prologue. *Henri Bayliff ostlyer* (hotelier) appears in Southwark records in 1380; he had represented the borough in Parliament.

754   *Chepe* ('market') was the market-place of the City of London, a more respectable place than Southwark.

756   The Host's *manhod*, manliness, becomes a topic in the Tales.

768   The Host's proposal *To doon yow ese* costs all but one of the pilgrims the price of another supper at the Tabard on their return.

794   *othere two* Thus each pilgrim would tell four tales.

805–6   *withseye/Shal paye* Another condition that is not met.

819–20   The *wyn* is a nightcap but perhaps a pledge also.

823   The *cok* The male bird whose call awakens humans – and who leads forth the flock of hens.

826   *the Wateryng* A stream where pilgrims could water their horses at the second milestone on their way to the shrine of St Thomas.

830   *even-song and morwe-song* . . . Proverbial: if you haven't changed your minds.

835   *draweth* The first of four polite plural imperatives.
       cut Probably cut straws held in the hand.

837   *Sire Knyght* The Host cajoles, but observes rank.

844   *aventure, or sort, or cas* The philosophical alternatives offered are near-synonyms. If the Host has fixed the draw, there is no luck about it.

THE KNIGHT'S TALE

The Knight's Tale is based on Boccaccio's *Il Teseida delle nozze d'Emilia* (*The Story of Theseus about the Nuptials of Emily*). Chaucer never mentions Boccaccio, though he elsewhere acknowledges Dante and Petrarch, senior and more serious Italian writers. There were many *olde stories* of Thebes in Latin languages, from the *Thebaid* of Statius (AD 45–100) onwards. The medieval versions added love to war, a balance reflected in the title of Boccaccio's tale, a martial epic about Theseus, as the *Aeneid* is about Aeneas; but concerning the marriage of Emily. Chaucer concentrates on love, cutting out three-quarters of the Italian, but adds an interest in destiny which is informed by the *De consolatione philosophiae* of Boethius (d. 524). The Knight's Tale is set in pagan antiquity, in a Greece which the Crusades had once more made interesting for the West.

PART I Chaucer passes over the story of the Amazonian war.

860   *duc* Athens had had a duke since the First Crusade. Theseus was king of Athens, but he is a duke in Boccaccio.

866   *Femenye* 'Feminia'?: a Latin name for Amazonia, the land of women without men.

875–85   The Knight often mentions what he is leaving out, a rhetorical figure known as *occupatio*.

884   *tempest* may mean tumultuous welcome.

886   *ere* Writing verse is traditionally likened to the art of the plough – parallel lines linked by a turn (Latin *versus*). A claim to inadequacy is traditional also.

889   The knight is being courteous to other tellers.

925   The Roman goddess Fortuna was depicted in the Middle Ages turning her wheel of prosperity and misery. Here the conqueror's triumph is spoiled by the widow.

928   In the sources the suppliants wait in the Temple of Clemency within the city.

932   *Cappaneus*, one of the Seven Against Thebes, boasted that nothing could stop him scaling the walls of Thebes; Zeus slew him with a thunderbolt. The Seven supported the right of Oedipus' son Polynices to the throne, which his brother Eteocles had agreed to share with him. The brothers killed each other in single combat. See 1177–80n.

938   *Creon*, Jocasta's father, resumed the throne he had surrendered to Oedipus. He commanded that the bodies of Polynices and the Seven should remain unburied.

951   To pity and succour women in *sorwe* or distress is a sign of *gentillesse* (920) and knighthood (959). Froissart tells how in 1346 a pregnant Queen Philippa had knelt before her wrathful husband Edward III outside the gates of Calais to beg (successfully) for the lives of the burghers of Calais.

980   The slaying of the *Mynotaur* in the Cretan labyrinth was Theseus' most famous feat.

990   *rente adoun* Theseus shows the redness of Mars in destroying the city, to avenge Creon's treatment of the slain.

994   *al to longe for to devyse* For another (pagan) funeral *occupatio*, see 2919ff.

1007   *pilours* Taking the armour of the dead was approved practice.

1013–14   The names *Arcita/Arcite* and *Palamon* are derived from Boccaccio.

1018   *the blood roial* The royal house of Thebes had been cursed by Oedipus.

1024   The growing practice of exchanging a captive enemy for *raunsoun* was regarded as unchivalrous and mercenary.

1030   *in angwissh and in wo* Compare 1028.

1034   *in a morwe of May* May day ceremonies to greet the Spring were popular at court and are made much of by Chaucer. See 1510ff.

1074ff *And so bifel* In Boccaccio Arcita sees Emilia first, and both cousins think that she is Venus. Emilia knows that the youths are watching her. (See the picture on the front cover of this edition.)

1087ff *disposicioun* Position of a planet affecting its astrological influence; Saturn's is usually malign. The Thebans blame any misfortune on the gods or the stars.

1131–2 *brother/Ysworn* The cousins are blood-brothers, who have (unluckily) vowed not to hinder one another in love.

1165 *Love is a gretter lawe* A saying taken from Boethius, where it refers to the love of the supreme Good, not to earthly love.

1167 Arcite argues that the law of nature (which compels love) overrides any *positif lawe* men may make.

1177–80 *the houndes for the boon* A fable whose lesson is lost upon its teller.

1191ff Pirithous and Theseus, who tried to get Proserpine out of hell to be Pirithous' bride, were proverbial friends – who helped one another in love, unlike the Theban pair. Line 1200 follows *Le Roman de la Rose*, the thirteenth-century French poem translated by Chaucer, in claiming that Theseus tried to rescue the dead Pirithous from hell.

1201 *write* and 1209 *endite* neglect dramatic propriety.

1226 *purgatorie* Not a pagan idea.

1251–67 Though Arcite's complaint against *purveiaunce* is derived from Boethius, he does not distinguish God's Providence from Fortune. The acceptance of this distinction is the way to the Consolation of Boethius' Philosophy.

1260–1 A descent from the Epistle to the Romans 8:26 ('for we know not what we should pray for as we ought') to a homely figure. Though the man too *dronke* to find his way home is in Boethius, the humour is Chaucer's.

1266 *felicitee* Chaucer often recurs to the question of where true happiness is to be found.

1274 *I nam but deed* Compare 1122.

1279 *grete* Better taken with *fettres* than with *shynes*.

1302 *boxtree* pale yellow.

1303–27 Palamon's eloquent complaint at the *crueel goddes*, like Arcite's at 1251–67, is modelled on those of the imprisoned Boethius, whose protests at the injustice of Providence are answered by Philosophy.

1308 The *sheep that rouketh in the folde*, like the drunken *mous* at 1261, is not in Boethius.

1329–31 *Juno* is *jalous* towards the blood of Thebes because of Jove's adultery with Semele, daughter of Cadmus, founder of Thebes. The Theban cousins harbour *jalousie* (1299, 1333) and are perhaps, like Juno at 1329, *eek wood*.

1347 *this questioun* Such cases had been debated in the Courts of Love of twelfth-century Provence, and imitated in Italy, France and England. In romances, such Questions of Love were often put to *yow loveres* in the audience.

PART II Significant differences from Boccaccio's tale here are that in *Il Teseida* Emilia sees through Arcita's disguise as a servant, and that she is alone when she discovers the rivals fighting.

1359 *sorwe* Love-sickness was a mental disease described in medical text-books. Arcite has most of the symptoms.

1374 The word *hereos* was derived not only from the Greek *Eros*, sexual love, but also from the Latin *hero*, hero. The disease of *Amor hereos* could lead to *mania*, a madness which could prove fatal. *Mania* could affect the front cell of the brain so that the imagination could perceive no image other than that of the beloved. Melancholy could affect the middle cell, the seat of judgement.

1379 *daun* from Latin *dominus*, lord, a title of respect.

1385ff *Mercurie* is not in Boccaccio. In Virgil, Mercury prompts Aeneas to leave Dido (as he does in Chaucer's *Hous of Fame*, l.429). Chaucer brings him in to prompt the next move, though this move is more 'hereotic' than heroic. Mercury's words are oracular. He appears in the guise in which, in Ovid's *Metamorphoses I*, he first puts *Argus* to sleep with his wand, then kills him. Argus had been posted by Juno to guard Io, a nymph of whom Juno was jealous.

1422 *hewen wode* . . . Compare Joshua 9:21.

1428 *Philostrate* A name borrowed from Boccaccio's *Il Filostrato* (source of Chaucer's *Troilus and Criseyde*), supposed to mean 'laid low by love'. See 1558.

1459 *Who koude ryme* Chaucer has previously apologized for the rude language he has to report, and the shortness of his wit, and now for the defects of English rhyme. Line 1461 (like 1458) deploys anti-climax.

1462-3 *May/The thridde* The third of May, a date specified twice elsewhere in Chaucer's work, may be unlucky for lovers. *Il Teseida* does not mention a date here; there are no *olde bookes*.

1472 *Thebes* in Egypt is meant.

1494 *That al the orient laugheth of the light.* An image from Dante: *faceva tutto rider l'oriente* (*Purgatorio* I.20).

1529 Lines 1510-12 could be the opening of a *roundel*.

1537 *Friday* is Freya's day, translating Latin *Veneris dies*.

1539 Proverbial, like 1524 and 1531.

1543ff For the *crueltee* of *Juno*, see 1329-31n. *Cadmus* founded Thebes with warriors sprung from the dragon's teeth he had sowed; Amphion raised the walls of Thebes with the music of his lyre.

1559   Mars is *felle* because Thebes has suffered in war.

1585–6   *byjaped* Trickery and disguise: 'hereotic' rather than heroic.

1592   The righteous Palamon owed his escape to *nercotikes* (1472) as much as to *grace*.

1625–6   *love ne lordshipe/Wol . . . have no felaweshipe* A classical maxim.

1636ff   *This Arcite and this Palamon ben met* In Boccaccio Arcita stuns Palemone, revives him, and renews the fight; which is discovered first by Emilia, then by Teseo.

1660   *Up to the ancle* This may not be a hyperbole, if the ankle is inside a metal boot.

1663ff   *The destinee, ministre general* In the theology of Boethius the course of events is attributed by the human mind to Fortune or Destiny, but is eternally present to the divine mind as Providence. Destiny delivers what Providence has foreseen.

1712   *Withouten juge* 'Theseus objects to the irregularity of the duel' (R).

1761   *For pitee renneth soone in gentil herte* A maxim quoted five times by Chaucer: true *gentillesse* is readily prompted to mercy, a doctrine of the Trecento. Compare 3089.

1771   *wepen* could be taken in the present not past tense.

1785   *The god of love* In this speech, which is Chaucer's addition, Theseus speaks of Cupid ironically but with rueful respect, and treats his 'servants' with sympathy.
        Latin *benedicite* bless you (plural). In English it can have three, four or (as here) five syllables.

1796   *maugree hir eyen two*: 'in spite of what is manifestly obvious'.

1799   *Who may been a fool but if he love* True folly must include love.

1802   *the god of love* A reprise of 1785.

1809   *she woot namoore* Boccaccio's Emilia was aware of her admirers. Chaucer makes Emily unaware, and her unawareness strikes Theseus as comic. Laughter leads to clemency.

1810   In proverbs the *cokkow* is foolish, the *hare* mad.

1814   *a servant was I* The love of Ariadne for Theseus got him out of the labyrinth; he abandoned her on Naxos.

1838   *pipen in an yvy leef* Proverbial, like *blow the bukkes horn* (3387).

1880   The walls of Thebes are *wyde* but also (1331) *waste*.

PART III Chaucer omits much that occurs in the *Teseida* in the year before the tournament.

1885–6   *swich a noble theatre . . . ther nas* A justified claim: the amphitheatre is three times greater in circumference than the Roman Colosseum, and could hold the *c*.35,000 inhabitants of Chaucer's London six times over. Chaucer has Theseus build it specially for the tournament, and puts the oratories inside the theatre. After he had written the

Knight's Tale, Chaucer, as Clerk of the Works, had to construct (wooden) scaffolds for the lists at Smithfield in 1390.

1918   *temple of Venus* The description follows a tradition as old as Homer's account of the Shield of Achilles. The temples are 'historiated', covered with painted or carved images of stories from myth, legend and history, an encyclopaedia of curious examples, often moral or allegorical. The temples display the destructive power of Venus and Mars over their devotees. Chaucer had borrowed stanzas from *II Teseida* to describe the Temple of Venus in *The Parliament of Fowls*.

1925–8   *Plesaunce et al.* Personages from *Il Teseida*, except for Hope and Bisynesse, who come from the *Roman de la Rose*.

1929   *yelewe* is the colour of jealousy.

1930   The *cokkow* is a symbol of cuckoldry.

1936   *Citheroun* Venus was born from the sea near the Aegean isle of Cythera, confused by medieval writers with Mt Cithaeron near Thebes.

1940   *Ydelnesse* is the porter of the Garden of Love in Chaucer's *Romaunt of the Rose*, where we also meet the fair *Narcisus*. When Echo died of love for him, he fell in love with his own reflection and died of despair.

1942   *Salomon* the wise king was also love's fool: he had a thousand wives.

1943   *Ercules* is a victim of love in the *Teseida*.

1944   *Medea* tried to hold Jason by magic, as did *Circes* Odysseus.

1945   *Turnus* fought Aeneas for the love of Lavinia, and was killed.

1946   It is not clear how *Cresus* was laid low by love.

1955   *The statue of Venus* Anadyomene rises from the waves, with musical instrument, a rose garland and doves, symbolic of her amorous attractiveness.

1963   The properties of *Cupido* suggest the randomness of his devastating power.

1969ff   The inner wall of the temple of *Mars* is painted with a picture of his temple in Thrace. The description draws on Boccaccio and Statius.

1987   *northren* The orientation of the temple in Boccaccio.

1990   *adamant* The hardest of stones.

1995   *Ther saugh I* The Knight did not see the temple, but Chaucer makes us see it.

2007   Jael killed Sisera by driving a nail into his head (Judges 4:17–22).

2017   *shippes hoppesteres* ship's dancers: dancing (bobbing) ships. The ships in Statius are *bellatrices* (warlike); Chaucer may have read *ballatrices*.

2030   *Hangynge by a . . . threed* Perhaps an allusion to the sword of Damocles.

2031–2   *Antony* was a *sleere of hymself*, as was *Nero*. In medieval Christianity, self-slaughter is classed as murder. Antony and Nero are thus not only victims, like *Julius* Caesar, but murderers, like Brutus and Cassius (whom Dante places with Judas in Satan's jaws in the lowest pit of hell).

2045   *Puella* and *Rubeus* Figures in geomancy or divination, linked to unfortunate and fortunate horoscopes of Mars, the ruby planet.

2048   *of a man he eet* The man-eating wolf may image the etymology that derived Mars from Mavors: *mares vorans*, devouring of males.

2051   *the temple of Dyane* Boccaccio gives no details of the temple of Diana. Chaucer shows her at first as the 'Queen and huntress, chaste and fair' of Ben Jonson, but later as Luna and Lucina.

2056–61   *Calistopee* Ovid and Boccaccio tell how Diana punished the nymph Callisto for her unchastity with Jupiter by turning her into a bear, the Great Bear constellation. Her *sone* Arcas was turned into the Lesser Bear constellation. Chaucer confuses constellations with stars; the pole star or *loode-sterre* is in fact in the Lesser Bear.

2062   *Dane* Daphne, turned into a laurel (the meaning of the Greek word *daphne*) by her father Peneus, to prevent her rape by Apollo. In the *Metamorphoses* Ovid has Daphne call upon Diana for help.

2065   *Attheon* The *Metamorphoses* also tell how Actaeon, for having seen Diana bathing, was turned by her into a stag and eaten by his own hounds.

2070   *Atthalante* In the *Metamorphoses*, Atalanta and Meleager hunt a wild boar sent by Diana.

2075–80   Her *hart*, green colour, and bow associate Diana with hunting; the moon under her feet signifies her role as Luna, changing in her monthly course.

2085   In heaven the goddess Luna, Diana is on earth a huntress, and in Hades, Pluto's *derke regioun*, she is *Lucyna*, patroness of childbirth and women in labour.

2129   *Lygurge . . . kyng of Trace* Chaucer makes Lycurgus of Nemea (from the *Teseida*) king of Thrace (like Lycurgus in the *Thebaid*). His physiognomy is saturnine.

2133   The *grifphon*, a heraldic beast, has the head and wings of an eagle and the body of a lion.

2156   *Emetreus* (from Demetrius?) is not in the sources. His physiognomy is martial.

2215   *Citherea*, so called because she rose from the sea near the island of Cythera (see 1936).

2217   *hir houre* Each of the hours was ruled by a planet. Each day the hour beginning at sunrise belonged to the planet for which the day was named. Thus the hour at which Emily rose on Monday (Moon-day) belonged to the Moon, Luna (Diana). The hours were assigned to the planets in order of distance from earth: Saturn, most distant, first; and the Moon, nearest, last. Arcite rose on the third hour on Monday, ruled by Mars. Palamon rose on the twenty-third hour of Saturday, ruled by Venus: her man rises in her hour.

2224 The love of Venus for Adonis is told in *Metamorphoses* 10.

2271 *houre inequal* Unlike the hours of the clock, the planetary hours, twelve of the day and twelve of the night, vary in length, and are unequal except at the equinox.

2313 For the *thre formes* of the goddess, see 2082n.

2325 *desireth* desires. Is Emelye in two minds?

2340 The *blody dropes* betoken Arcite's death.

2367 *The nexte houre of Mars* on a Monday would be the fourth after sunrise.

2389 *Vulcanus*, the smith of the gods, made a net in which he trapped Mars in bed with his wife Venus, as recounted in the *Roman de la Rose* and the *Metamorphoses*.

2443 *Saturnus* is not in Boccaccio. Chaucer puts him in charge of the dirty tricks department. In tradition he is not always malign.

2447–9 Proverbs on *elde*.

2453 *doghter* Form of address to a young woman.

2456–62 *Myn is the drenchynge* Chaucer's chill list of disasters due to Saturn is not original; but 2459 is taken as a reference to the Peasants' Revolt of 1381.

2462 Saturn's aspect is most malign in *the leoun*, Leo, the astrological sign or 'house' opposite his own, Aquarius.

2466 *Sampsoun* In the Biblical book of Judges, Samson brings down the pillars of the temple of the Philistines, killing them and himself.

2475 *compleccioun* See GP333n.

PART IV A severe compression of books 7–12 of the *Teseida*, omitting many speeches, ceremonies and divine appearances, and especially the marriage of Arcita to Emilia and her vow never to remarry.

2489 *the grete fight* Such mass tournaments were rare in Chaucer's day.

2491 The *morwe* was Tuesday, Mars's day, auspicious to Arcite.

2529 *a god in trone* Theseus is more godlike than Boccaccio's Teseo.

2549 *But o cours* Teseo likewise tries to minimize bloodshed.

2605 *shyveren shaftes* Alliteration (and mimetic language) are rare in Chaucer, but conspicuous in this passage of action, 2601–16. Alliteration also features in his account of the Battle of Actium in *The Legend of Good Women*.

2614 *a bal* Football was a popular game in medieval England.

2626 *Galgopheye* The vale of Gargaphia in Boeotia, where Actaeon was killed by his hounds (see 2065n).

2630 *Belmarye* Morocco, where the Knight has *riden* (57).

2652–3   *Who sorweth now* Echoed by the Miller in MT 3747–9.

2680   *freendlich ye* Emelye prefers Arcite as soon as Palamon is taken.

2681–2   This comment on *wommen . . . in comune* and *Fortune* is not in the best MSS. Chaucer, if he wrote these lines, may have cancelled them.

2683   *And was al his chiere, as in his herte.* Probably from a sentence in the *Teseida* which says that Emilia's heart turned towards Arcita, rather than that his heart turned towards her.

2684   *a furie infernal sterte* This horse-frightening fury comes from Statius via the *Teseida*, where it is sent by Venus, not Saturn.

2713   *save* is sage, Latin *salvia*. A decoction of sage was a common remedy or 'salve'.

2747   *veyne-blood* Blood let by opening a vein.
ventusynge drew blood away from the affected part by applying a cupping-glass from which air had been evacuated by heat.

2749–50   *vertu . . . animal . . . natural* Galen taught that the body had three virtues: the natural, in the liver; the vital, in the heart; and the animal, in the brain.

2751   *venym* If blood *corrupteth* (2746) and is not expelled from the body it turns into *venym*, poison.

2775   *my wyf* In the *Teseida*, Arcita and Emilia marry before he dies.

2809   *his spirit chaunged hous . . .* In the *Teseida* the soul of Arcita ascends to the eighth sphere, an account which Chaucer had borrowed for *Troilus and Criseyde* to describe what happens to the soul of Troilus, who looks down on his own funeral with a smile. Thus the Knight cannot give any account of where Arcite's soul has gone, as he has never been there. He is no *divinistre* (probably divine, theologian, rather than diviner, futurologist). There is nothing in his book about souls; nor does he wish to retail what *divinistres* may have written about where they dwell. He leaves the conduct of Arcite's soul to Mars. Chaucer's switch from pathos to bluff military humour covers the hole he has made in his source, and avoids the difficult question of the destiny of the (? virtuous) heathen.

2817–20   *Shrighte Emelye* The Knight follows his jokes about Arcite's soul with a shrieking Emelye and a howling Palamon. Chaucer's sense of propriety may surprise modern readers. Perhaps he seeks relief after the pathos of Arcite's dying words. Certainly his Knight is fond of bathos. Then, an unrestrained display of public grief is not in itself comic: look at the widows at 903, 949, 995. Palamon had yowled earlier, in prison: *the grete tour/Resouneth of his youling and clamour*; though this is in private. It is safer to suspect irony in some later lines, for example 2826 and 2836, and (less certainly) 2850.

2847–9   *a thurghfare ful of wo* Christian commonplaces central to the Middle Ages.

2919–64 *But how* This immense sentence – a record example of the rhetorical device of *occupatio* – lists all the things about the funeral that Chaucer is *not* going to describe.

2921–23 *ook, firre, birch* . . . The catalogue of trees is adapted from Boccaccio.

2925 *the goddes ronnen* The Knight stands back from the pagan funeral, and smiles at the confusion of the unhoused tree-spirits.

2987–3089 *The Firste Moevere of the cause above* Theseus' final speech commanding marriage to Emelye and Palamon is drawn from Boccaccio, but is framed in a perspective derived from Boethius' *Consolation of Philosophy*. The *faire cheyne of love*, the succession of species, and the way God returns everything inevitably to its source – these are Boethian doctrines, Platonic and Stoic in their derivation, yet silently Christian in their tendency. Theseus has a political purpose (the obedience of the Thebans), and a practical human one (presented as the making of two sorrows into one joy). Nevertheless, his practical and humane desire to put an end to mourning, and bring order into emotional chaos, seems to enjoy the approval not only of the Knight (who much resembles Theseus) but perhaps of the Knight's elusive creator.

3017 *Loo the ook* The examples of transience and of the fates of men are from Boccaccio, as is the value of heroic fame.

3089 *For gentil mercy oghte to passen right* This emphasis on mercy is *gentil*, chivalrous, Christian. Not all modern critics are convinced of the adequacy of Theseus' arguments.

THE MILLER'S PROLOGUE

3115 *unbokeled is the male* The tale-telling game has begun.

3118 *sir Monk* The Monk is the senior male present after the Knight, and the Host wishes to observe precedence.

3120 *for dronken* Sometimes taken as *fordronken*, totally drunk. Later, the Pardoner is drunk, and much later the Cook is so drunk that he falls off his horse.

3124 *Pilates voys* The first of several references in MP & T to the mystery plays, in which the medieval trade guilds ('mysteries') enacted episodes of Biblical history which had been dramatized by clerics in a popular style. Pilate was often a loud ranting tyrant, like the overbearing Miller.

3125 *By armes* The Miller's villainous swearing is both physical and blasphemous.

3134 *Tell on* The Host concedes. He has now lost control.

3140   *Wyte it* Chaucer kills two birds with one stone: the Miller's 'apology' for any mistakes is also an insult to the Host's ale.

3141   *a legende and a lyf* suggests a saint's life. A dig at the Monk, who could be expected to tell a holy tale.

3142   *of a carpenter and of his wyf* Another dig, this time at the Reeve, who is a carpenter by trade. Legendary married carpenters were Noe and Joseph.

3143   *set the wrightes cappe* See GP586 and n.

3152   Cuckoldry is a theme of the Tales of the Reeve, Shipman, Summoner and Merchant. Sexual misdemeanours feature in several other tales, notably the Wife of Bath's.

3164   *pryvetee* is a theme in this Tale full of puns: God's secrets (the mysteries of providence); Nicholas's privacy; a wife's secrets; and the lovers' privy parts.

3165   *Goddes foyson* God's plenty. The theological doctrine of God's generosity was commonplace enough to be proverbial. It was so still for John Dryden, who said of the *Canterbury Tales*, 'Here is God's plenty.' Here the Miller gives it a vulgar application.

3167–86   *What sholde I moore seyn* An extended apologia for ribaldry. Compare GP 725–42 and 3139.

3177   *Turne over the leef* Advice to a reader, inconsistent with the fiction of open-air tale-telling. Chaucer is no slave to dramatic propriety.

THE MILLER'S TALE

3187   *Oxenford* A market town which since the early twelfth century had been the seat of a university famous for logic (GP286). For Chaucer's knowledge of Oxford and Oxford men, see J.A.W. Bennett, *Chaucer at Oxford and Cambridge*, a rich commentary on this Tale and the next.

3188   *riche gnof* The victim in a *fabliau* is normally rich (John has two servants) and often keeps lodgers.
Gnof: compare Scots *gnaf*, a low and foolish person.

3190   *poure scoler* A formula. Compare this portrait with that of the Clerk of Oxenford (GP285ff), a genuine clerk who is genuinely poor.

3191   *art* Arts, especially logic.

3192   *astrologye* also·comprising astronomy, a clerical hobby in which Chaucer was interested. Nicholas makes money out of the gullible by providing weather forecasts and other small operations; the weather-forecasting comes in handy.

3199   *hende* Nicholas is generally *hende*, a conventional epithet for a hero of romance: 'gracious', but also 'deft' and 'handy'.

3200   *deerne love* Secrecy was famously necessary to 'courtly' love. See *pryvetee* (3164n and 3278).

3204   *compaignye* Compare especially KT2779, but also GP461 and 3839.

3208   *Almageste* The Arabic title of the great treatise on astronomy by Ptolemy (second century); hence, a textbook of astronomy.

3209   *astrelabie* astrolabe, an elaborate astronomical instrument. Chaucer wrote a *Treatise on the Astrolabe.*

3210   *augrim stones* counters with arabic numerals, for use on an abacus.

3211   *shelves* Compare the Clerk at GP293.

3213   *sautrie* psaltery, stringed instrument like a small harp.

3216   *Angelus ad virginem* 'A song on the Annunciation beginning . . . "The angel, secretly entering her chamber, softly overcoming the virgin's fear, says to her 'Hail!' " ' (R). The mismatch between this song and Nicholas's approach to Alison has raised comparisons with the Mystery plays on 'Joseph's Trouble'.

3217   *Kynges Noote* An unidentified song.

3218   'To anyone who has had to live in the proximity of students, this line seems clearly ironical' (Gray in R).

3220   *After his freendes fyndyng* Compare the Clerk at GP302.

3227   *Catoun* The Maxims of Cato were an elementary school primer, so not to know them is not to know the first thing.

3231   The *snare* may not be unequal marriage but marriage itself.

3248   *pere-jonette* The early-ripe pear is sometimes given an erotic suggestion in literature. See the end of the Merchant's Tale.

3251   *latoun* See GP699n.

3253   *thenche* imagine. Alison is a dream, better than the most attractive girl a man could imagine.

3263   *colt* See 3282.

3268   *prymerole, piggesnye* Common wild flowers, terms of appreciation and endearment, like *popelote* at 3254.

3271   *Now, sire, and eft, sire* Comic patter.

3274   *Oseneye* Osney, a village near Oxford, with an Abbey of Augustinian Canons.

3276   *queynte* Gray in R sees *queynte* as an example of the adjective *queynte*, pleasing, used absolutely: the pleasing thing. It is also a euphemism for a noun which it resembles.

3286   *out, harrow* Cries for help. See 3825.

3305   The *sawtrie* is linked to sexual excitement.

3313   *Absolon* This parish clerk is named after the Old Testament Absalom (2 Samuel 14:26), a type of male beauty, whose long hair was his undoing.

3317   *His rode was reed . . .* Beauties in a girl.

3318   *Poules wyndow corven* The uppers of his shoes are fashionably cut into patterns like the Gothic windows of Old St Paul's Cathedral.

3326–7   *laten blood* ... Absalom is a barber-surgeon who also does legal work; parish clerk was not a full-time job.

3341   *Sensynge* One duty of the clerk is to sanctify the congregation with incense from the thurible he swings. Absalom enjoys censing women, and is too smitten to take from them the offerings which it was his duty to accept on behalf of the priest at the Offertory of the Mass.

3369   *Yis* The emphatic form of assent. The modern yes is equivalent to Chaucer's *ye* (R).

3370   *what wol ye bet than weel* A catch-phrase?

3384   In the mystery plays, *Herodes*, like Pontius Pilate, was a tyrant's part, for which Absalom's high treble might not be appropriate. Bennett thinks that the *scaffold hye* was the upper part of a pageant wagon.

3404   *sely* is John's epithet, *hende* Nicholas's, *jolif* Absolon's.

3449   *Frydeswyde* Eighth-century virgin patron saint of Oxford. Her church became Christ Church Cathedral.

3451   *astromye* Probably a mistake for *astronomie*, repeated at 3457. Compare 3818n.

3454   *Men sholde nat knowe of Goddes pryvetee* A theological doctrine popular in the Middle Ages, when the limits of human knowledge were appreciated.

3456   *bileve* Knowledge of the Creed was sometimes held to be sufficient for salvation.

3460   *marle-pit* Pride comes before a fall, and star-gazers fall into pits; Plato tells such a story about Thales. It is John's own belief in *astromye* that leads to his fall and *agonie*.

3466   *the dore* See the Miller's portrait at GP545–51.

3478   *Cristes passioun* is a remedy for despair.

3479   *I crouche thee* The sign of the cross wards off evil spirits.

3480–86   *nyght-spel* Popular religion: John's spell is a charm banishing spirits from the demarcated area; a similar one is found in a mystery or miracle play, the Towneley First Shepherds'. The Life of St Benedict is full of miracles against evil spirits. The *white pater-noster* (not black magic) is found in the rhyme: 'Matthew Mark Luke and John'. We are less familiar with the *nyghtes verye* and St Peter's sister.

3494   *thyng that toucheth* A double entendre.

3512   *harwed helle* John would have seen Christ descending into and 'harrow-ing' (despoiling) hell in mystery plays and painted on the church wall.

3529   *Salomon* was credited with most of the wisdom of the Old Testament. Ecclesiasticus 32:24: 'My son, do thou nothing without counsel, and thou shalt not repent when thou hast done.'

3534   *Noe* John claims to have heard *how saved was Noe* 'ful yoore ago'. He

clearly has forgotten God's promise that there would be no second
flood 'to destroy all flesh' (Genesis 9:15).

3539   *The sorwe of Noe* A 'clear reference to the comic scenes in the mystery
plays in which Noah's wife refuses to enter the ark . . . Noah's Flood
took place on the seventeenth day of the second month (17 April,
March being the first month . . .), the date traditionally assigned to
the first day of the Canterbury pilgrimage' (R). Noe was often
shown as a carpenter, and the Ark with ladders.

3590   *no synne* It was believed that there was no copulation on the Ark, as it
was human lechery that had made God send the Flood.

3611–13   *Lo, which a greet thyng is affeccioun!* A Boethian reflection, made
elsewhere by Chaucer. Compare Theseus' speech at KT1785ff.

3637   A *furlong way* is the time it takes to walk one-eighth of a mile.

3645   *corfew: couvre-feu*. Fires had to be covered at dusk.

3652–4   The lovers' *bisynesse* (compare 3643) is alluded to in positive
terms (*revel, melodye, myrthe, solas*) compared to the grossness of the
Tales of the Reeve and others.

3655–6   *belle of laudes . . . synge* In this tale set firmly in time and space, this
chronographia is a reminder of the existence of another *melodye* attended
to by other clerics in Oxford.

3682–3   *mouth hath icched . . . kissyng* A popular superstition.

3692   *trewe-love* 'A four-leaved sprig of herb paris (*Paris quadrifolia*) in the
shape of a fourfold true-love knot' (R).

3698–707   *cynamome* Absalom's rhapsody at the window borrows, ludi-
crously, from the Song of Songs: *honycomb, bryd, cynamome, turtel,* and
other details.

3709   *pa* may be a nursery word for a kiss.

3720   *I come* Chaucer's version of this tale is the first to have the woman
perform the trick.

3726   *Lemman, thy grace* 'The whole line may be meant to sound hackneyed'
(R).

3742   *berd* means beard. Its rarer sense of joke is possible but not probable
here.

3743   *By Goddes corpus* The oath adds blasphemy to other forms of
profanity.

3747–9   *Who rubbeth* may parody the rhetorical questions at KT1454–6,
1870–1 and 2652–66.

3757   *maladie* Quitting the *loveris maladye/Of Hereos* at KT 1373–5?

3762   *in his forge* The *couvre-feu* did not apply to the fires of blacksmiths.
Gerveys, getting ready for the day's work, is surprised to find
Absalom about at this illegal hour.

3770   *viritoot* Of the guesses at this unknown word, that from Old French
viretost, early rising, sounds best.

3771   *Seinte Note* St Neot by tradition encouraged King Alfred to found the university at Oxford.

3774   *tow on his distaf* business on hand. Proverbial. There is also evidence that persons convicted of sexual misdemeanours in London had to carry, on the way to the pillory, a distaff with tow on it.

3807–8   *thonder-dent/yblent* A parody of the epic simile of Palamon versus Arcite at KT1637ff.?

3818   *Nowelis flood   Nowel* is Noel, Christmas, confused by the half-awake John with *Noe*, of whom he had heard so long ago. His howler is laughed at by Nicholas and Alison at 3834. Like *astromye* at 3451, this is not a drunken slip of the Miller's tongue, but shows John's ignorance. January awakes similarly confused at the climax of the Merchant's Tale. As these slips of the tongue are the first in English literature, malapropisms might be called Carpenterisms.

3821–2   *foond . . . to selle* John found nothing to detain him on his way from the roof of the hall to the floor (*celle*), a fall of two storeys. He breaks the arm (3829), which had made him rich enough to marry Alison.

3842   *turned al his harm unto a jape* Compare *Sir Gawain and the Green Knight*, 2514: *laghen loude thereat.*

3848   *The man is wood* The opinion of every clerk underlines *wood*: the carpenter is not only mad, but a wooden-head.

3850   *swyved* From Old English *swifan*, to move quickly to and fro.

THE REEVE'S PROLOGUE

3857   *Diverse folk . . .* A proverb.

3860   The *Reve* (see GP587–622) comes from Norfolk, and his speech is touched with northernisms. *Oswold* is a saint of the north, and the clerks in the Reeve's tale are very northern.

3864   *theek* incorporates *ik*, the Northern form of I.

3865   *bleryng* tricking; a bleared eye cannot see properly.

3867   *ik am oold* The Reeve presents himself as a type: 'We old men are lecherous.' He is also sententious, and his speech is stuffed with proverbs.

3868   *gras tyme* The Reeve favours country comparisons; here he is a horse reduced from grass to winter feed.

3871   The medlar apple is an *open-ers* because it has a split. It is left to go mushy, and is then edible.

3877   The *nayl* that sticks up to hinder his desire may be a version of Paul's 'sting in my flesh' (2 Corinthians 12:7).

3890–7   *the tappe of lyf . . .* A life is a barrel of wine. At birth Death bores a tap into it, and turns it on. At first the *streem of lyf* pours out vigorously, but it is eventually reduced to a few drops onto the rim of the cask. Lechery is then a matter of hollow talk and reminiscence rather than of deeds.

3902   The Reeve's moralizing is scarcely *hooly writ*. See 3920n.

3904   *of a soutere a shipman . . .* A proverb.

3906   *Depeford* is five miles from London, *Grenewych* half a mile further. Chaucer lived there at about this time. *Half-wey pryme* is half-way between prime and terce, about 7.30 a.m.

3911   *sette his howve* rearrange his hood, make him look foolish. Compare *set the wrightes cappe* (MP3143).

3912   *with force force of-showve* A legal maxim.

3915   There could often be conflict between a miller and a reeve on a manorial estate. Chaucer adds to this friction by making the Reeve a carpenter, on whom a miller would have to rely for repairs.

3916   *quite* A word coming to mean repay rather than match. Compare MP3119 and 3127.

3917   *cherles termes*. Another apology for rudeness. Compare MP3168.

3919–20   *stalke/balke* 'And why seest thou the mote in thy brother's eye: but the beam that is in thy own eye thou considerest not?' (Luke 6:41). The Reeve does not apply this saying to himself. His anger against the Miller is irrational, as in his prayer that God will break the Miller's neck.

THE REEVE'S TALE

The plot of the tale is a traditional *fabliau* with a 'cradle-trick', a Miller and two students. It is a coarser parody of the Miller's Tale.

3921   Trumpington is a village three miles from Cambridge.

3924   *sooth* There was a mill, and is still a bridge over a brook, at Trumpington.

3927–8   *Pipen* and *wrastle* are aimed at the pilgrim Miller, as are other details of this heavily-armed, coarse-faced, bullying thief.

3928   *turne coppes* turn cups on a lathe; *sheete* shoot with a bow.

3933   *Sheffeld* Sheffield is famous for steel.

3934   A *camus* nose is broad, flat and concave.

3941   *deynous Symkyn* A form of Symond, Simon; *deynous* is his nickname.

3943   *hir fader* The clergy were celibate. The parson of Trumpington 'was in 1343 succeeded by his son' (R).

3944   *many a panne* To endow an illegitimate daughter might make her marriageable. Compare the Friar, GP212–14.

3945   *allye* ally, but also alloy: a joke about the brass pans which came with her hand to encourage Symkyn's alliance with the parson's 'noble' blood.

3948   *ynorissed* educated; also, fed.

3954   *gyte of reed* an upper-class colour, affected also by the Wife of Bath (GP456) and Absalom (MT3212).

3961–2   *perilous* Another gibe at the Miller: any heavily-armed man is (a) jealous, (b) less tough than he would like his wife to think.

3964   *water in a dich* is not good to drink: stinking with pride?

3968   *lerned in the nonnerie* The nuns had taught her to be proud?

3973   *ygrowen* Compare *ynoryssed*, 3948n.

3974   *kamus* Like her father's at 3934.

3983–5   *hooly chirches good* The parson's words reported. Holy, the normal adjective for Church, is repeated to draw attention to the parson's insistent desire to leave church property to the child of his illegitimate daughter, whom he thinks *feir* enough to catch a husband.

3990   *soler* a room open to sunlight. *Soler Halle*, a name for the King's Hall, a Cambridge hall, part of Trinity College.

3991   *hir malt* their barley. Colleges brewed their own beer.

3993   *maunciple* See GP567.

3999   *wardeyn* master (of Soler Halle).

4000   *tare* A miller can tell tares from wheat.

4002   *povre scolers* See MT3190n.

4014   *Strother* Recognizably a Northern place-name. There is a Castle Strother in Northumberland, but identity cannot be shown.

4022   *Al hayl* John and Alan are heartier and plainer than Nicholas and Absalom. As soon as they open their mouths, the clerks announce themselves as from the North of England, by forms such as *ik* for *ich*, *gas* for *goes*, *heythen* for *henne*, *taa* for *take*, and dialect words like *boes*. Bennett found that no college had so many Northerners as King's Hall. This is the first use of dialect for comic/dramatic purposes in English; London English was becoming standard.

4036   The corn is fed into the mill through the *hopur* and ground into flour. The clerks watch the milling process to see that Symkyn does not 'lose' some of their corn.

4038   *by my fader kyn* An oath which reminds us of the family pride of *deynous Symkyn*. At 4041 a tonsured clerk swears *by my crown*, as does the bald miller at 4099, and at 4049 Symkin swears *by my thrift* – he thrives by dishonesty.

4050   *philosophye*: Brawn's contempt for brain. Compare GP574 and MT3455 and next note.

4054   '*The gretteste clerkes* . . .' An ancient proverb, here put into the mouth of a mare. She tells a wolf, who wishes to buy her foal, that the price is written on her hind foot. When he tries to read it, she kicks him.

4065   *wilde mares* There were wild mares in the fens of Cambridgeshire, then undrained.

4066   '*wehee*': a call to the *wilde mares*.

4079   *The wyf cam lepynge inward with a ren.* For these animal high spirits, compare the coltish Alison (MT3282) and the *wilde mares* at 4081.

4093   *half a busshel* Compare *half a pekke* (4010).

4096   *make a . . . berd.* See 3742n.

4115   *Bayard* A horse's name, found three times in Chaucer.

4122   *ye han lerned art* The miller celebrates his victory with a gibe against the intellectual claims of mind over matter; *space* turns out to be important in the Tale.

4127   *Cutberd* St Cuthbert, the favourite saint of the far North-East of England, is given a Northern pronunciation.

4130   *Slyk as he fyndes . . .* This proverb turns out not to be true: the clerks take both what they find and what they had brought.

4134   *With empty hand . . .* A proverb.

4140   *chalons* blankets, as made in Châlons-sur-Marne.

4149   *vernysshed* A *vernissage* (French) is figuratively a drinking session; but as the miller is bald, the effect of drink might be to make it shine.

4155   To wet your *whistle* is to have a drink.

4164   *his tayl* Another horsy detail.

4166   *two furlong* a quarter of a mile.

4167   *compaignye* See MT3204n and 3839.

4171   *complyn* Compline is the last liturgical office of the day. The Symkyn family are a kind of animal choir.

4172   The *wilde fyr* Alan wishes on the Symkyn family is probably the skin disease erysipelas.

4174   *flour* flower; the most perfect (of bad deaths). A play also on the *flour* that ends up badly (for the miller).

4179–86   *lawe* provides the terms in which the clerks justify their retaliation. They may be law students.

4210   '*Unhardy is unseely*' Another proverb.

4233   *the thridde cok* The third cock-crow, traditionally an hour before dawn.

4236–48   *Fare weel, Malyne . . .* The Trumpington Mill version of the *aube*, the lovers' dawn parting of romance.

4253   *toty* The unique occurrence of this dialect word.

4257   *twenty devel* Compare 3713.

4264   *Jame* Presumably St James the Great, the apostle honoured at Santiago.

4271   *disparage* dishonour. The miller's first thought is of his daughter's social status.

4285   *out of hir sleep she breyde* The climax is precipitated by a mistake made by someone awaking bleary-eyed from sleep, as in the Miller's Tale (and the Merchant's).

4286 *hooly croys of Bromeholm* A supposed relic of the True Cross, brought to Norfolk from Constantinople in the early twelfth century, famous for its miracles.

4287 *In manus tuas* A prayer used before sleep or death, imitating Christ's 'Father, into thy hands I commend my spirit' (Luke 23:46).

4313–24 *Thus is the proude millere wel ybete* The traditional recipe for ending such a tale: a plot summary, a simple moral, with a proverb or two; the second of these would fit most *fabliaux*. After a prayer for the company, the Reeve boasts of his revenge.

THE COOK'S PROLOGUE

4325–6 *The Cook of Londoun* is tickled pink; towards the end of the Tales he is so drunk that he falls off his horse.

4327 *For Cristes passion* The lower the speaker, the worse the oath.

4328–9 *conclusion/Upon his argument* This jocular use of scholastic language recalls Symkyn's jokes at RT4122–4.

4330–31 'Bring not every man into thy house: for many are the snares of the deceitful' (Ecclesiasticus 11:31). Hebrew wisdom attributed to Solomon.

4336 *Hogge*, a familiar form of Roger (Old English Hrothgar). Ware marks the start of the Great North Road, 30 miles north of London, in Hertfordshire. The name of Roger of Ware occurs in records. See GP379ff.

4346 *many a pastee* The Host's mockery of the bad practices of cooks reflects trade rivalry between innkeepers and caterers. Chaucer's family were in the drink trade.
laten blood drawn off the juice from unsold pies to preserve them.

4347 *Jakke of Dovere* A reheated meat pie?

4350–52 *many a flye loos* may have got into the *percely* stuffing for the *stubbel*-fed *goos*.

4354 *wroth for game* The Host asks the Cook not to be angered by his jokes about cooks. Compare the Miller's taunting of the Reeve in MP.

4357 *quaad* is Flemish for bad. Chaucer's wife was the daughter of a Flemish knight.

4358 *Herry Bailly* The Host's name, the name of a historical innkeeper of Southwark. See GP751ff.

THE COOK'S TALE

The Cook's tale of Perkyn Revelour, the riotous London apprentice to the catering trade, stops short after only 40 lines.

4365   *A prentys* Apprenticeships lasted seven years, the junior living in his master's house, a situation in which 'youth and elde often at debaat' (MT3230) was proverbial.

4367   *goldfynch* A lively, pretty, noisy and companionable little bird.

4371   *Perkyn* A pet form of Peter, Peterkin.
       Revelour A nickname on the way to becoming a surname.

4377   *Chepe* Cheapside, the chief market of the City of London (as distinct from Southwark), and a main street on which processions took place, including the processions at festivals and of criminals going to Newgate (see 4402n).

4392   *dys, riot, or paramour* See the scene at the beginning of the Pardoner's Tale.

4396   *he* Probably the apprentice, but possibly the master.

4402   *lad with revel* Criminals were taken in public procession to Newgate prison, with minstrels proclaiming their disgrace.

4406   The *roten appul* is still familiar in proverbs. The Fragment becomes increasingly proverbial.

4413–14   *leve/leve* An instance of *rime riche*. Compare GP17–18.

4422   The *shoppe* is a front for the real business of *swyving*. The scribe of the Hengwrt MS wrote in the space he left after this line: 'Of this cokes tale maked Chaucer na moore.' Why? What would happen next? We do not know. Chaucer has left the appetites for sex and money triumphant over age, authority, propriety, social and religious order, and chivalry. The number of characters is reduced to three. Unlike the households in earlier tales, the knocking-shop contains no older man but only two young men and one young woman. Earlier tales show how rivals can be eliminated. Chaucer stops at a point where reductiveness can go little further, though in a later Fragment the Pardoner's Tale shows how three can become zero: three young thieves kill each other for a pot of gold.